Putting Poor
People to Work

PUTTING POOR PEOPLE TO WORK

HOW THE WORK-FIRST IDEA ERODED COLLEGE ACCESS FOR THE POOR

KATHLEEN M. SHAW
SARA GOLDRICK-RAB
CHRISTOPHER MAZZEO
AND
JERRY A. JACOBS

RUSSELL SAGE FOUNDATION,
NEW YORK

The Russell Sage Foundation

The Russell Sage Foundation, one of the oldest of America's general purpose foundations, was established in 1907 by Mrs. Margaret Olivia Sage for "the improvement of social and living conditions in the United States." The Foundation seeks to fulfill this mandate by fostering the development and dissemination of knowledge about the country's political, social, and economic problems. While the Foundation endeavors to assure the accuracy and objectivity of each book it publishes, the conclusions and interpretations in Russell Sage Foundation publications are those of the authors and not of the Foundation, its Trustees, or its staff. Publication by Russell Sage, therefore, does not imply Foundation endorsement.

Library of Congress Cataloging-in-Publication Data

Putting poor people to work : how the work-first idea eroded college access for the poor / Kathleen
  M. Shaw . . . [et al.]
      p.   cm.
    Includes bibliographical references and index.
    Contents: The emergence of the work-first prescription — Welfare reform ad access to post-
secondary education — The implementation of welfare reform: consistency and change — The
workforce investment act: investment or disinvestment? — The implementation of WIA: does
the rhetoric match the reality? — The power of work-first: implications and future trends.
    ISBN 10: 0-87154-775-9
    ISBN 13: 9780871547750
    1. People with social disabilities—Education (Higher)—United States.   2. Poor—
Education (Higher)—United States.   3. Public welfare—United States.   4. United States.
Workforce Investment Act of 1998.   I. Shaw, Kathleen M.
    LC4823.P88   2006
    378.1'986942—dc22

                                                                                    2006043946

Text design by Genna Patacsil.

RUSSELL SAGE FOUNDATION
112 East 64th Street, New York, New York 10021
10 9 8 7 6 5 4 3 2 1

CONTENTS

ABOUT THE AUTHORS

KATHLEEN M. SHAW is associate professor of urban education and chair of the Department of Educational Leadership and Policy Studies at Temple University.

SARA GOLDRICK-RAB is assistant professor of educational policy studies and sociology at the University of Wisconsin-Madison, and faculty affiliate of the Wisconsin Center for the Advancement of Postsecondary Education.

CHRISTOPHER MAZZEO is a New York City–based independent consultant.

JERRY A. JACOBS is Merriam Term Professor of Sociology at the University of Pennsylvania and editor of the *American Sociological Review.*

ACKNOWLEDGMENTS

THIS BOOK would not have been possible without the assistance and support of many people and organizations. We would first like to thank Atlantic Philanthropies, the Russell Sage Foundation, and the Annie E. Casey Foundation for their generous support of our work.

A legion of extremely talented graduate students assisted us on various aspects of the project (many of whom are no longer students). We would like especially to thank Susan Eachus and Emanique Joe for conducting excellent field work in a number of our states; and Ann Boulis, Emanique Joe, Sarah Winslow, Scott Brooks, Suzanne Sublette, May Wang, Angelina Castagno, You Geon Lee, and James Benson for critical support in a number of other aspects of the research and writing process. In addition, Andrea Forton, Alex Breland, Catherine Lewitt, Elena Poiata, Melody Meyer and Suzanne Smith, all of them University of Pennsylvania undergraduate students, provided excellent transcription services.

We were also fortunate to benefit from the feedback and support of many professional colleagues and friends, who listened, reviewed, and provided critical perspective during the life of the project. Among them were Kevin Dougherty, Brandon Roberts, Davis Jenkins, Tom Bailey, Julian Alssid, Marya Sosulski, Lisa Matus-Grossman, Regina Deil-Amen, James Rosenbaum, Erin McNamara Horvat, James Earl Davis, Joan Shapiro, and Erika Kates. We are especially thankful to Mark Greenberg and Julie Strawn from the Center for Law and Social Policy, who provided data and counsel as we chose our states. And family members—in particular John Noakes, Liam Goldrick and Geraldine and Isaac Youcha—supplied much-needed perspective, along with incisive editing.

We received important feedback from presenting earlier versions of our work in a variety of settings. We thank Gary Orfield and Cathy Horn for the opportunity to present our research at a meeting of the Harvard Civil Rights

Project; and the Sociology Department of the University of Pennsylvania, the College of Education at Temple University, and the University of Wisconsin Department of Educational Policy Studies for providing us with forums to discuss initial research findings.

Because so much of our work depended upon gaining access to a wide variety of venues across multiple states, we are thankful for the generosity of many individuals in state and local government who fitted us into their busy schedules; and to the faculty, students, and administrators at the community colleges that we visited as well. We are particularly indebted to those who helped us to obtain state-level quantitative data, including David Prince in the State of Washington; Jenni Lee Robins, Bill Hudgins, Sidonie Squier, Duane Whitfield; Jenny Wittner of Women Employed in Chicago; Whitney Smith and Rose Karasti at the Chicago Jobs Council; Steve Becker, Kim Fuiten, Bill Branham, Ken Durst, and Barb Payne in the Illinois Department of Human Services; Karen Carroll and William Box in Pennsylvania; Elaine Frawley, Claire Ghiloni, and Ed Sanders-Bey in Massachusetts; Jeannette Cabral in Rhode Island; and David Stevens and Sang Truong, of the Jacob France Institute, for access to data in a number of states.

Finally, we are grateful as well for the feedback and guidance of Suzanne Nichols at the Russell Sage Foundation. Her encouragement and flexibility was much appreciated. We are also particularly indebted to our anonymous reviewers, whose extraordinarily thorough and constructive comments greatly increased the quality of this manuscript.

CHAPTER ONE

INTRODUCTION

IN THE 1996 commencement address he delivered at Princeton University, President Bill Clinton declared, "It is clear that America has the best higher education system in the world and that it is the key to a successful future in the twenty-first century. It is also clear that because of costs and other factors not all Americans have access to higher education. I want to say today that I believe the clear facts of this time make it imperative that our goal must be nothing less than to make the thirteenth and fourteenth years of education as universal to all of Americans as the first twelve are today."[1] He then proceeded to describe his "college opportunity strategy," which included the biggest expansion of college aid since the GI Bill, which funded college attendance for thousands of veterans after World War II.

Later that same year, Clinton signed the Personal Responsibility and Work Opportunity Reconciliation Act (otherwise known as welfare reform), which was designed to "end welfare as we know it." He declared, "This bill will help people to go to work so they can stop drawing a welfare check and start drawing a paycheck." There was no mention of college, nor even education, in his speech. That is because, as he put it, "We are saying with this bill that we expect work."[2]

The difference in President Clinton's rhetoric in those two speeches demonstrates a new attitude toward poor Americans that became a widely accepted tenet of popular discourse by the mid-1990s: an idea that is often referred to as the "work-first" approach to social welfare policy. The title of his campaign book labeled Clinton the *Putting People First* president. But work-first does not put people first, and it differs significantly from the "college for all" ethic Clinton talked about at Princeton; in fact, it stands in stark contrast to it. According to the work-first perspective, college is for some, not for all. For those at the bottom of the income distribution who have turned to the government for support, work—and work only—is deemed most appropriate.

"Work-first" is a simple idea. In fact, its strength lies in its simplicity: poverty can be alleviated by moving the poor off welfare and into work as quickly as possible. This notion powerfully capitalizes on the American ideals of individualism and hard work, focusing squarely and exclusively on employment as the route out of dependency. This shifting emphasis decouples education and work, despite increasing evidence that they must be linked. In so doing, it effectively ignores the critical role that high-quality education and training play in achieving self-sufficiency, especially for the most vulnerable populations. Consequently, work-first policies and practices have further weakened this country's already-fraying social safety net, effectively ensuring that the poor will remain in poverty or be sorted into low-paying jobs with little chance for advancement.

This book examines the ascendance of the work-first idea—its emergence at the federal level, its dominance in policy and practice at the state level, its impact on access to education and training generally and, more specifically, on the institutions that serve as the entryway to postsecondary education for the disadvantaged—community colleges. We focus on exploring work-first as it is embodied in two policies: welfare reform and the Workforce Investment Act (WIA). By tracing the emergence and the implementation of work-first from the broadest federal level to the most localized communities and educational institutions, we demonstrate how it has usurped human-capital ideals, which link the economic well-being of the poor with education and training. We also show the very real impact this shift has had on the institutions and individuals most directly affected by it.

Our argument about the far-reaching effects of the work-first idea is three-pronged, and is based on an extensive array of both quantitative and qualitative data collected over the course of four years (2001 to 2005) and across six states (Illinois, Massachusetts, Florida, Washington, Pennsylvania, and Rhode Island). First, we argue that the ascendance of the work-first ideology challenges a human-capital approach that links economic self-sufficiency with access to high-quality postsecondary education. Contemporary policy harbors a contradictory set of notions that discredit education as a viable route out of poverty for the poor, even as it promotes education for the non-poor. Second, as embodied in welfare reform and WIA, work-first reduced both the quantity and the quality of education and training available to low-income adults. It did so via a set of policy signals, incentives, and laws that result in policies that are squarely work-first in their implementation, despite variations in formal, official policies at the state level. And third, welfare reform and WIA discouraged community colleges from serving low-income populations, thereby contributing to their more general movement away from serving these populations. In short, our evidence clearly indicates that welfare reform and WIA cemented a "sea change" in national thinking about the role of education in the lives of poor people. Whereas education is commonly acknowledged to be a sure and consistent route to self-sufficiency, recent federal policy has effectively removed this pathway for our poorest citizens.

It is hard to exaggerate how successfully the work-first approach acted as an organizing principle for the reform of these policies. The emphasis on putting poor people to work as quickly as possible leveled everything in its path. It overcame a generation of social-science research on poverty which produced clear evidence that such an approach provides no long-term benefits to the poor. It succeeded in states regardless of whether the governor was a Democrat or a Republican, whether there was an effective advocacy community or not, and whether there was support for this approach from state officials. Whereas most implementation studies seek to understand how and why policies have failed to reach their intended goals, in the case of this new generation of welfare-reform and job-training programs, the work-first philosophy was implemented more fully than anyone could have realistically expected. Thus, our challenge in this book is to understand how this idea came to dominate the policies and practices of poverty programs, despite the fact that the work-first approach contradicts a widely held acceptance of the importance of education and training for success in the contemporary labor market.

In the remainder of this chapter, we provide the scaffolding for examining the ways in which the work-first idea became embodied in welfare reform and WIA, and how it took tenacious hold of the implementation of these policies, despite significant variation across states in their formal policies. We begin by situating this idea within the broader context of American beliefs about the value of postsecondary education, followed by a discussion of the distinction between education and training, which points out how they differ in terms of content, delivery, and outcomes. Next we provide a brief overview of how work-first operates in each of the two policies, providing a foundation for our more in-depth examination of this topic later in the book. We then introduce our analytical framework, which utilizes recent social science theory regarding the power of ideas and their role in the formation and implementation of policy. Our particular focus on community colleges in our study of these policies is also discussed. Finally, we provide an overview of our research methodology.

THE PARADOX OF "WORK-FIRST"

A clear and consistent narrative permeates American discourse regarding education. A college education is increasingly viewed as the gateway to the American Dream—a necessary prerequisite of social mobility. Indeed, recent polls indicate that fully 98 percent of American citizens believe that all people, regardless of race, ethnicity, social class, or gender, should have equal opportunity to attend college (National Forum on Higher Education for the Public Good 2003). Most acknowledge that postsecondary education yields both private and public benefits, providing an opportunity to overcome poverty and increase one's social standing, greater access to well-paying jobs, a steady stream of well-trained workers, reductions in crime and incarceration, and increasing civic engagement in activities such as voting.

Thus, in the public imagination college attendance increases human capital—neutralizing all manner of initial social disadvantage and positioning its recipients as viable members of the economy and of society more generally. These beliefs are sensible ones, as confirmed by numerous recent studies on the economic benefit of higher education, which report a 5 to 12 percent annual increase in income for every full-time year of postsecondary education completed, and even more if a credential is earned (Grubb 2002b). They also provide the intellectual and moral underpinnings of numerous public-policy efforts toward improving the stock of human capital among all Americans, including an array of sources of assistance for those who wish to attend college, such as federal and state financial aid, state subsidies to public higher education, and state savings plans to assist parents in saving for their children's education.

Yet for the most disadvantaged the policy picture is quite different. The work-first ideology now driving federal and state policy directed at the poor ignores, and effectively contradicts, the human-capital approach characterizing most postsecondary educational policy. The two major pieces of federal legislation that have emerged in the past decade—the Personal Responsibility and Work Opportunity Reconciliation Act (PRWORA), known to all as welfare reform, and the Workforce Investment Act (WIA)—embody a work-first approach to the needs of low-income populations. According to the Department of Health and Human Services, at the "heart of the [welfare reform] statute is the expectation that, in exchange for flexibility in designing appropriate programs and services, each State be held accountable for moving families from welfare to self-sufficiency through work" (U.S. Department of Health and Human Services, n.d.). Likewise, WIA is a mechanism that, paradoxically, encourages an "employment-first approach to job training," in the words of one U.S. Representative (U.S. House of Representatives 1998).

By de-emphasizing postsecondary education in favor of rapid labor-force attachment, these two policies establish a double standard for our poorest and our better-off adults. A variety of policies and practices encourage and even assist in providing access to postsecondary education for Americans generally; but at the same time, federal welfare and workforce policies erect barriers to access for the mostly low-income individuals who are the targets of the policies. Explaining this paradox and its effects on low-income adults and the community colleges that serve them is the central task of this book.

WHY ACCESS TO EDUCATION AND
TRAINING MATTERS

At the heart of the work-first idea is a debate over who deserves access to education and training. But the terms denote quite different things in the context of welfare reform and the Workforce Investment Act. What, exactly, is characterized as "training," and how does it differ from more traditional notions of "education"? What are the relative benefits of education versus training?

Generally speaking, "getting an education" means going to college and pursuing either an associate's or bachelor's degree. In contrast, the term "training" is often used to characterize short-term occupational learning that typically does not lead to a certificate, degree, or credit toward a degree. Training is usually vocationally oriented, and can occur in a classroom or on the job; but even activities that do not include training, such as job-search assistance and resume writing workshops, are often identified as "job training." W. Norton Grubb (1996) has argued that job-training programs are commonly "one-shot efforts to get individuals into employment rather than the beginning of a long period of education and job training" (73). As such, these programs often ignore the need for long-term resources that would increase cognitive and vocational competencies. In and of itself, training is not always a dead end; training can, and sometimes does, provide an entry to credit-bearing college-level course work, especially when it occurs at community colleges (Jenkins 2002). Yet the vast majority of training remains disconnected from a career or educational pathway.

Given these shortcomings, it is not surprising that evaluations of the job-training programs that preceded welfare reform and WIA—the Job Training Partnership Act and the Job Opportunities and Basic Skills Training program—revealed that their benefits were modest at best. In the only JTPA evaluation based on a randomized controlled experiment (now considered by the U.S. Department of Education to be the "gold standard" for evaluations of educational programs), researchers found relatively small gains for job-training participants when compared to a control group that qualified to receive these services but did not enroll (Orr et al. 1996). Earnings gains for all job-training participants were about $2,000 or less annually, and the biggest earnings gains for both men and women were derived from on-the-job training and job-search assistance rather than classroom training (Orr 2004).

Other nonexperimental studies of job training (for example, Raphael, Stoll, and Melendez 2003; Hamilton 2002) suggest that integrated job-training strategies, those comprising a combination of job search, job training, and basic education and training, result in the highest employment and earnings gains. Yet the provision of integrated job training is an exception rather than the rule. For example, in one study, fewer than 20 percent of individuals participating in a job-training program in Massachusetts received integrated services (Raphael, Stoll, and Melendez 2003). As we later illustrate in our analysis of the implementation of educational and job training under welfare reform and WIA, this pattern has been reinforced and even exacerbated in recent years. As a result, the vast majority of job-training programs do not address the long-term educational or occupational needs of their participants, although they could serve as an important first step in achieving this goal. Indeed, recent evaluations of high quality training programs in Missouri and North Carolina suggest that although earnings losses may result immediately after completion of training, over the long run most welfare recipients experience significant earnings gains from such programs (Dyke et al. 2005).[3]

In contrast to training, the term "education" most often refers to programs based at postsecondary institutions that are delivered in traditional classrooms. While education at the postsecondary level may or may not lead to a certificate or a degree, it is generally distinguished from training by the fact that it carries college-level credit, and it can at least potentially be credited toward a recognizable certificate or degree. Compared to the negligible impact of training, the economic returns to postsecondary education are substantial. Returns to the equivalent of even one year of full-time enrollment at a community college (approximately thirty credits) increases earnings 5 to 11.3 percent for men and 11.8 percent for women (Grubb 2002a, 2002b). In fact, as former President Clinton himself noted, the thirteenth and fourteenth years of education are especially important. Individuals with an associate's degree earn approximately $7,000 more annually than do high school graduates, and those with bachelor's degrees earn close to $12,000 more annually (U.S. Bureau of the Census 2003). Credentials are particularly valuable for women. In a study of displaced workers attending community college in Washington State, Louis Jacobson, Robert J. LaLonde, and Daniel G. Sullivan (2001, 2005) found that women who completed an associate's degree experienced a significant increase in earnings, which they did not experience if they took only a few courses. This finding echoed results of previous research (Kane and Rouse 1995, 1999). In short, a substantial body of empirical evidence indicates there is a clear, positive relationship between years of education (and credentials in particular) and annual earnings. Moreover, in real terms, the earnings for educated skilled workers have risen while those of less-educated workers have declined. In the last thirty years, workers without a high school degree experienced an 18.5 percent decline in real wages, while those with a college degree experienced an increase of 15.9 percent (Karoly and Panis 2004). The implications are clear: those who do not acquire a degree or some postsecondary credential will remain at the bottom of the economic ladder.

Indeed, recent results from studies of those who have left the welfare rolls bear this out. Although many welfare recipients who left the rolls early during implementation did find jobs, this is less common among more recent leavers. The number of families leaving welfare without a steady income and support system is rising, and their unemployment rate has increased. Moreover, most studies of leavers find that they enjoy little to no income growth in the years following departure from the rolls. In other words, welfare recipients pushed off the rolls and into work stay poor (Fremstad 2004).

ACCESS TO EDUCATION AND TRAINING UNDER WELFARE REFORM AND WIA

As our subsequent analyses demonstrate, the ascendance of work-first resulted in a decrease in access to both the quantity and the quality of education for low-income adults. Not only are fewer individuals accessing postsecondary education or training via these policies, but when they do, they are increasingly directed toward the most ineffective forms of training rather than toward higher-quality college-level education.

Part of this story is about the importance of numbers. The overall number of welfare recipients receiving education or training declined dramatically following welfare reform in large part because far fewer people were on the rolls. Since 1996, caseloads have dropped by over 64 percent, and with them the absolute number of individuals for whom welfare has provided access to education and training. There were over 12.6 million people on welfare in 1996; as of 2005, that number was just over 4.5 million (U.S. Department of Health and Human Services 2005). Caseload reduction is thus a significant aspect of how work-first manifests itself in welfare reform. The sooner individuals obtain jobs the more rapidly they can be removed from the welfare rolls. Poor women with young children make up the vast majority of welfare recipients, and the health-care and child-care benefits that can be accessed via welfare are critically important factors that can determine whether this population has in place the supports needed to pursue postsecondary education. Thus, the massive drop in caseload must be seen as an important mechanism in eliminating welfare as a pathway to postsecondary education.[4] As Jason DeParle has written with regard to welfare reform, "Putting people to work [is] a discretionary activity. The core curriculum [is] getting them off the rolls" (2004, 129).

Yet federal welfare programs were never a significant route to postsecondary education for a large proportion of the poor. Prior to welfare reform, it was rare for more than 10 percent of recipients to enroll in college; following reform that proportion became even smaller, as we detail in later chapters. Clearly, the rate of participation in education and training in this population has never been high, and welfare reform has resulted in still lower rates of participation. But belief in the power of education remains alive and well in the minds of many poor women, who do, despite popular belief, often desire to attend college (Sosulski 2004). In a recent study, a group of California welfare recipients reported, "Nothing can replace an education. . . . It's the best thing anyone can do. . . . Education provides the greatest access to the pathway out of poverty. . . . I [don't] just want a job, I want a future, a career, a life for my daughter—attending college will give me that" (Jones-DeWeever 2005, 26–27).

Work-first in welfare reform not only reduced access to postsecondary education but also diminished access to the most important type of postsecondary education—specifically, the credit-bearing higher-education courses that lead to long-term economic benefits. Under welfare reform, a significantly higher percentage of recipients participating in any type of education or training pursue only short-term, noncredit training. Thus, when we disaggregate the types of education that are available, we see that the quality of the education that is available to welfare recipients has been significantly reduced. More detailed analyses of federal and state level welfare data are provided in chapters 3 and 4.

Access to all forms of education and job training dropped even more precipitously in the wake of WIA. Federal workforce-development policies that antedated WIA, such as the Job Training Partnership Act (JTPA), provided ample entrée to job training—over 90 percent of clients received some kind of training or education, albeit usually the kind of short-term, noncredit training activities that lead only to modest income or employment gains (Grubb and Lazerson 2004). WIA clients, however, are much less likely to obtain access to either job training or postsecondary education than those served by previous federal programs. Under WIA, both the quantity and the quality of education available were significantly reduced. Moreover, because this policy contains a multitude of onerous reporting requirements, it also effectively reduces the participation of the institutions that have consistently delivered the highest-quality training to the poor—community colleges.

THE POWER OF IDEAS: ANALYZING THE IMPACT OF WORK-FIRST

Welfare reform and the Workforce Investment Act do not reduce access to postsecondary education simply by forbidding it through federal law. Rather, this effect is achieved via a complex set of formal and informal rules, incentives, and signals that work to restrict the range of responses of state and local implementers to the needs of clients by making education and training a less attractive and feasible option. In short, the work-first idea is expressed most powerfully and visibly via the policy-implementation process.

In recent years, a diverse and rich body of literature has emerged across the social sciences on the role of ideas in public policymaking (Campbell 2002; Goldstein 1993; Goldstein and Keohane 1993; Hall 1993, 1997; Kingdon

1984; Somers and Block 2005; Weir 1992, 1993). Research on ideas provides an alternative to interest-based explanations of political and social phenomena that is more nuanced than the latter. Yet heretofore, researchers in this area have been primarily interested in the causal impact of ideas on policy adoption—that is, the process by which ideas become embodied in law and formal policy—while relatively little work has explored the ways ideas can subsequently influence policy implementation processes. Yet, as recent scholarship has shown (see Goldstein 1993; Hasenfeld 2002; Lin 2000; Maynard-Moody 2003; Roe 1994; Spillane, Reiser, and Reimer 2002; Stein 2001, 2004; Weir 1992), policy ideas, once institutionalized, can strongly influence "implementing agents to think differently about their behavior . . . and encourag(e) them to construct alternative ways of doing business" (Spillane 2004, 12).

Ideas assert their power over policy implementation via two major institutionalization mechanisms. The first mechanism is through law and incentives (Goldstein 1993; Pierson 1993; Weir 1992; Weir and Skocpol 1985; Weiss 1990). Policy ideas are generally enacted through legislative processes and formalized through statute and legal interpretation. Statutory law creates rights and obligations and builds in a set of formal rules that govern the behavior of state and local implementing agencies. Implementers will not always comply with rules, of course, but laws create powerful incentives to do so, even for those who do not believe in the ideas (Goldstein and Keohane 1993). In short, when policy ideas become laws they change the interest calculations of those who must implement them. In the case of welfare reform and the Workforce Investment Act, work-requirement thresholds for states, along with new and complicated sets of accountability measures and outcomes tracking, were developed to keep caseworkers clearly and consistently focused on concrete measures of success that operationalize the work-first idea.

Policy ideas can also become institutionalized through their role as focal points or signals (Garrett and Weingast 1993; Mazzeo, Rab, and Eachus 2003; Moore 1988). Ideas are powerful political forces because they can cause people to think and act differently (Roe 1994; Spillane 2004; Spillane, Reiser, and Reimer 2002). Political actors and policy entrepreneurs are aware of this and seek to frame policy ideas in ways that are marketable and resonant with other politicians and the general public. Policy ideas that are adopted widely are thus likely to be those that are easily understandable, simple to describe, and commanding of broad support. As John L. Campbell (2002) put it, "The most successful [policy ideas] are those that provide the clearest road maps out of troublesome or uncertain policy situations" (29).

Policy models built around a central slogan or animating principle, such as "work-first," are particularly powerful. The work-first slogan provides a simple, straightforward precept that is appealing to politicians and the public. Work is a central value in American political culture, and appeals to that value have historically influenced social policy in this country (Skocpol 1992). Furthermore, once an idea such as work-first becomes law it is also deceptively easy to implement—work before welfare, work instead of education. As embodied in federal statute, it sends a simple but potent signal to states and implementing agencies about the preferred approach to welfare and workforce policy. An alternative slogan (such as self-sufficiency or poverty reduction) is both harder to sell and harder to implement.[5] Putting people to work is seen as a mere problem of will; pulling people out of poverty requires resources and training and implementers with strong skills and a high level of professional authority.

In sum, recent scholarship in the public-policy literature provides a framework for understanding how federal welfare and workforce policy might powerfully influence the multiple and disparate actions of thousands of state and local political officials and implementing agencies. Through the mechanisms of law and incentives, and via its power as a focal point for policy implementation, the work-first idea provides a powerful cognitive template for state and local policymaking. Put differently, the state welfare and workforce-policy processes we describe in this book involve the "making, interpreting and enforcing of meaning" (Maynard-Moody 2003, 9). While, as argued above, we can predict with some confidence the outcomes of these processes, we can also surely expect the surprises and variability characteristic of federal policy implementation in the United States.

COMMUNITY COLLEGES: WHERE WORK-FIRST IDEAS BECOME PRACTICE

Policy implementation is a lengthy and complex process that can result in impacts—even unintended consequences—on seemingly uninvolved parties. In the case of welfare reform and WIA, community colleges, while not directly involved in the formation of these policies, have nevertheless been sharply affected by the work-first agenda. Indeed, we argue that the signals sent by the work-first message have reduced incentives for community colleges to provide education to the poor, and have raised barriers to their efforts to do so.

The community college sector is unique in American higher education because it holds at its core an equity agenda focused on providing access to postsecondary education for those who have traditionally been denied entry. As growing numbers of Americans seek a postsecondary education and college tuition simultaneously skyrockets, the community college remains the single most affordable and accessible option for disadvantaged individuals. Today there are 1,085 community colleges in the United States serving 5.7 million students, including 45 percent of all first-time freshmen. The community college population is disproportionately female (58 percent), and serves more minority students than any other postsecondary institution, including 46 percent of black undergraduates and 55 percent of Hispanic undergraduates (Bailey, Jenkins, and Leinbach 2005a, 2005b).

For the poor and working class, the community college is the most accessible point of entry to the postsecondary system. Sixty percent of low-income first-year students begin their undergraduate careers at community colleges (G. Winter, "Junior Colleges Try Niche as Cheap Path to Top Universities, New York Times, December 15, 2002, p. 1); see also David T. Ellwood and Thomas J. Kane 2000). Over one-third (37.8 percent) of community college students qualify for and receive some form of financial aid, even though the average annual tuition is a low $2,076—because for the lowest-income families that tuition represents approximately 12 percent of their annual income (American Association of Community Colleges 2005; National Center for Public Policy and Higher Education 2002). Yet community college tuition remains the least expensive postsecondary option. On average, it is less than half the tuition at public four-year colleges and one-tenth that at independent four-year institutions (Philippe 2000).

Community colleges, acting as comprehensive "second chance institutions" (Grubb 2001, 284), provide much of the education and skills training taking place in the United States today. Each year they award more than 579,000 associate's degrees and nearly 200,000 two-year certificates (National Center for Education Statistics 2003; Philippe 2000). In one industry, health care, 65 percent of new workers get their training at community colleges (Philippe 2000). Because community colleges offer a wide variety of courses and programs, ranging from remedial to academic, flexibility in response to employer needs; and credentials with economic values, they are particularly well positioned to serve the low-income population, which possesses less information about college programs and fewer financial resources and thus faces much more uncertainty than middle-class students. But perhaps even more important, because they have traditionally functioned as educational rather than training institutions—connected to learning and concerned with quality instruction—community colleges serve the poor not only educationally but also by offering a real route to social mobility (Grubb 2001). Therefore, if access to education via the community college is reduced, the most feasible route to higher education for the vast majority of low-income adults is obstructed.

The work-first ideology emerged at a time of rapid change for community colleges, and as a result its effects are particularly potent. In recent years, the mission of the community college has grown increasingly complex. As Kevin Dougherty notes, "The community college is a hybrid institution, combining many different and often contradictory purposes" (1994, 8). Historically community colleges held their academic mission as primary, but now there is mounting pressure on them to adopt a workforce-preparation mission, which

11

includes varied curriculums blending vocational and academic programs, short-term, certificate-oriented training programs, and an increasingly entrepreneurial approach toward education and training (Bailey and Averianova 1999; Dougherty 2003; Dougherty and Bakia 2000a, 2000b; Grubb, Badway, and Bell 2003; Grubb et al. 1997; Gumport 2003).

This trend flows from a shift in the economic, educational, and policy environment in which community colleges operate. First, competition is emerging in the form of a growing number of private, two-year or less "occupational colleges" focused on narrow training in vocational areas and offering quick, attractive training options for low-income students (Deil-Amen and Rosenbaum 2003). In addition, community colleges are increasingly dependent upon public funding (federal, state, and local) compared to other sectors of higher education, which can generate more funds from higher tuition, endowments, and alumni support. More than half of community college revenue comes from public funding (Hebel 2003). Moreover, this funding is increasingly being linked to strict performance-based outcome measures such as transfer rates, degree-completion rates, and other outcomes that are difficult to attain when serving highly disadvantaged student populations.

In the face of increased competition for low-income students and funding formulas that are a disincentive to serving this population, community colleges are having a difficult time maintaining their commitment to serving poor and disadvantaged adults. As Alicia Dowd notes, "Against the din of calls for efficiency, productivity, and accountability, concern for the vitality of the community college's democratizing role is barely evident in the policy agenda" (2003, 93). It is therefore unsurprising that some community colleges show signs of turning their attention away from serving this community and toward more lucrative niches, such as business and community education programs and honors programs targeted to middle-class students (Bailey and Averianova 1999; Bastedo and Gumport 2003; Shaw and Rab 2003).

This trend is exacerbated by the emergence of work-first. Through the power of law and the informal influence of ideas, community colleges face even greater pressure to shift from their historic mission of serving low-income individuals. Under the influence of work-first, community colleges are both less willing and less able to address the needs of either welfare reform or WIA clients.

FOLLOWING IMPLEMENTATION
ACROSS MULTIPLE STATES

Although welfare reform and the Workforce Investment Act are federal policies, both emerged in a context of "devolution," in which states received a relatively high degree of autonomy in responding to federal legislation in exchange for meeting relatively strict performance measures. As a result of this policy context, states have the potential to vary considerably in terms of their response to both policies. Because of these factors, we felt that it was important to closely compare the implementation of both welfare reform and WIA across several states.

Our goal was to investigate states whose responses to these policies varied significantly, and we collected an array of data to assist us in our selection. During the state selection process, we conducted telephone interviews with state officials, examined state Internet sites, reviewed published reports by research and policy houses, and consulted with the Washington D.C.–based Center for Law and Social Policy (CLASP); we were able to make critical use of CLASP's typologies of states and their responses to welfare reform in our decisionmaking process. Our assessment of welfare reform policy determined our choice of states to study for several reasons. First, this project was originally focused solely on welfare reform but expanded within the first year to include an analysis of the Workforce Investment Act. Second, high-quality work by CLASP and others had been done to typologize states in terms of their response to welfare reform at the time that we were choosing our sites. And finally, when we examined state-level WIA policies specifically in terms of formal policy regarding access to education and training, we found very little variation. Thus, although states had enacted WIA policies that were quite similar, our group of states purposefully includes variation along a number of factors related to welfare reform.

In making the final selection of our six states, we sought to assemble a sample that varied in terms of general approaches to welfare reform and of the level and quality of access to postsecondary education afforded welfare recipients. We also wanted to achieve some level of geographical diversity as well. Although each state's approach to welfare reform and WIA is quite complex, it was possible to place them initially into broad categories according to the amount of access to postsecondary education that is allowed in the states' formal welfare policies. As table 1.1 shows, two states—Massachusetts and Washington—could be categorized as low-access states when our sample was selected in 2001. At that time, Massachusetts required students to do twenty hours of work while attending college, although this requirement has subsequently been relaxed so that recipients can attend college without work for twelve months or less—a change that we examine in more detail in chapter 4. Washington did not allow recipients to attend college unless a mandated job search did not result in employment; and they were restricted to vocational education.

In contrast, both Florida and Pennsylvania were categorized as moderate-access states. Though quite different in their approach to postsecondary education, both allowed college attendance for some period of time without a work requirement, and they did not restrict the type of education available to

Table 1.1   Welfare Reform: Six States' Policies Regarding Access to
Postsecondary Education and Training under TANF

State	Access to Postsecondary Education
Massachusetts	Low. College attendance without working is not allowed. Recipients must work twenty hours a week while attending college.
Washington	Low. Recipients may attend college for twelve months without working, but only vocational education is allowed. They may attend college only if mandated job search fails.
Florida	Moderate. State has forty-eight-month lifetime limit of college study. Recipients may attend college for twelve months without working, and in some instances may continue past this point.
Pennsylvania	Moderate. Recipients must conduct job search. If search unsuccessful, they may attend college for twenty-four months without working.
Rhode Island	High. State employs a human-capital approach to welfare reform. Recipients may attend college for twenty-four months without a work requirement and may continue full-time postsecondary education if necessary after this point.
Illinois	High. Recipients may attend college full-time for thirty-six months without working. To continue after that time, they must work twenty-nine hours per week. State uses Maintenance of Effort funds to "stop the clock" for recipients pursuing postsecondary education.

Source: Compiled by authors, drawing on Greenberg, Strawn and Plimpton (1999).

recipients. Rhode Island and Illinois were chosen because they allowed a relatively high level of access to postsecondary education. Welfare recipients in these states could attend postsecondary education for more than twenty-four months without a work requirement. In sum, the six states appeared to represent a broad range of responses to welfare reform—multiple contexts within which to examine WIA—and provided a rich and fertile field from which to conduct our analyses.

Within each state we collected data that allowed us to examine how each policy was implemented at various levels of analysis—at the state and local levels, and also within individual community colleges. We utilized a nested comparative case-study design, which is based on the methodological thinking of Charles Ragin, Howard Becker, and others (Ragin 1987; Ragin and Becker 1992) that explores ways in which comparative case-study methods can be used to examine complex social phenomena. We strove to develop a pool of data that would allow us to do meaningful comparisons of the effects of these policies across different state and institutional contexts. This approach is in keeping with the recommendations of Stephen H. Bell's *New Federalism and Research: Rearranging Old Methods to Study New Social Policies in the States* (1999), which suggests that variation within and across states resulting from devolution requires intensive, detailed case-study analysis.

Data were collected at several different levels. First, we interviewed a total of one-hundred-ten state-level officials in relevant departments (for example, education, human services, employment and training), and analyzed formal policy development and implementation utilizing existing policy documents and policy analyses provided by a number of policy-research houses as well as the agencies themselves. Next, we identified one to three community colleges in each of the six states. These community colleges varied in terms of size and urbanicity, but we chose institutions that had historically served a significant number of low-income students, including welfare recipients. In this way, we hoped to be able to gauge the effects of WIA and welfare reform among community colleges that were most likely to be impacted by shifts in these policies. We interviewed a total of ninety-six faculty members and administrators at thirteen different colleges. We also conducted eleven individual interviews and interviewed four focus groups with low-income workers such as welfare recipients and WIA clients. Finally, we interviewed thirteen welfare and WIA caseworkers. Our interviews were "in-depth," meaning that we followed a topical script rather than a survey instrument, and these conversations often lasted an hour or more. We also visited each state multiple times over the course of a two-year data collection period (2001 to 2003), and conducted numerous follow-up interviews as our analysis proceeded through 2005. This extended period of time in the field allowed us to analyze the implementation of both policies over time.

All interviews were tape-recorded and transcribed. We utilized Hyperresearch, a qualitative data-analysis package, to code and analyze the interviews. As is true in most qualitative research, our analytic framework became increasingly specific as analysis unfolded, leading us to focus more carefully on how conceptions of the work-first idea influenced the implementation of welfare reform and WIA as it became clear that there was far less variation in the implementation of these policies than written, state-level policy would suggest. We were also particularly interested in discerning both the intended and the unintended effects of these policies as they were implemented at the local and institutional levels.

In addition, we collected an extensive amount of secondary data regarding the implementation and outcomes of both policies, including reports generated by states, research institutions, advocacy organizations, and community colleges. These data sources were used to verify and expand upon information culled from the interviews, and to develop interview protocols as the study unfolded.

We complemented our detailed case studies with original analyses of micro-level data on postsecondary education enrollment. Specifically, we examined the degree and type of change in postsecondary education participation that occurred in the wake of welfare reform and WIA. National analyses of welfare reform and postsecondary activities were conducted utilizing the Current Population Surveys (CPS), the National Household Education Surveys (NHES), the Surveys of Income and Program Participation (SIPP), and the National Postsecondary Student Aid Surveys (NPSAS). State-level analyses of changes in education and training activity pre- and post-WIA were drawn from state reports that used standardized program data. In addition, descriptive state-level analyses of enrollment in postsecondary education pre– and post–welfare reform were conducted using data provided by state officials at the relevant departments in each state.

In all, our data allow us to paint a detailed and comprehensive picture of how the implementation of welfare reform and WIA is affecting access to postsecondary education and training for low-income populations. A framework that includes multiple levels of analysis, as well as cross-state and cross-policy comparisons, provides us with a rare opportunity to examine the implementation of two major federal policies simultaneously.

OVERVIEW OF THE BOOK

We begin our close examination of welfare reform and WIA in chapter 2, where we lay the foundation for our argument by providing an analysis of the emergence of the work-first idea, as we trace shifts in federal social policy from a historical perspective and identify a critical set of factors that provided a fertile environment for the work-first idea to take hold. Specifically, the chapter examines the role that training and education have historically played in federal and state welfare and workforce development initiatives and describes how work-first emerged as a potent policy idea in the late 1980s.

The next four empirical chapters trace the ways in which these policies filtered down from state-level policy to practices that occurred within individual community colleges and local one-stop career centers. In chapter 3 we analyze the development of welfare reform, focusing specifically on the policy elements that restrict access to postsecondary education. We provide a detailed analysis of the ways in which work-first is embedded in the details of federal welfare reform, pointing to aspects of the policies that create barriers to postsecondary education participation. And we present statistical analyses to provide the most comprehensive assessment that exists today on the effects of welfare policy on college access.

Chapter 4 provides a more fine-grained analysis of the implementation of welfare reform by exploring the mechanisms through which the policy is enacted at the state and local level. We begin with an analysis of state data that demonstrates the extent to which implementation of welfare reform resulted in variation in access to education, across all six states. Then, by utilizing an array of data from our case studies we examine how various actors, agencies, and institutions reacted to and shaped welfare reform in their states. Our case studies include states that have implemented a work-first policy despite variations in formal legislated policy, as well as examples of states that have not allowed work-first to completely dominate welfare reform. Our analysis looks closely at the roles of state officials, welfare advocates, and community colleges themselves in explaining how access of welfare recipients varies across these states.

In chapter 5 we turn our attention to the Workforce Investment Act. This chapter pays particular attention to devolution and its effects on local WIA policy, and examines the myriad of accountability measures that are an integral part of WIA federal policy. Quantitative data provide evidence of the overall effect of WIA on access to education and training. Utilizing data from several states, in chapter 6 we further illustrate how access to education and training was reduced by WIA, through its effects on one-stop career centers and education and training providers. Several aspects of WIA contribute to this trend: burdensome reporting requirements; a relative drop in funding for training; and a work-first orientation among one-stop career center caseworkers who failed to send their clients to college. These details about the processes of WIA implementation provide a greater understanding of the ways in which a work-first training policy actually affects access in practice.

The book concludes with a chapter that synthesizes our findings regarding the power and influence of the work-first idea, examining how welfare reform and WIA work in combination to erect sizable barriers to postsecondary access in a number of arenas. We also explore the implications of welfare reform and WIA within several broader contexts. What lessons can we learn from considering these two policies together? What is the cumulative effect of these policies on the ability and willingness of community colleges to continue to serve low-income populations? How can the grip of the work-first idea be loosened from federal policy directed at the poor?

Although the genius of work-first lies in its simplicity, this book does not tell a simple story. Welfare reform and the Workforce Investment Act are complicated pieces of federal legislation, and their emergence and implementation at the federal, state, and local levels has been a complex and sometimes maddeningly contradictory process. But whereas the details of their implementation varied in some important ways, the overarching theme that emerges from our analyses is this: the work-first ideology that drove first welfare reform and then the Workforce Investment Act has had a remarkably pervasive and consistent effect—a marked decrease in access to quality higher education for low-income populations. Clearly, college is only for some, not all, in the United States.

CHAPTER TWO

THE EMERGENCE OF THE WORK-FIRST PRESCRIPTION

WHERE DID "work-first" come from? How did this particular philosophy gain such overwhelming acceptance and power among policymakers at all levels and with the general public? How did it displace the human-capital ideas that animated much of social policymaking in the late twentieth century and are still powerful in mainstream educational policymaking circles? Why did work-first begin to dominate discourse and practice in welfare and workforce policy? This chapter tackles these difficult questions.

Ideas are powerful actors in the policy process. The ideas present in formal policy, more so even than formal language or mechanisms, may be reified, so that they come to exert their own independent influence apart from the policies in which they emerged. They act as signals and focal points, even spreading their message beyond their originally intended scope. Work-first is such an idea. Once work-first became ascendant, its principles became "hardwired" into federal policy through a series of policy mechanisms. Thus, an understanding of how this idea emerged will help us to assess its full impact.

WELFARE, JOB TRAINING AND THE HUMAN-CAPITAL NARRATIVE

The American welfare system extends back to 1911, and its history has been extensively documented and analyzed (see, for example, DeParle 2004; Gordon 1994; Katz 1986, 2001; Piven and Cloward 1993; Skocpol 1992; Somers and Block 2005). Our intent is not to reproduce all of the arguments or findings of these studies, but rather to explain the context from which the work-first perspective emerged. To do so, we selectively review this history, using a dual focus: ideas regarding investments in skills and training on the one hand, and reducing welfare rolls through rapid employment on the other.

Three important themes emerge from this literature. First, "welfare" as it is identified in the public imagination has rarely enjoyed consistent, enthusiastic support from either policymakers or the general public. David Ellwood (1988) put it most succinctly: "Everybody hates welfare" (4). Second, historically, training and education have not played a central role in welfare-policy debates. Although the concept of providing job training and public employment for the poor first emerged in the 1930s during the Great Depression, welfare, education, and employment policy mostly steered clear of each other until the 1960s. Last, issues of work and the obligations of recipients increasingly became a central, and often contested, aspect of welfare policy as welfare moved from an entitlement to a temporary support system (Katz 2001; Mead 1986; Rogers-Dillon 2004). These changes corresponded with changes in women's workforce participation, shifts in the racial composition of welfare rolls, and growth in both teenage childbearing and the number of women bearing children out-of-wedlock.

Welfare policy has its origins in the "mothers' pensions" movement in the early twentieth century. Pensions were designed to allow widowed mothers to support their children at home without having to work (Youcha 2005). Initial programs were state-based and designed both to support mothers and to encourage suitable child-rearing practices (Skocpol 1992). Many states established child-care and home-management standards for recipients to encourage them to conform to middle-class social standards (Abramovitz 1996). By 1929 all but four states had passed some form of mothers' or widows' pension program, although the states varied significantly in their generosity (Teles 1996).

In 1935 the state pensions were subsumed under the Social Security Act and the new program was renamed Aid to Dependent Children, or ADC (Skocpol 1992; Gordon 1994). Because women were not expected to work outside the home while raising young children, and because the children of these women usually were not born out of wedlock, ADC—though not overwhelmingly politically popular—was generally supported by the public. But over time changes in the ADC population and women's labor-force participation undermined support for the program. In 1939, Congress removed most widows from ADC, and instead made them eligible for the more generous Old Age Insurance program if their deceased husbands were eligible for benefits. Henceforth ADC would be populated primarily by a politically vulnerable population of unwed single mothers (Katz 1989; Skocpol 1992; Teles 1996).

Beginning in the 1940s, eligibility criteria for ADC were tightened and work was more often promoted as a viable option for single mothers. Caseworkers began to refuse ADC to women they judged to be potential workers, particularly women of color or women who failed so-called moral criteria (Abramovitz 1996). In some cases, low-wage work was enforced by a cut in benefits when caseworkers judged that seasonal work was available.[1] Southern states in particular refused assistance to black women on the grounds that they were needed to work in the fields or as domestics (Reese 2005). These exclusionary practices were generally ignored by federal policymakers until the early 1960s, when media attention over egregious practices in Louisiana and Newburgh, New York, spurred the federal Department of Health, Education, and Welfare (HEW) to act. When ADC was reauthorized in 1962—it was renamed Aid to Families with Dependent Children (AFDC)—these and many other restrictions on eligibility were banned. The new law also called for increased obligations for recipients that included work or voluntary employment and training (Patterson 1986; Teles 1996).

A combination of court decisions and administrative-policy changes continued to shape the debate over the eligibility criteria for welfare receipt. A series of rulings built the foundation of a right to public assistance and curtailed state discretion to deny assistance to "undeserving" mothers (Melnick 1994; Rogers-Dillon 2004; Teles 1996). Meanwhile, HEW, the federal agency administering AFDC, shifted its policy direction away from a social-service orientation toward an emphasis on income maintenance. Ongoing concerns about discrimination against prospective black recipients and new concerns about payments to ineligible recipients led to tighter bureaucratic controls on local welfare offices. Caseworkers now had as their primary goal to "determine eligibility and hand out checks," rather than to make independent judgments about the worthiness of a welfare applicant (Rogers-Dillon 2004, 54).

Thus began the reframing of welfare as an entitlement for poor mothers, which led to an explosion in the numbers of women receiving AFDC. Between 1960 and 1974, the number of Americans on welfare increased from 3.1 to 10.8 million. From 1967 to 1972 alone the numbers of recipients grew by an average of nearly 17 percent a year. Advocacy groups emerged to encourage poor women to apply for welfare, legal assistance sought to protect the rights of welfare recipients from arbitrary loss of benefits, and a substantial body of case law developed around the legal rights of welfare recipients (Patterson 1986; Piven and Cloward 1977, 1993; Rogers-Dillon 2004). Efforts to decrease the stigma of welfare and encourage participation were so successful that by 1974, over 80 percent of low-income single mothers with children were receiving welfare.

Yet a counternarrative was emerging as well. By the mid-1960s, talk of a "welfare crisis" was common both in both Washington, D.C., and the popular press. Perhaps most significant, the enrollment boom cemented a lasting change in the public perception of the typical welfare recipient. No longer was she thought to be a white widow; now she was a never-married black woman with multiple children born out of wedlock (Quadagno 1994; Patterson 1986; Rogers-Dillon 2004). The 1965 release of the Moynihan Report (Moynihan 1965) detailing a "crisis" in the black family structure cemented this inaccurate perception. According to federal reports, common belief, and media outlets, the "problematic behaviors" associated with welfare recipients—teenage childbearing, out-of-wedlock births, poverty—were more common among African Americans (Gilens 2003; Schram, Soss, and Fording 2003) than among other social groups. This depiction grew more explicit in the 1980s with President Ronald Reagan's repeated references to the seemingly ubiquitous "welfare queens." This mismatch between rhetoric and reality had significant consequences, as Sanford Schram and his colleagues have demonstrated: for decades welfare policy has been less generous in states with small percentages of white recipients (see also Goldrick-Rab and Shaw 2005). In short, welfare recipients were fast becoming the "undeserving poor," a change in perception that would pave the way for a series of welfare-policy reforms aimed at reducing welfare dependency, rather than reducing poverty itself.

WELFARE MEETS TRAINING: WIN, CETA, AND THE "WAR ON POVERTY"

Education and training would come to be seen as among the most important tools in achieving this goal, but the link between them did not emerge overnight. Where AFDC has historically been targeted at disadvantaged women and their children, job training and employment policy has historically targeted men who through economic dislocation or other disruptions were unable to find suitable employment. The modern job-training system first emerged, albeit briefly, in the early 1930s.[2] The Great Depression left hundreds of thousands of workers unemployed, and "poverty lost much of its moral censure as unemployment reached catastrophic levels" (Katz 1989, 15). In response, President Roosevelt created a series of training and employment programs as part of his New Deal. For the most part these were public jobs programs that provided subsidized paid employment in public works programs such as that of the Works Progress Administration (WPA), the Civilian Conservation Corps (CCC), and the National Youth Authority (NYA). The Federal Relief Emergency Administration (FREA, created in 1933) and the Civil Works Administration (CWA, 1934) continued the American tradition of providing "outdoor relief" to the poor and economically disadvantaged. These efforts were termed "outdoor" because they lay outside the realm of traditional public institutions such as poorhouses, asylums, and schools. At its peak, the CWA employed 4.26 million workers, or 22.2 percent of the potential workforce; the WPA employed 3 million workers in 1936, its second year of operation (Katz 2001).

Training and education were relatively minor components of these programs, which were instead oriented toward subsidized work. These programs mostly disappeared as attention turned to World War II; indeed job training was largely absent from the policy agenda for the next twenty years. One important legacy of the New Deal programs, however, was that they were administered through local community-based organizations, not the public school system, because the Roosevelt Administration believed the federal Office of Education and states and local school districts could not be trusted to run the new programs effectively. Thus, whereas educational ideology has played a important role in the development of job training since World War II, its implementation has been and continues to be divorced from the public school and university system (Grubb and Lazerson 2004).

Of course, the end of the Second World War brought the Servicemen's Readjustment Act of 1944, otherwise known as the GI Bill. All returning veterans were provided with tuition assistance and supportive funding to attend the college of their choice. The underlying motivation of this act was not only to reward those who had served the country but also to keep them out of the labor market: there were not enough jobs to absorb them and they were likely to be unemployed. At the time, this was perhaps the federal government's biggest intervention into education ever, and it opened the doors to college for millions of men (and some women) who otherwise might have never been able to afford it (Bowen, Kurzweil, and Tobin 2005). One historian went so far as to call the GI Bill an "entitlement" program "with no limits on the number of participants" (Thelin 2004, 264–68). For many, this bill held out the promise that higher education was truly no longer the bastion of the privileged. In the long term, it also served effectively to prevent poverty and unemployment among millions of men. In short, the GI Bill cemented the human-capital notion that economic well-being was best achieved through investing in education and training.

Job training (as distinct from the more traditional postsecondary education that was the focus of the GI Bill) reentered the federal policy scene in the early sixties with the Manpower Development Training Act (MDTA) of 1962. As had occurred during the Depression, training policy again gained political salience in the context of economic woes (in this case, the recession from 1960 to 1961), a pattern that would continue to the present day (Grubb and Lazerson 2004; Lafer 2002). The MDTA was designed to reduce unemployment via short-term (ten- to fifteen-week) training courses that focused on readying participants for entry-level work. Once again, education and training (although extremely short-term in this instance) were emerging as the preferred solutions to unemployment.[3]

The MDTA was also a response to increasing concerns with poverty among policymakers and the general public. Michael Harrington's searing 1962 book, *The Other America*, brought widespread attention to the problem of rural and urban poverty and helped focus the attention of the Kennedy administration on the problems of poor Americans. What eventually came to be called the War on Poverty was initiated through a request by President Kennedy to his cabinet and Council of Economic Advisers (CEA) to look into ways federal policy could attack the problem of poverty. Kennedy's initial inquiry culminated after his death in President Lyndon Johnson's Economic Opportunity Act of 1964, which formalized the War on Poverty in federal law. The next decade saw the establishment of most of the programs that came to make up the modern U.S. welfare state, including Medicaid, Medicare, and a number of education and training programs (Katz 2001; Patterson 1986; Weir 1992).

It is particularly notable that many of the War on Poverty programs were designed to provide education and training to the poor. The programs that delivered such services were quite disparate, ranging from the early-childhood-education focus of Head Start to financial aid programs designed to provide access to college for low-income students, but the dominance of the human-capital notion was clear (Stein 2004). The corresponding rapid expansion of the community college sector—and of higher education more broadly—was yet another sign that education was an increasingly important route to middle-class status.

But education and training were soon reframed as a means through which to reduce welfare dependency, and work emerged as a legitimate component of welfare as well. The Work Incentive Program (WIN) was created in 1967 as a supplement to AFDC. There were mounting pressures to move welfare mothers off welfare rolls and into employment—outcomes that could be achieved without actually reducing poverty but nevertheless did not directly contradict that goal. WIN was the first federal welfare policy to make the connection between welfare and training explicit—training, and by extension education, were essential tools in welfare policy. WIN offered at least the prospect of generous job training for some, and also mandated work for a subgroup of welfare recipients with older children (Grubb and Lazerson 2004). Still, the work component of the program was not as dominant as the training component, which had been incorporated at the behest of Department of Labor. Both Labor Department and White House officials were increasingly concerned with the "sub-employment," or underemployment, of women (Katz 2001, 64). With WIN, the focus of welfare policy also shifted back from being exclusively on income maintenance toward what W. Norton Grubb and Marvin Lazerson (2004) call a "services strategy" that used training and complementary supports such as child care and transportation to "enable recipients to work their way out of poverty" (110–11). The "services strategy" reached its peak—and endpoint—in the aftermath of the Family Support Act of 1988.

At the time this shift to "services" was both lauded and limited. On the positive side, it reflected the optimistic view at the time that poverty could be

23

overcome through government action. On the other hand, training and education could also be defined as the limits of government action to reduce poverty, and thus could be framed as a cheaper and more palatable alternative than such strategies as a guaranteed income and public jobs. This new emphasis on education and training became increasingly popular through the 1970s and early 1980s. At the time, job training was seen as a limited step to help people out of poverty—certainly more limited than direct interventions to restructure opportunities for work in the labor market. Today education and training strategies are advocated only by the most liberal politicians, although a short generation ago they seemed like rather mild and limited measures.

Even so, workforce policy was not yet fully linked to welfare policy. Harking back to the New Deal, in 1973 Congress passed the Comprehensive Employment and Training Act (CETA) as an old-fashioned federal jobs program. Although the program included a small training component that provided funds to local governments to support "manpower planning," CETA's more important public-service employment (PSE) program sought to address unemployment through the provision of short-term federal jobs. CETA focused on "unskilled and semi-skilled positions like clerks, typists, guards, and road crews, along with jobs in maintenance, repair and warehouse work . . . [while not] provid[ing] any training" (Katz 2001, 65). Public-sector employment was promoted rhetorically by supporters of CETA—mostly Democrats—as part of an explicit macroeconomic strategy to move toward full employment. Over time, PSE came to dominate the implementation of CETA: its share of the CETA budget nearly doubled between 1973 and 1978. At its high-water mark, PSE supported over 725,000 adults in public employment (Grubb and Lazerson 2004). Education and training were seen as secondary, but nevertheless important, tools for reducing unemployment.

The emergence of CETA indicates that as recently as the early 1980s, job training and education still played a relatively minor role in federal workforce policy. However, rhetoric included in both WIN and CETA to the effect that training was a means out of poverty for welfare recipients and the poor was gaining currency among experts and policymakers (Patterson 1986; Teles 1996). As noted earlier, this rhetoric emphasized the individual causes of poverty and the potential for transformation through job training. The rising popularity of skills-building strategies served to undermine the support for PSE. Public jobs were never popular among Republicans and conservative Democrats and job training was a solution both parties could more easily support. As a result, CETA was dismantled in 1982.

In its wake emerged the Job Training Partnership Act, a skills-based workforce development policy that passed easily into law in 1982 with strong support from both parties. JTPA reflected a growing consensus that viewed training and skills building as a legitimate approach to alleviating poverty. But the policy was popular for another reason as well: the country was in the midst of a major recession and the Republican leadership wanted to have something it could tout to show concern over the economy. Democrats went along, even those who supported public jobs, because training was an easy sell politically—at a minimum it showed that government was doing something about unemployment and poverty. The law signaled a new approach to employment policy: eschewing public jobs, JTPA sought to enhance skill building through a greater focus on improved training outcomes and the stronger "involvement of the private sector in shaping programs to meet the needs of local employers" (Lafer 2002, 89; see also Weir 1992).[4]

JTPA was the embodiment of a human-capital approach to workforce development, but between 1982 and 1998, when JTPA was discontinued, the ideology driving welfare debates grew increasingly conservative and the poverty problem—no longer seen as a reflection of a lack of training and skills—was reframed as one of inadequate workforce attachment and dependency upon government handouts. As a result, the human-capital notion at the root of JTPA was quickly replaced with a work-first idea that held rapid job placement and reduction of the welfare rolls as its primary goals.

THE EMERGENCE OF A CONSERVATIVE APPROACH TO POVERTY POLICY

Conservative arguments about welfare dependency took hold among both right-leaning intellectuals and the general public by 1980, despite a decade of research that punctured such arguments. Then a new wave of writing upped the ante. The first significant missive was George Gilder's 1981 book *Wealth and Poverty*, a favorite of President Reagan. Gilder argued that redistributive programs such as welfare and CETA only served to keep the poor dependent; indeed, by subsidizing paid employment at attractive wages, programs like CETA "deprive[d] the poor of an understanding of their real predicament: the need to work harder than the classes above them in order to get ahead" (Gilder quoted in Lafer 2002, 164).

Gilder's critique was followed to its logical conclusion by Charles Murray in his influential 1984 book, *Losing Ground*. Focusing on the welfare state in its totality, Murray argued that all forms of public assistance had perverse effects—subsidizing those already on welfare and encouraging the lazy and indolent to seek similar benefits. The solution was to provide incentives for the poor to get ahead—carrots for good behavior such as working, and sticks when necessary, including revoking assistance (Murray 1984; Teles 1996).

Gilder and Murray had enormous influence on debates over welfare and social policy in the next two decades. More immediately, the conservative critique was successful in moving the discussion about poverty rightward in the

25

1980s, so that the reduction of welfare caseloads was a principal policy goal in itself. If dependency on welfare was defined as the problem, then reducing dependency was the solution.

Recipients had to take responsibility for their poverty, argued Lawrence Mead, a political scientist. In *Beyond Entitlement: The Social Obligations of Citizenship* (1986), he contended that welfare ought to be a matter of "mutual obligation" between poor parents and the state—"a balance of rights and duties" (2) rather than an entitlement. Under such an arrangement, the state would provide temporary financial support and other services, but in return recipients had a responsibility to support their families through paid and unsubsidized employment. Though Mead saw himself as an advocate of "big government conservatism," he was not a fan of training and education. At the time, he helped cement the notion that welfare policy needed to "integrate the obligations of work into welfare" (Teles 1996, 150).

Analysts and researchers on the progressive end of the political spectrum had their own critique of welfare policy. Liberals focused on efforts to reduce poverty rather than to reduce welfare caseloads. They felt that benefit levels should be increased, opportunities for education and training expanded, the minimum wage raised, job opportunities expanded, career ladders from entry-level jobs encouraged, and employment and housing discrimination ended. The liberal perspective emphasized the importance of expanding opportunities for the poor. The conservative agenda, in contrast, named the poor as the problem, and the moral failings of the poor as the central set of behaviors that needed to be changed.

For example, the sociologist William Julius Wilson took up the issues raised by Gilder and Murray in his 1987 book, *The Truly Disadvantaged*. Wilson sought to shift the debate to the general inadequacy of welfare as a strategy to fight poverty. Yes, incentives were a problem, Wilson argued, but a problem less of the welfare system itself than the consequences of structural unemployment and the limited availability of jobs in the inner city (Wilson 1987). The solution, though, was not public jobs nor increased cash assistance but general-purpose programs that promoted economic development in cities and provided extensive and intensive training and education for the poor. Wilson's critiques of welfare and his support of aggressive human-capital building strategies among the poor were influential among liberal thinkers and policymakers.[5] Like their more conservative colleagues, they too believed that welfare was deeply flawed. But they also believed that the state could play a role through job training and other strategies in building the skills of the poor. Still, the work-first idea continued to gain strength, and it was buttressed by results from the first round of state welfare experiments, which showed that work-oriented welfare reform could increase work efforts and even the earnings of recipients under certain circumstances (Rogers-Dillon 2004).[6]

In 1988, Congress passed the Family Support Act (FSA) by large margins in the House and Senate and with strong leadership from the states through the lobbying of the National Governors Association (Teles 1996). The FSA aimed squarely at the work-first goal of "moving welfare recipients into the work-place" (Rogers-Dillon 2004, 59), but it also reflected some of the arguments put forth by liberal thinkers. First, the FSA made all two-parent families eligible for AFDC under federal law, rather than at the discretion of states. Second, the law amended AFDC by expanding education and training options through the Job Opportunity and Basic Skills program (JOBS). JOBS enabled participants to meet work requirements through adult, remedial, or other forms of education and training while providing matching funds to the states for these and other services (Grubb and Lazerson 2004). Although there were no direct work requirements for single-parent families, two-parent families were required to have at least one parent participate in sixteen hours or more of "community work experience" (workfare). And single-parent families received a series of incentives for the parent to work, including job training, child care, and income disregards (Weaver 2000, 78). In short, the FSA and JOBS allowed for work-oriented and training-oriented approaches to alleviating poverty to coexist.

In reality, the FSA reflected a compromise among different political and intellectual currents, and its stability was fundamentally a function of political circumstance. The work-first idea, although present, had not yet become dominant. Indeed, even when Congress reauthorized JTPA in 1992, it agreed to revisions in the act that strengthened its education and skills-training components. Responding to evaluation results showing that participants who enrolled in skills training had greater earnings increases than those who merely enrolled in job search or referral (U.S. Department of Labor, Office of the Inspector General 1998), the reauthorized JTPA "banned local governments from providing job search assistance, 'job readiness' programs, resumé writing or interview training without also providing substantive education or skills training" (Lafer 2002, 196). But in less than five years, these lessons would be turned on their heads as federal policy shifted away from education and training toward a new policy paradigm, work-first—one that embraced the very approaches discredited in 1992.

THE ASCENDANCE OF THE WORK-FIRST IDEA

What happened? First and foremost, the politics changed. The JTPA reauthorization was passed in the last months of President George H. W. Bush's presidency. By 1993, Bill Clinton had taken office, and unlike his recent predecessors this president promised to tackle the welfare issue head-on (Clinton 1992).[7] He did just that, in the midst of rapid changes in the political and intellectual climate that took place between 1992 and 1996. It is in this context that the human-capital ideals that were vital parts of the 1980s consensus on poverty became increasingly discredited, and it is in this context that work-first emerged and began to take hold.

In the early 1990s, conservatives and other social-policy critics renewed and intensified their attacks on welfare. Arguing that the FSA trapped poor families in a perverse cycle of dependency on the government, Charles Murray and others spoke openly about the proposal Murray first floated in *Losing Ground*—that the federal government should eliminate welfare and end all forms of public support for poor mothers (Bennett and Wehner, ". . . And a Skeptical View of Welfare," *Boston Globe*, January 27, 1994; Murray 1984; Teles 1996).[8] Employing what Albert Hirschman (1991) called the "the rhetoric of perversity," they again made the case that programs such as welfare, although nominally designed to reduce poverty, can create incentives that actually increase dependency and exploitation, rather than ameliorate them. In this way, Murray and others now turned the issue of income maintenance on its ear, arguing that even the modest income support of AFDC discouraged a strong work ethic by providing a basic income floor for the poor that shrank more, the more they worked (Massing 2000). As Margaret Somers and Fred Block (2005) point out, "The logic behind the rhetoric is impeccable—if assistance is actually hurting the poor by creating dependence, then denying it is not cruel but compassionate" (9).

Even as congressional Republicans were considering new proposals to reform AFDC in 1994 by coupling more generous benefits in the public sector with work requirements, conservative intellectuals and Republican presidential candidates were proposing the abolition of AFDC for unwed mothers. These proposals reflected continued public distress over welfare, and the increasing political potency of the issue of out-of-wedlock births. Moreover, they asserted that the old consensus regarding the means of alleviating poverty was misguided; as William Bennett and Peter Wehner of Empower America put it in their *Boston Globe* article, "The point is not tougher work provisions and job training; rather it is to go after a system that fosters illegitimacy and its attendant pathologies" (". . . And a Skeptical View of Welfare," *Boston Globe*, January 27, 1994, p. 11).

This critique of training also helped resuscitate Lawrence Mead's earlier warning that education and training were unacceptable and irrational steps toward employment, at least as practiced under the AFDC system. Rather, they acted as impediments to work, shielding the poor from the realities of the labor market and permitting them to aspire to jobs that were beyond their reach, rather than accept the "menial jobs actually available to them." Even policies that required work but allowed work preparation, such as CETA, were faulty because they shielded recipients "from the need to accept available

jobs" (Mead 1986, 65). Furthermore, programs such as the 1967 Work Incentive Program (WIN), though it required "employable" welfare recipients
to work, failed, according to Mead, because in practice few worked, since
most women were either allowed to enroll in education or training or were
defined as not employable.

The conservative critique of welfare was often inconsistent with the facts.
Perhaps most striking of all was the "cycle-of-poverty" myth, according to
which generation after generation of women remained mired in welfare. The
data clearly indicated otherwise. Roughly half of welfare recipients in 1995
had been on the rolls for less than two years. This pattern was typical
throughout the 1970s, 1980s, and 1990s. Moreover, only a small fraction—
less than 5 percent—had been on welfare for more than ten years. Long-term
welfare dependency was not completely fictitious, but it represented only a
small fraction of the caseload. Perhaps most relevant from the vantage point
of the five-year lifetime limit on benefits that was included in the 1996 welfare reform legislation, the data indicated that only 20 percent of the current
caseload at any time had been on the rolls for more than five years. Panel
studies, such as the nationally representative Panel Study of Income Dynam-
ics based at the University of Michigan (Duncan 1984) and local studies such
as Frank Furstenberg's (1976) research on teenage mothers in Baltimore, had
shown that most welfare mothers had small families and most did not remain
on welfare for long periods of time.

In reality, among Republican politicians the conservative critique of illegitimacy and training was mostly about finding a way to outflank President
Clinton with respect to welfare. Their goal was either to deny him victory or
to force him further to the right than he wanted to go. After all, Clinton had
come to Washington vowing to "end welfare as we know it" and planned on
introducing his reform bill in the 1994 session of Congress. After extensive
meetings of his welfare-reform task force, Clinton produced a bill in the summer of 1994 that was basically a modified version of the now frayed consensus. The new twist was a two-year time limit on cash assistance, after which
recipients were required to work. Throughout the two-year assistance period,
recipients would be provided generous education, training, and child-care
benefits. If the two-year limit was up, recipients without a job would be guaranteed public-sector work until a private-sector job could be found (DeParle
2004; Rogers-Dillon 2004; Weaver 2000).

The response to Clinton's proposal confirmed that any consensus regarding welfare policy had evaporated. Some liberals in the House and Senate attacked the bill for providing minimum-wage public-sector jobs as opposed to
wages that would raise recipients out of poverty; other Democrats attacked
the notion of time limits itself. For their part, Republicans quibbled about
small details while holding out hope for a bill that would move the debate

"further to the right" (Representative Tom DeLay, quoted in Teles 1996, 157). A few months later Republicans would get their wish, as the midterm elections brought a historic turnover of the House majority from Democrat to Republican.

But politics are only part of the story of welfare reform and the emergence of work-first. As noted earlier, since the early 1980s states had been implementing innovative welfare-reform proposals under the approval of a "waiver" from federal regulations that exempted states from some aspects of the federal legislation. Waivers were first used as a policy strategy by the Reagan administration as a way to reform welfare without new federal legislation (Rogers-Dillon 2004; Teles 1996). This move allowed states to apply for waivers to an interagency board, the Low-Income Opportunity Advisory Board, which had been given the discretion to approve state waiver requests subject to several conditions, including the requirement that the waiver policy be revenue-neutral and that any new programs undergo rigorous evaluation. Many of the waiver experiments tested the contrasting strategies of voluntary education and services versus work requirements as means to move welfare recipients into paid employment and off of welfare. The states developed different approaches to these strategies that struck somewhat different balances, and independent research organizations (most notably Manpower Demonstration Research Corporation, now known as MDRC) were contracted to determine the effectiveness of various state experiments.

The use of waivers accelerated after 1992, the last year of the Bush administration and an election year. Waivers became a way for states, particularly governors, to take on welfare reform in their states; they also provided the federal government a chance to say it was doing something about welfare in the absence of a congressional consensus on new legislation. The first wave of waivers, in 1992, tended to focus on enhancing human capital and increasing work effort among recipients. But after 1992, the character of the waivers changed: they began to focus more on family structure and dependency, as proposals for "family caps"—designed to provide a disincentive for recipients to have additional children by capping benefits at the family size recipients had when they entered the program—and time limits on benefits became increasingly common. Most of these were proposed by Republican governors as a means to put pressure on a new Democratic president. By 1995, the political climate had changed such that Governor William Weld of Massachusetts, a Republican, could propose a waiver for the state's Employment Support Program that would limit cash assistance for most clients to sixty days, after which recipients would be required to perform forty hours of community service and job search to continue to receive benefits (Teles 1996, 141).

How did the state waivers come to influence federal welfare reform as it was ultimately formalized in the Personal Responsibility and Work Opportunity Reconciliation Act 1996 (PRWORA)? Not through the hypothesized model of experimentation, research and dissemination of results that made up the public ideology of the state waiver program. Both Kent Weaver (2000) and Michael Katz (2001) maintain that public-policy research and evaluation played only a minor role in the eventual adoption of PRWORA. In fact, findings regarding the efficacy of various combinations of education and work for welfare recipients were sufficiently varied that a clear consensus did not emerge on the relative merits of human-capital building strategies and more restrictive approaches such as time limits. In any event, argues Robin Rogers-Dillon (2004) in her book *The Welfare Experiments*, focusing on the influence of evaluation results on PRWORA underestimates the influence of the waiver policy. She contends that the very existence of welfare waivers that allowed states to implement time-limited welfare, work-first, and other previously untested ideas paved the way for the passage of PRWORA:

> The pilot programs from 1992 to 1996 redefined what welfare means in the United States. They did not simply tinker with welfare-to-work programs or make small changes in the incentive structure within welfare. These programs redefined welfare as a temporary program rather than an entitlement. They abolished the entitlement to welfare in the public mind well before Congress ended it. . . . Pilot programs are most powerful before research is complete, when they have been removed from politics but are not yet mired in empirical results. (Rogers-Dillon 2004, 6)

By providing concrete instances of new welfare ideas being implemented, welfare experiments in the years leading up to welfare reform redefined what was possible politically and made more extreme ideas viable in the eyes of the public. The very existence of these experiments was thus in many ways more important than their actual results.

One clear example of this phenomenon is MDRC's evaluation of California's GAIN program (Greater Avenues to Independence) in the early 1990s. Evaluations of GAIN indicated that individuals who participated in a strongly enforced "work-first" approach to welfare earned more than those who did not participate in some stances. At a time when many states' JOBS programs emphasized education and training, "The study had the effect of turning the conventional wisdom—train first, then work—on its head" (DeParle 2004, 112). To be sure, the gains in earnings did not lift these families out of poverty, and results varied depending upon the level of skills that recipients had when they entered the program, the local job market, enforcement, and expenditures. Furthermore, the lessons drawn from these studies differed markedly depending upon the political persuasion of the observer: whereas

GAIN seemed to demonstrate to liberals the need for a significant investment in supports to ease the transition to employment, conservatives saw programs that were too lenient and argued for more dramatic changes in the welfare system to produce changes in behavior among the poor (Weaver 2000). But perhaps most important, the existence of the program itself proved that a work-first approach to welfare was possible and did not lead to disastrous results. Thus, regardless of the outcomes of MDRC's evaluation, GAIN legitimized work-first as a real possibility in broad-based welfare reform.

Overall, evaluations in the 1980s and 1990s found small but statistically significant effects for many experimental programs, regardless of their relative emphasis on education versus work (Manski and Garfinkel 1992). If this research contributed to any sort of common view, it was one centered on the conviction that the existing welfare policy had a number of fatal flaws. Thus, both policymakers and the general public came to believe that the current system was "broken."

CRITIQUING EDUCATION AND TRAINING

By the end of 1994, President Clinton was increasingly pressured to support a more "radical" welfare reform than the states' waiver requests from a newly empowered Republican Congress. The Republicans' "Contract with America" (created as part of the campaign for the midterm election) had included a proposal to cut off welfare entirely to the majority of unwed mothers. As the conservative Robert Rector put it, "We are not going to have a debate about AFDC, we are going to have a debate about the 'War on Poverty'" (Teles 1996, 159; see also DeParle 2004).

Somers and Block (2005) argue that these political and intellectual shifts set the stage for welfare reform and were a necessary precursor. "Before any major institutional change was possible [in welfare reform], the hard work of ideational regime change was necessary. Once the hard fought battle of ideas was won, policy transformation took place almost effortlessly" (15). The old consensus about poverty had been overthrown, but what was left in its place? As noted earlier, nearly all policymakers involved agreed on the centrality of work and shared some common ground on the importance of time-limited assistance, but they were at odds over most everything else. Clinton and the Democrats supported a modified version of a welfare entitlement that would use incentives, work requirements, and generous supports to provide a safety net. The Republicans were fixated on illegitimacy, hard time limits, and ending the entitlement (Weaver 2000).

In both parties, the debate had undoubtedly moved to the right. Where in the 1980s the majority of Republicans still supported a skill-building approach, by 1996 most shared the views of conservative thinkers such as Murray who argued that training programs were of little value and that the primary problem of welfare recipients and other poor Americans was not a skills deficit but that they had "never been socialized into the discipline of the workplace" (Murray 1984, 214).

The Democratic party also shifted its thinking. As noted earlier, the role of work in welfare policy occupied an increasingly prominent position during the years preceding the 1996 welfare-reform legislation. The Work Incentive Program of 1967 stated that employable welfare recipients must work or be moving toward work in order to receive their benefits; and the 1988 Family Support Act (FSA) required work from at least one parent in two-parent families and included a range of incentives to encourage all welfare recipients to work.

Yet despite the increasing weight Democrats gave to work, chief among the work incentives was the availability of education and training. Within the context of the FSA, education and training and employment were seen as compatible elements of welfare policy—a natural pairing whereby employment preparation led to long-term, stable employment. Up until the late 1980s, Democrats supported these educational incentives and supports vigorously, especially in states whose waiver programs paired education and employment in trying to build the skills of recipients.

But by the early 1990s, the emphasis of the Democrats had changed perceptibly. An example of this new thinking can be seen in the 1992 book *Reinventing Government*, by David Osbourne and Ted Gaebler. Like David Ellwood, a Harvard professor, the authors were advisers to the Clinton administration and helped shape the administration's welfare-reform proposal. Along with the requisite support of work and critique of dependency, the volume makes the case that the kinds of education and training AFDC clients participated in—usually basic education and short-term training—were expensive and often ineffectual. In one way this shift is not surprising: most research and evaluation findings from the 1980s and 1990s did show that adult basic education programs were often of low quality and had little economic or educational impact on participants (see, for example, Beder 1999; D'Amico 1997, 1999; Pauly and DeMeo 1996; Strawn 1998; Strawn and Echols 1999).[9] But this was not the only way to read the evidence. Basic education programs as they operated under AFDC and the state waivers often had some telling weaknesses that limited their impact. For one thing, these programs had weak or nonexistent links with advanced certificate and degree programs. For example, in the San Diego GAIN program, clients who successfully completed basic education went on to job search rather than to working toward a General Equivalency Diploma (GED) certificate or to a community college degree. Given the positive role that credentials play in increasing earnings (Berg 1970; Strawn 1998; Strawn and Echols 1999), it is not surprising that merely completing basic education did not translate into any significant earnings gains in the San Diego GAIN program (Martinson and Friedlander 1994).

Similar findings were reported in the evaluation of the New Chance program, a MDRC national demonstration project combining education, vocational training, and college classes: women who just obtained a GED showed no positive earnings effects from the program, but women who earned a postsecondary training certificate increased their average monthly earnings by $121. In other words, the effects of education in this program were not felt until participants achieved a postsecondary level of education (the sample consisted of 2,079 women, and the follow-up period lasted forty-two months). Johannes M. Bos (1996), part of the MDRC evaluation team, concluded that "participants should be made aware that basic education has little value by itself and [they] should be strongly induced to pursue post-GED training and credentials" (16).

Other experimental evidence provided similar supporting evidence. A series of evaluations, the National Evaluation of Welfare-to-Work Strategies, conducted by MDRC, compared the success of JOBS programs using employment-focused strategies with those using education-focused strategies (Brock et al. 1997). A significant point was that programs using the latter model were focused on increasing participation of single-parent welfare recipients in adult basic education, preparation for the GED, and ESL (English as a second language) classes, but not in postsecondary education. In these programs participation impacts "resulted primarily from large increases in attendance in basic education; only small increases in attendance in postsecondary education or vocational training were found for the education-focused programs, and they were generally among only high school graduates or GED holders" (Friedman 1999, 15).[10]

One program in particular, Steps to Success, in Portland, Oregon, was unusually successful in increasing employment and earnings and GED attainment. The program took an employment-first approach but did not push recipients immediately into job search. The strong labor-force attachment message in the Portland program was combined with high-quality education and training services, which may have contributed to the program's success. Individuals who were deemed by case managers to have a good chance of getting a GED were offered the opportunity to do so as their first activity instead of immediate job search. Portland's program "produced the largest, most consistent increases in employment stability and job quality during the follow-up period (Friedman 1999, 30). Participants worked more, earned higher wages, and had a higher rate of finding jobs that offered health insurance than nonparticipants (Strawn and Echols 1999, 7–8).

In short, the research on education and skills training for welfare recipients provided mixed evidence of the efficacy of education and training strategies. However one chose to interpret it, the research provided no clear road map for either Democrats or Republicans to advocate a workforce-attachment model with limited options for education and training. Yet this is exactly what happened. There appear to be three primary reasons for this shift. First and foremost, both the political and intellectual center shifted rapidly after 1992 and the Democrats, particularly the President, were quickly forced to move away from the kinds of skill-building strategies they had supported through the 1980s and early 1990s, and had pushed hard to incorporate into the reauthorization of JTPA. Secondly, ideas that had hovered at the margins over the years were now widely accepted parts of the new thinking on welfare. Policymakers and a large portion of the public now increasingly believed that skills were less important to the economic fate of the poor than what might be called "cultural" values—punctuality, attitude, and discipline (Lafer 2002). They also increasingly believed that any job was better than no job at all; that even a low-paying job was a foothold in the marketplace.[11] Whether these ideas had basis in fact was beside the point; because they were accepted as true, they structured the discourse around welfare reform and later the Workforce Investment Act.

Last but not least, governmental fiscal realities had also changed. The budget deficit, and the Democratic party's desire to reduce it, undermined the desire of its political leadership to experiment with high-cost approaches such as education, particularly in a welfare program that was unpopular with the public and was viewed by many as costly and inefficient (Weaver 2000). These fiscal realities were also factors in the states. In California, for example, the state GAIN program had been initially designed to contain a strong educational remediation and basic-skills component based on client assessments. Yet despite the completed assessments, the state modified the legislation to remove the remediation component and shift the focus to immediate workforce attachment. The reason: The state had budgeted money for only 8 percent of GAIN clients to receive remedial education (Lafer 2002, 197).

In sum, between 1992 and 1996 the terms under which welfare would be "reformed" had changed radically. The traditional supports for increasing workforce attachment among recipients—education and skills training, child care, health insurance—all fell by the wayside. In their place arose the work-first idea (more accurately, a work-only idea), characterized by firm time limits, strong work requirements for both clients and states, and strong disincentives for human-capital building strategies. Devolution was also a central part of the discussion. Block grants of welfare dollars to states gave governors greater control over welfare reform—a control that they had gained a taste for after the state waivers—and gave Congress a way to avoid difficult debates over such issues as illegitimacy (Teles 1996).

The Republican Congress sent President Clinton three bills for reforming welfare that followed this rough template. Heeding advice from his political advisers that it would clinch his victory in the 1996 election over Bob Dole, Clinton ultimately signed the third bill, but he did so over the objections of his advisers in the Department of Health and Human Services. AFDC had been consigned to history; in its place was a new time-limited welfare program, Temporary Assistance for Needy Families, called TANF for short (DeParle 2004).

EXPANDING WORK-FIRST: THE WORKFORCE INVESTMENT ACT

The triumph of the work-first idea in the welfare arena clearly paved the way for its acceptance in the development of the Workforce Investment Act of 1998. WIA and the job-training programs that preceded it were nowhere near as extensively reviewed and debated as those surrounding welfare. In fact, most of the rhetoric surrounding the reform of this country's largest federal job-training program focused on issues of efficiency and the need to develop a system that was more "market-driven" than its predecessors. Yet as welfare and workforce policies have become more closely aligned philosophically, the linkages to welfare reform are unmistakable. WIA is designed to funnel clients into employment quickly and minimize their opportunities to obtain education and training. Like welfare reform, it is designed to be an efficient policy that employs mechanisms meant to ensure that only "cost-effective" programs are used and that participants are accountable for their actions. Putting people to work without first providing any education or assistance certainly reduces both the amount of time they are served and the money spent on them. Time-limiting and restricting access to services cuts the number of people on the rolls. Finally, both welfare and WIA policies embrace work-first as a quick solution to a "broken" system, one where AFDC encourages "dependency" and JTPA lacks "market-responsiveness."

In many ways WIA's embrace of the work-first philosophy illustrates the power of the work-first idea. Its influence expanded far beyond welfare reform and into the massive federal job training programs that were, at least in theory, designed to fuel the nation's economy as it expands and changes. As we have demonstrated in this chapter, this idea grew slowly, developing over time and sinking its tentacles into American politics. It has its roots in struggles over race and class, in debates about the poor and the meritorious, the worthy and those to be pitied. Thus, it is deeply entrenched in today's political ideology and rhetoric and affect policymaking beyond the seemingly narrow scope in which it was conceived. In the next chapter, we examine how this idea has affected a parallel movement to increase college access for the general population. Challenging the very notion of "college for all," work-first has effectively closed more doors to higher education than it has opened.

CHAPTER THREE

WELFARE REFORM AND ACCESS TO POSTSECONDARY EDUCATION: NATIONAL TRENDS

WHEN EXAMINED within a broader context of beliefs about higher education and its role in American society, it is quite remarkable that federal welfare reform so clearly discourages access to college. Postsecondary education leads to a wide array of individual and collective benefits, both monetary and non-monetary. Scholars have found that postsecondary education is linked to higher levels of happiness and satisfaction in an array of life factors such as family, home, job, and community (Astin et al. 1997). Postsecondary education is also related to increased levels of citizen involvement, particularly with regard to voting and volunteerism (Putnam 2000). Increased college access for minorities has resulted in the gradual creation of a black middle class (Hochschild 1995, 43), and recent court decisions regarding access to selective institutions of higher education put in sharp relief the value placed upon college attendance among the general populace (Bowen and Bok 1998).

The evidence regarding the relationship between education and employment and income outcomes is even more clear-cut. Those with more education are more likely to be employed, and to earn more when they are employed. Recent data supporting this conclusion are presented in table 3.1. Those without a high school diploma are much more likely to be unemployed than those with more education. Of women who had not completed high school in 2004, 8.5 percent were unemployed, compared with 5.0 percent of high school degree recipients. Those with some college, even if they had not completed a degree, fared better, as did those with an associate's degree. Needless to say, those with a bachelor's degree were the least likely to be

Table 3.1   Unemployment Rate and Earnings by Educational Level

Educational Level	Unemployment Rate in 2004	Median Annual Earnings in 2003
No high school diploma	8.5	$22,939
High school graduate or equivalent	5.0	$30,766
Some college, no degree	4.5	$35,714
Associate's degree	3.7	$37,605
Bachelor's degree	3.0	$49,889

Source: U.S. Census Bureau, Bureau of Labor Statistics.

unemployed (their unemployment rate was 3.0 percent). The same pattern holds for earnings. Associate's degree recipients earned more in 2003 ($37,605) than did those with some college but no degree ($35,714), who in turn earned more than those with a high school diploma ($30,766), while those without a high school degree earned the least ($22,939). In comparison, the median earnings for bachelor's degree recipients in 2003 were $49,889.

Scholars seek to refine these statistics by attempting to correct for the possibility that those with the most education might have earned more even in the absence of additional schooling, perhaps because they are more ambitious, are quicker learners, or have stronger connections to the employment sector. The clear conclusion of research in this area is that statistical adjustments to the raw figures presented in table 3.1 reduce but do not eliminate the employment and earnings benefits of additional schooling (see, for example, Grubb 1997; Kane and Rouse 1995; Levy and Murnane 1992; Mayer and Peterson 1999).[1] In short, postsecondary education has a real and concrete impact on quality of life in terms of happiness, employment, and income; and traditional postsecondary education leading to certificates or degrees is particularly valuable.

Notwithstanding empirical evidence about the relationship between education and earnings, the 1996 Personal Responsibility and Work Opportunity Reconciliation Act (PRWORA), otherwise known as welfare reform, explicitly shifted federal welfare policy toward a work-first philosophy (Gais et al. 2001; Greenberg, Strawn, and Plimpton 2000; Weaver 2000). This shift, as we will demonstrate with both quantitative and qualitative evidence, curtailed access to postsecondary education in several ways. First, the policy is explicitly designed to reduce the size of the welfare caseload—to move individuals as quickly as possible from welfare receipt to work, which often does not lift them out of poverty. In reducing the caseloads, welfare reform has reduced the raw number of individuals who receive access to postsecondary education as welfare recipients. This is important, since welfare receipt provides a set of supports and benefits critical to the health and well-being of a poor woman's family. Moreover, a greatly reduced number of welfare recipients enrolled in college provides little incentive for community colleges to devote resources to meet the unique needs of those few recipients. Second, welfare reform imposes a set of work requirements and other policies that make it difficult for those remaining on welfare to pursue postsecondary education. Third, those who do receive access to postsecondary education are increasingly enrolled part-time in short-term non-degree-granting programs, rather than the degree-oriented postsecondary education that dominated prior to welfare reform.

In this chapter we explain how the work-first idea is built into welfare-reform policy, and how the law produced mechanisms and incentives that structure access to education and training for recipients. We also discuss why devolution functions as a key mechanism of welfare reform, and how state policies can vary from federal policy with regard to educational access as a result of devolution. Finally, we carefully examine the impact of the shift from Aid to Families with Dependent Children (AFDC) to PRWORA as it affects access to postsecondary education for welfare recipients, first using existing quantitative studies and then presenting new descriptive and inferential analyses based on three national data bases.

WORK-FIRST MECHANISMS OF WELFARE REFORM

Temporary Assistance for Needy Families (TANF) does not expressly forbid states from allowing welfare recipients to pursue postsecondary education. Instead it lays out a number of rules and incentives that strongly discourage states from enrolling recipients in two- and four-year colleges, and in degree-granting programs in particular (Greenberg, Strawn, and Plimpton 2000). Under TANF, states receive a block grant designed to provide temporary cash assistance and support to help families move into the workforce quickly. TANF required states, by 2002, to have 50 percent of all families on cash assistance participate in thirty hours a week of work activity or face fiscal penalties. Although, according to the federal rules, "vocational educational training" can count toward work requirements, it can only count for up to twelve months, and for no more than 30 percent of the caseload. All recipients are also required to "engage in work" within twenty-four months of receiving cash assistance (Golonka and Matus-Grossman 2001). In short, TANF sends a clear signal to states that workforce attachment is the guiding principle of the new welfare law, with caseload reductions as the ultimate measure of state and local policy success (Gais et al. 2001).

As discussed briefly in chapter 1, welfare reform was part and parcel of a broader federal movement to decentralize the development and implementation of large social programs. Devolution affected the development and implementation of welfare policy in concrete and far-reaching ways. The federal government continues to provide guidelines to states such as those noted above, but the ways in which states achieve the goals and adhere to the requirements of the federal government can vary significantly. Despite its clear work-first message, the 1996 federal welfare law gave states significant discretion to support and even promote postsecondary-education access for low-income adults. For instance, states have latitude in defining the activities that can count toward work participation and activity requirements. If a recipient participates in a minimum of twenty hours of work, the remainder of his or her work requirements can be filled through "job skills training related directly to employment" (Golonka and Matus-Grossman 2001, 7). These federal rules govern how states count their overall participation rates, but states are free to set different rules for individual recipients (Greenberg, Strawn, and Plimpton 2000). For example, in Pennsylvania if a recipient is unsuccessful at obtaining a job she can be referred to education and training, at which point she can count education as filling her work requirement for up to twenty-four months. However, the average recipient of an associate's degree is enrolled in school for thirty-four months before earning that "two-year" degree, largely because two-thirds of community college students attend primarily on a part-time basis and many have significant family responsibilities (Berkner, Horn, and Clune 2000; Hoachlander, Sikora, and Horn 2003, 31).

To date, states have had little trouble meeting their required overall work participation rates even when they allow activities that do not count under federal rules. States are also required to spend their own Maintenance of Effort, or MOE, funds on welfare programs, and these monies are not subject to the restrictions attached to federal TANF dollars. States can, and many do, allow these funds to provide support for welfare recipients who wish to pursue education or training of some type.

As a result of the discretion accorded to states under welfare reform, state policies regarding access to postsecondary education for welfare recipients vary widely. Table 3.2, which has been reproduced from a report published by the Center for Law and Social Policy (2002), illustrates that variation. As of 2002, twenty-nine states and the District of Columbia allowed participation in postsecondary degree programs to count toward work requirements for longer than twelve months. Fourteen of these states allow participation in postsecondary education to completely meet work requirements.[2] Five of these states sometimes allow participation in postsecondary education to fulfill the work requirement, but may require that it be combined with other work activities.[3] In eleven states, college enrollment can fully or partially meet work requirements, but only for up to twelve months. In four states, postsecondary degree programs cannot count toward meeting state work requirements, save the 30 percent of the caseload allowed to participate in vocational education (Center for Law and Social Policy 2002).[4] Clearly, states have taken advantage of the autonomy afforded to them via devolution to craft welfare policies that vary significantly in terms of access to postsecondary education.

CREATING ADDITIONAL BARRIERS

Yet it is not enough simply to examine those aspects of welfare policy that explicitly address access to postsecondary education. Welfare reform touches many aspects of recipients' lives, and the ability to attend college is determined to a large degree by factors that fall outside the realm of education.

Issues of access and equity in postsecondary education intersect very clearly with gender in the realm of welfare reform. This becomes visible when we examine the demographics of welfare recipients. Welfare reform is clearly a gendered piece of social policy: women make up the vast majority of the nation's welfare recipients, 96.4 percent of the caseload. Moreover, nearly all of them have children, and most of these children (72 percent) are under school age. Eighty-five percent of welfare recipients are single parents, 41 percent have not obtained a high school diploma, and another 36 percent ended their formal education with a high school diploma or a General Equivalency Diploma (GED) (Urban Institute 2002). Clearly, welfare recipients are an extremely vulnerable population, and their ability to obtain or retain living-wage employment is complicated not only by their lack of formal education but also by other defining aspects of their lives such as their marital status and their parenting responsibilities.

This constellation of factors that define most welfare recipients requires us to look more closely at welfare reform, and identify which aspects of policy erect barriers to college that extend beyond those aspects that directly curtail the pursuit of higher education. None of the following elements of welfare reform can be defined as educational policy in the strictest sense, yet they have particular import when analyzed within the context of a poor single mother's life. Four elements of welfare policy in particular can affect the decision of a welfare recipient to attend college:

Time limits. Nearly all states have adopted a five-years or less lifetime limit for citizens to receive welfare benefits (Greenberg, Strawn, and Plimpton 1999). These limits have very clear implications for how a woman receiving welfare benefits decides to spend her time. Time limits have the potential to discourage welfare recipients from pursuing post-secondary education, since in most instances states do not stop the time clock while a recipient attends college or obtains training. Thus, even in states that allow women to attend college while receiving welfare, a woman must engage in a gamble of sorts: Should she let the time clock tick as she pursues education, or should she stop the clock by obtaining

Table 3.2   Education Allowance and Time Limits for Welfare
             Recipients, by State

Education Allowance			
Allowed as a Stand-Alone Activity	Allowed in Combination with Work	Not an Authorized Work Activity	Policy Set by County
Alaska	Alabama	Connecticut	Colorado
Florida	Arizona	Idaho	Montana
Georgia	Arkansas	Mississippi	New York
Illinois	California	Oklahoma	Ohio
Iowa	Delaware	Oregon	
Kentucky	District of Columbia	South Dakota	
Maine	Hawaii	Washington	
Minnesota	Indiana	Wisconsin	
Nevada	Kansas		
Pennsylvania	Louisiana		
Rhode Island	Maryland		
Utah	Massachusetts		
Vermont	Michigan		
Wyoming	Missouri		
	Nebraska		
	New Hampshire		
	New Jersey		
	New Mexico		
	North Carolina		
	North Dakota		
	South Carolina		
	Tennessee		
	Texas		
	Virginia		
	West Virginia		

Time Limit		
Twelve Months	Twelve to Forty-Eight Months	No Time Limit
Alaska	California	Alabama
Arizona	Illinois	Arkansas
Florida	Iowa	Colorado
Indiana	Kentucky	Delaware
Kansas	Maine	Georgia
Louisiana	Maryland	Hawaii

Table 3.2   (*continued*)

Twelve Months	Twelve to Forty-Eight Months	No Time Limit
Michigan	Minnesota	Massachusetts
Nevada	Missouri	Montana
New Mexico	Nebraska	New Jersey
North Dakota	New Hampshire	Ohio
Texas	North Carolina	Tennessee
	Pennsylvania	West Virginia
	Rhode Island	Wyoming
	South Carolina	
	Utah	
	Vermont	
	Virginia	

Source: Compiled by the State Policy and Documentation Project, July 2000.
Note: These classifications are based on formal state-level policies.

full-time employment and exiting welfare as soon as she can, so that she can "bank" time in case she needs to utilize welfare again in the future?

Rules on exemptions for new parents. As of 2003, federal law permits but does not require states to exempt single parents from work requirements while caring for an infant up to one year old. According to the Urban Institute, half of the states have taken this option; four have enacted more generous approaches; and fourteen states impose even harsher restrictions on parents with infants, such as imposing a twelve-month lifetime limit on exemption from work requirements. Moreover, the infant child-care exemption does not stop the clock on the five-year lifetime limit on TANF (Finegold and Weil 2002). If a woman with a young child is required to spend considerable time away from her infant due to work requirements, then she is less likely to extend her absence by attending college. Moreover, even if a woman has been exempted from work requirements during the first year of her baby's life, the fact that the lifetime limit time clock is still running during that year makes it less likely that she will take additional time to pursue postsecondary education.

Monetary benefits. Monthly welfare benefits are quite small; in 2001, the average monthly benefit per recipient was $137, a slight decline (in constant dollars) from 1996, when it was $152. The decline in benefits for families was greater—in 1996, the monthly benefit per family (not reduced by child support) was $410 (in 2001 dollars); in 2001, it was $351 (U.S. Department of Health and Human Services 2003). Yet when compared with AFDC, under welfare reform a relatively generous amount of income is allowed to enter the household before welfare benefits begin to be reduced. Since it is quite unlikely that welfare benefits alone will provide adequate financial resources for a family, there is a strong incentive for recipients to pursue additional work (Edin and Lein 1997). And of course, working additional hours is more lucrative in the short term than is education or training. Thus, because welfare benefits generally are not sufficient to provide adequate housing and care, women who decide to pursue postsecondary education instead of working are doing so at great economic sacrifice.

Child care. There is no guarantee of adequate child care for the children of welfare recipients. Prior to welfare reform, welfare recipients were entitled to child care as specified by the Family Support Act of 1988. However, PRWORA fundamentally changed program eligibility for child-care assistance by eliminating the child-care entitlement for families receiving welfare or transitioning off welfare. In its place, Congress created the Child Care Development Fund (CCDF), which consolidated into a separate funding stream a variety of programs that provided child-care subsidies to low-income families. The CCDF allows states considerable flexibility in deciding how much families are required to contribute toward child-care expenses, how long they remain eligible for assistance, how much to reimburse providers, and which populations receive priority for subsidies. As a result, states have greater flexibility in allocating child-care funds across both the welfare and non-welfare populations (U.S. Government Accountability Office 1998).[5]

The lack of high-quality affordable child care is perhaps the most significant barrier to the pursuit of either postsecondary education or employment for poor women with young children. According to the Center for Law and Social Policy (CLASP), individuals with child-care needs are among the most difficult to move off of the welfare rolls (Mezey 2004).[6] The prevalence of jobs that require work at night and on weekends makes the task of obtaining child care that much more difficult. Harriet Presser (2003) has documented the fact that Americans are increasingly likely to work at night and on weekends as the economy moves toward a 24–7 schedule. She notes that there is little child care available for those who work in the evenings, at night, and on weekends.

Clearly, welfare reform makes it difficult for recipients to utilize education and training to advance their long-term economic interests. In fact, there are multiple barriers to obtaining postsecondary education and training. Many of the barriers to education are explicit regulations regarding the amount and type of education that is available. Another set of barriers is erected by policies that force women to choose between education and other factors that are equally if not more important in her life—income, child care, the risk of complete loss of benefits as lifetime time limits approach. As a piece of formal policy, then, welfare reform contains numerous regulations that would render the pursuit of education difficult for any individual receiving welfare. But these regulations are particularly onerous for the poor women who make up the vast majority of welfare recipients, because they are insensitive at best to the complexities of these women's lives and their multiple roles as mothers, providers, and, at least potentially, students.[7]

QUANTITATIVE EVIDENCE OF THE EFFECTS OF WELFARE REFORM ON ACCESS TO POSTSECONDARY EDUCATION

Clearly, welfare reform had the potential to significantly reduce participation in postsecondary education for welfare recipients. Yet since the passage of PRWORA in 1996 it has been difficult to document in a comprehensive way the effects of this legislation on college enrollment among welfare recipients at a national level. This is due to a number of factors. First, there is no systematic federal-level mechanism through which college enrollment data for welfare recipients is collected; data collection at the state and institutional level is also limited in this regard. Before TANF, the federal government collected data on enrollment in educational and training programs. Among the many changes introduced by TANF was elimination of many reporting requirements, including those pertaining to enrollment in school and training. This change has had the unfortunate result of making it difficult to track the consequences of TANF on access to higher education. But in addition, as a result of the "new federalism" there is so much planned and unplanned variation in policy that a true picture of the effects of welfare reform on college attendance cannot be arrived at easily. Indeed, even when variations in policy are incorporated into quantitative analyses, they do not fully capture the complexity of the effects that these policies have on college attendance.

Despite these difficulties, it is critical to describe and summarize what is known about postsecondary education access and attainment for welfare recipients. To do so, we first present existing analyses of college enrollment under welfare reform. These data present a broad, descriptive picture of enrollment trends pre- and post–welfare reform, and allow us to synthesize what is currently known about how national trends in postsecondary enrollment have shifted in the wake of welfare reform. Next, we present our own analyses of four large national databases—the Current Population Survey, the National Household Educational Surveys, the Survey of Income and Program Participation, and the National Postsecondary Student Aid Survey. These analyses allow us to develop a more finely honed portrait of the effects of welfare reform on postsecondary enrollment and attainment. Specifically, we address the question of whether reductions in postsecondary enrollment among welfare recipients are due merely to the reduction of the overall number of welfare recipients; whether enrollment varies significantly in states due to variations in their policies regarding access to postsecondary education; and whether the type of postsecondary education that is accessible to welfare recipients has shifted under welfare reform.

ACCESS TO POSTSECONDARY EDUCATION: PRE- AND POST-TANF

In the decade or so prior to the 1996 welfare reform legislation, college attendance among welfare recipients (and indeed, among the rest of the population) was increasing. Figure 3.1 indicates that the number of recipients engaged in higher education through the Employment and Training Program under AFDC, rose steadily during the early 1990s, reaching a peak in 1994. In fact, the number of recipients enrolled in college tripled from 1989 to 1993, yet there was no corresponding increase in welfare-enrollment rates. But by the mid-1990s AFDC was already constricting access, as several large states were granted waivers to experiment with work-first approaches to welfare and other ways to restrict caseloads and access to education and training (for example, Wisconsin, Florida, and California). Therefore, our intent is not to contrast TANF to an idealized version of experiences under AFDC. Rather, we are comparing the early years of TANF to the last years of AFDC, recognizing that AFDC was not a static system but itself was experiencing significant changes during the 1990s. One can only speculate on what opportunities for AFDC recipients might have become, had the trends during the early 1990s been allowed to continue.

The available federal program enrollment data, which pertain to the late 1990s, suggest that nationally about 136,000 welfare recipients were enrolled in some form of postsecondary education through the JOBS program in 1995. In contrast, post-PRWORA data for fiscal year 1997 indicate that only 54,000 recipients were engaged in any type of activity that could include postsecondary education. This was a decline of 82,000 people, almost a two-thirds reduction, in the enrollment of welfare recipients in higher education following implementation of welfare reform.[8]

Only a few studies of national survey data have examined the college enrollment of welfare recipients before and after the adoption of TANF.

Janice Peterson, Xue Song, and Avis Jones-DeWeever (2002), using data from the Survey of Income and Program Participation, found that the proportion of low-income single parents with some college education declined from 24 percent to 17 percent after the implementation of TANF, particu-

Figure 3.1   Welfare-Recipient Participation in Postsecondary Education, 1989 to 1997

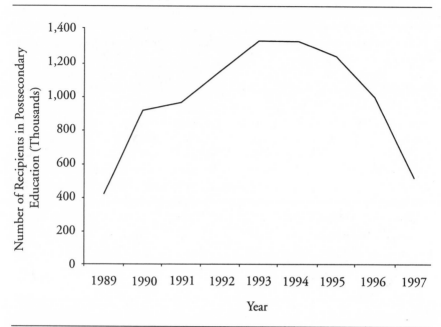

Source: AFDC Microdata, available at: http://afdc.urban.org.

larly among welfare recipients. This finding suggests that the most-educated welfare recipients were the most likely to leave the welfare rolls, but the authors also maintain that it is consistent with the fact that welfare recipients have limited access to higher education.

The National Urban League's multivariate analysis of data from the 1997 and 1999 waves of the Urban Institute's National Survey of American Families found a decline in college enrollment of welfare recipients (Cox and Spriggs 2002). When comparing welfare recipients pre– and post–welfare reform, the analysts found that although welfare recipients were 13 percent more likely than other poor women to attend college before welfare reform, they were 7 percent less likely to attend college than were other poor women after welfare reform. An examination of the effects of variation in state policies revealed that they "account for 13 percent of the drop in the probability that welfare recipients would enroll in college relative to other poor women after the implementation of TANF" (15).

Marya Sosulski's (2004) analysis of data on 686 poor women in the Illinois Families Study focused only on women on welfare post-TANF, but even without a pre-TANF comparison her data provide some interesting insights into predictors of college enrollment in this population. Women who had worked for more than 25 percent of their lives were significantly less likely to be enrolled in college, as were women who had been on welfare for more than five years. However, whether or not a poor woman was actually receiving TANF at the time of the survey did not influence the odds of her being enrolled.

Another source of information about college enrollment trends are statistics drawn from financial aid applications. Between the academic years 1996 to 1997 and 1998 to 1999, the number of applicants for Title IV student aid who reported receiving AFDC or TANF benefits fell from 580,000 to 359,000, a 38 percent decline. In the same time frame, the overall number of student aid applicants increased from 9.3 million to 9.6 million (Friedman 1999). This is not a perfect indicator of enrollment, since not all those who enroll apply for aid and not all those who applied for aid enrolled.[9] Nonetheless, the trend line for this indicator is down, and its slope is remarkably steep. We further explore this issue later in original analyses of the 1996 and 2000 National Postsecondary Student Aid Surveys (NPSAS), which allow us to consider in what type of programs students are enrolled.

A NATIONAL ANALYSIS

Despite the lack of uniformity, the data just discussed consistently suggest that PRWORA has resulted in significant reductions in the number of welfare recipients enrolled in postsecondary education. To achieve a more nuanced and accurate understanding of college-going activities among welfare recipients, we conducted a series of original analyses utilizing several different existing databases. These analyses were designed to determine the degree to which welfare reform affects access to college, the amount of time spent in college, the type of college courses available to welfare recipients, and the likelihood of enrolling full-time rather than part-time. We also examined whether welfare recipients in states with more generous policies are more likely to enroll in higher education than are recipients who live in states with more restrictive policies. Our analyses utilized several national data sets:

> *Current Population Survey (CPS)* The CPS is a large and consistent data source created by the U.S. Department of Labor that can be used to track enrollment trends. It includes basic demographic information such as age, parental and marital status, and family income. Our sample includes slightly less than 9,000 respondents in 1995 and slightly less than 8,000 respondents in 2000. By comparing enrollments in 1995 and 2000, we can ascertain what the impact of TANF has been on enrollments. The CPS also allowed us to examine the enrollment pat-

terns of all young single mothers in addition to welfare recipients. Finally, the CPS samples are large enough to allow examination of variation across states. The October CPS series has more detailed information on schooling patterns but unfortunately does not include information on family receipt of government programs. The March CPS data have more information on earnings and program receipt but less detail on schooling. Another important limitation of the March CPS data is that the school-enrollment question is only asked of respondents aged twenty-four and younger. Although this group of young welfare recipients is an important one, and includes the age group most likely to seek higher education, we sought additional data to examine enrollment trends across a wider age spectrum.

National Household Educational Surveys (NHES)   The National Household Educational Surveys were designed and administered by the National Center for Education Statistics, a division of the U.S. Department of Education, to track enrollment patterns for adult learners as well as for traditional-aged college students. The NHES was administered in 1995 and 1999 and thus provides enrollment data pre- and post-TANF. Slightly less than 11,000 respondents were surveyed in 1995 and slightly less than 4,000 were surveyed in 1999. Unfortunately, the public-access data that we analyzed do not indicate state of residence, and thus we were not able to examine the impact of state-by-state variation in access to higher education. In addition, the NHES data do not include a direct measure of parental status and thus are not ideal for examining the enrollment patterns of single mothers.[10] Nonetheless, we examined these data to corroborate the results of the CPS and see whether the patterns differ among those older than twenty-four.

Survey of Income and Program Participation (SIPP)   The SIPP data sets, created by the U.S. Census Bureau, are large and nationally representative surveys not directly focused on educational issues, and thus are similar to those collected in the CPS survey in many ways. SIPP collects more detailed information about the receipt of public assistance from various sources, and collects more detailed data on sources of respondents' incomes. For our purposes, the two main advantages of this database are that SIPP distinguishes full-time and part-time enrollment, and the SIPP data include information on enrollment of those over age twenty-four. SIPP is a panel data set, which means that the same individuals are followed over time. We focused on the first year of the panel, or group of individuals, that started in 1996 and the first year of the panel that started in 2001 to avoid any complications associated with sample attrition. In all, 40,155 households were sampled in 1996, and 36,700 were sampled in 2001, which provided data on more than

96,000 individuals aged fifteen and over in 1996 and over 91,000 individuals in 2001.

National Postsecondary Student Aid Survey (NPSAS) The National Postsecondary Student Aid Survey conducted by the National Center for Education Statistics collects detailed data on the financial aid status of college students. Since the NPSAS data only include individuals enrolled in school, we examined the proportion of college students who receive welfare and also drew on more detailed data on the changing program composition. Specifically, we analyzed data from the 1996 and 2000 NPSAS. These are two large surveys of students enrolled in college, with more than 30,000 respondents in 1996 and more than 40,000 respondents in 2000 (National Center for Education Statistics 1997, 2002b).

Our analysis proceeded as follows. In order to address the question of whether the rate of postsecondary enrollment among welfare recipients has declined, we began by comparing the enrollment rates of welfare recipients and nonrecipients before welfare reform (1995) and after welfare reform (2000) using the CPS data, and using 1996 and 2001 data from SIPP. We then conducted a multivariate regression analysis to assess the impact of welfare and other factors on enrollment. Since enrollment is a discrete (0, 1) outcome, we estimated logistic regression models.[11] We conducted the analyses separately for the pre- and post-welfare years and test for statistically significant changes between the years. We then replicated the CPS analyses using the NHES data set in order to provide additional data to support our conclusions, and because the NHES covers a wider age-span of respondents. The analysis was repeated a third time using SIPP. Finally, we drew on NPSAS data to glean more information about the nature, rather than the overall volume, of enrollments.

FINDINGS FROM THE CURRENT POPULATION SURVEY (CPS)

Individual-level factors contained in the analyses include age (broken into the following categories: sixteen to eighteen, nineteen to twenty, twenty-one to twenty-two, and twenty-three to twenty-four, with nineteen to twenty serving as the reference category in the regression analysis); marital and parental status (single mothers, married mothers, married women without children, and single women without children, which was the reference category); and race and ethnicity (dummy variables for African American and Hispanic, with non-Hispanic white as the reference category).

We also examined the impact of state-level policy variables on enrollment rates. We obtained a state-level measure of the dollar level of financial support for welfare recipients from data compiled by Robert Moffitt, a Johns Hopkins University economist and long-time student of poverty programs (2006). We used the real-benefit sum, which represents the maximum amount paid per month for a family of four. This total benefit is the sum of AFDC or TANF, Food Stamp Program, and Medicaid payments. In the regression analysis, we used the log of the benefit level, a standard statistical transformation used when income is included in multivariate models.[12]

We also constructed several variables to characterize state policies regarding access to higher education for welfare recipients. The first set of measures characterizes the formal state policy regarding access to postsecondary education for welfare recipients. As noted above, in some states education is not an approved work activity; in other states, education is allowed when combined with some work; in still others, education is approved as a stand-alone work activity. We consequently constructed one dummy variable for the states where education may be combined with work and another for those where education is approved as a stand-alone activity. States where education is not an approved work activity stand as the reference category. We also included a dummy variable indicating that the policy is set at the county level for states with their own decentralized policies.

A second variable was constructed for the time limits on education. States where education is an approved work activity have leeway in setting the amount of time for which education may substitute for or complement paid work. Some states allow welfare recipients to participate in postsecondary education for twelve months, while other states have a longer defined time limit (these generally range from eighteen to thirty-six months). Still other states, used as the reference category in our analyses, do not place a limit on the length of time during which education may fulfill the work requirement. Table 3.2 displays the classification of states for these two variables, which are from the State Policy Documentation Project, conducted by CLASP. We drew on the report issued in July 2000, which listed state policies as of October 1999.[13]

In table 3.3, we compare the enrollment patterns of female welfare recipients with non-welfare recipients. Welfare recipients who had graduated from high school were far less likely to be enrolled in postsecondary education than were other young women. In 2000, less than one-fifth (18.37 percent) of welfare recipients were enrolled in postsecondary education, compared with more than two-fifths (45.70 percent) of other women. These self-reports yield somewhat higher rates of enrollment than do official statistics, but this tendency to overreport should not affect the analysis of the trends over time in enrollment.

The enrollment rate of welfare recipients was roughly stable during this period: 20.68 percent were enrolled in postsecondary education in 1995, and

Table 3.3   Percentage of Young Female High School Graduates Enrolled in Postsecondary Education, by Year, Age, and Welfare Receipt

	Welfare Recipients		Welfare Nonrecipients	
	1995	2000	1995	2000
Age	Percentage Enrolled		Percentage Enrolled	
Sixteen to eighteen	68.21	51.84	57.32	61.78
Nineteen to twenty	17.32	19.1	56.14	60.13
Twenty-one to twenty-two	23.35	14.33	45.11	42.86
Twenty-three to twenty-four	17.89	16.41	23.14	21.24
Total (sixteen to twenty-four)	20.68	18.37	43.44	45.7

Source: U.S. Census Bureau, March 1995 and March 2000 *Current Population Survey* (Annual Demographic Survey).
Note: Statistics for welfare recipients aged 16 to 18 in both 1995 and 2000 are based on very small N's because few students in this age range have both graduated from high school and become welfare recipients.

18.37 percent were enrolled in 2000. (This change is not statistically significant in the CPS data, but the NHES data presented here do reveal a statistically significant decline in enrollment among welfare recipients.) We are not suggesting that welfare receipt per se reduces enrollment: surely there are many factors involved. Our principal concern is the trend over time, namely, whether the chances of pursuing higher education are lower after the adoption of TANF than before. We are also interested in examining whether enrollment is lower in states with more restrictive rules regarding access to higher education.

Table 3.4 presents regression analyses of enrollment using the 1995 and 2000 CPS data. These figures represent the results of logistic regression models that estimate the odds of enrollment from individual-level and state-level measures. For both years, we examine the impact of a variety of demographic attributes on enrollment and one policy variable—the log of total welfare benefits—that varies between states. In 2000, we add two more policy indicators that vary between states to assess the impact of interstate variation in TANF policies on enrollment. In both years, welfare recipients are less likely to be enrolled than are other young women. The size of the negative coefficient on receipt increases during this interval, but for the CPS data, this change is not statistically significant.

The regression analyses presented in table 3.4 also include several important policy indicators that vary across states. First, the level of financial support provided to welfare recipients per se does not appear to be related to en-

Table 3.4   Weighted Logistic Regression of Young Female High School Graduates College Enrollment, 1995 to 2000

	1995	Odds Ratio	2000	Odds Ratio	2000	Odds Ratio
Intercept	1.106 (1.487)		0.505 (1.576)		0.854 (1.843)	
Welfare receipt	−0.474** (0.167)	0.622	−0.562* (0.243)	0.570	−0.556* (0.243)	0.573
Log of total benefits	−0.087 (0.219)	0.917	0.040 (0.233)	1.041	−0.073 (0.270)	0.929
Age						
Sixteen to eighteen	0.006 (0.120)	1.006	0.080 (0.122)	1.084	0.082 (0.123)	1.086
Nineteen to twenty (reference)						
Twenty-one to twenty-two	−0.248** (0.079)	0.781	−0.514** (0.083)	0.598	−0.523** (0.084)	0.592
Twenty-three to twenty-four	−0.992** (0.089)	0.371	−1.348** (0.102)	0.260	−1.351** (0.102)	0.259
Single mother	−0.867** (0.116)	0.420	−1.178** (0.115)	0.308	−1.175** (0.115)	0.309
Married mother	−2.037** (0.149)	0.130	−2.128** (0.187)	0.119	−2.129** (0.189)	0.119
Married without children	−1.300** (0.120)	0.273	−1.230** (0.143)	0.292	−1.226** (0.144)	0.294
Single without children (reference)						
African American	−0.316** (0.092)	0.729	−0.415** (0.102)	0.660	−0.440** (0.103)	0.644
Hispanic	−0.259* (0.110)	0.772	−0.638** (0.118)	0.528	−0.675** (0.121)	0.509
White (reference)						

(*Table continues on p. 54*)

Table 3.4   (*continued*)

	1995	Odds Ratio	2000	Odds Ratio	2000	Odds Ratio
Two-year education allowance						
Not authorized (reference)						
With some work					0.496**	1.642
					(0.161)	
As a stand-alone					0.342*	1.408
					(0.174)	
Set by county					0.422*	1.525
					(0.163)	
Education time limits						
None (reference)						
Twelve months					−0.133	0.875
					(0.119)	
Thirteen to forty-eight months					0.115	1.112
					(0.113)	
R-squared	0.124		0.150		0.154	

Source: U.S. Census Bureau, 1995 and 2000 *Current Population Surveys* (March Annual Demographic Files).
*p < .05; **p < .01

rollment rates, either in 1995 or in 2000. However, policy measures more directly tied to enrollment opportunities do have a significant impact. Specifically, we examined whether postsecondary enrollment is not an authorized activity for welfare recipients (the reference category). As stated earlier, in some states, enrollment is an authorized activity when it is combined with some work, while in other states it is approved as a stand-alone activity. Finally, in some states—Colorado is one—the policy regarding authorization is set at the county level.

The results indicate that states that allow postsecondary enrollment as an approved work activity for welfare recipients have higher enrollment rates than states that do not allow enrollment. However, the data do not indicate that states allowing education as a stand-alone activity had higher enrollment than those requiring education combined with work.[14]

The data on time limits did not produce a statistically significant effect. In other words, states with longer time limits on enrollment did not exhibit higher enrollments than states with shorter time limits. These data suggest that the characterization of education as an allowable activity is more important in influencing college-going than the dollar amount of welfare receipt or the presence of enrollment time limits on the enrollment of welfare recipients in higher education. An alternative interpretation is that the time limits, imposed in 1999, had not yet had an impact on enrollment patterns in 2000.

Another important finding in table 3.4 is that the penalty of being a single mother on enrollment increased to a statistically significant extent during this period of time. Between 1995 and 2000, the odds that a single mother would be enrolled in college declined: in 1995, the odds of enrollment for single mothers were 42 percent of those for single women without children. By 2000, they were only 31 percent. In other words, these data indicate that young single mothers, some of whom might have been welfare recipients in the absence of policy changes that significantly reduced welfare rolls, are falling behind other women in accessing postsecondary education.

But married mothers are even less likely to be enrolled than are single mothers. Being married reduces the chances of women's enrollment relative to being single, even in the absence of children, but when combined with children, the effect of being married is intensified. Margaret Marini (1978) and Jay Teachman and Karen Polonko (1988) reported that being married has an inhibiting effect on enrollment, which indicates that the positive effects of added financial resources stemming from marriage are not sufficient to counterbalance the negative effects of additional role responsibilities. This effect may be accentuated among the younger groups (younger than age twenty-five) included in the CPS sample (Jacobs and King 2002).

A number of other notable findings are evident in table 3.4. African American and Hispanic women are less likely to be enrolled than their white counterparts, and this is particularly true following welfare reform, suggesting a disproportionate impact of the policy on minorities (for more on this issue, see Goldrick-Rab and Shaw 2005). The evidence also indicates that enrollment declines with age. Both of these effects are consistent with those of previous studies (see, for example, Jacobs and King 2002). It should be noted that these race and ethnicity "effects" may be a proxy for unmeasured variables, such as grades, test scores, and school quality.

ANALYSIS OF THE NATIONAL HOUSEHOLD EDUCATIONAL SURVEYS (NHES)

We repeated the demographic analysis using the 1995 and 1999 surveys. These results, shown in table 3.5, show a negative effect of welfare receipt on enrollment in 1999 but not in 1995. This finding is consistent with the expectation that the gap in enrollment between welfare recipients and other women has grown since the enactment of TANF in 1996. The odds ratio indicates that the odds of enrollment among welfare recipients were about three-quarters those of nonrecipients in 2000.

Table 3.5   Weighted Logistic Regression of College Enrollment, for
             Female High School Graduates, All Ages, 1995 and 1999

	1995	Odds Ratio	1999	Odds Ratio
Intercept	0.251**		0.365	
	(0.093)		(0.210)	
Welfare receipt	0.136	1.145	−1.315**	0.269
	(0.204)		(0.475)	
Age				
Under twenty	0.510**	1.665	0.037	1.037
	(0.171)		(0.261)	
Twenty to twenty-four (reference)				
Twenty-five to twenty-nine	−0.988**	0.372	−1.365**	0.255
	(0.133)		(0.268)	
Thirty to thirty-nine	−1.675**	0.187	−1.642**	0.194
	(0.123)		(0.216)	
Over forty	−3.196**	0.041	−3.240**	0.039
	(0.134)			
Single mother	0.372**	0.689	0.021	1.021
	(0.143)		(0.227)	
Married mother	−1.215**	0.297	−0.905**	0.405
	(0.131)		(0.238)	
Married without children	−0.577**	0.561	−0.822**	0.440
	(0.124)		(0.288)	
Single without children (reference)				
African American	−0.257*	0.774	−0.110	0.896
	(0.128)		(0.210)	
Hispanic	−0.295	0.745	−0.776**	0.460
	(0.165)		(0.290)	
White (reference)				
R-squared	0.253		0.268	

Source: 1995 and 1999 NHES data. See National Center for Education Statistics, 1996, 2001, for information on these surveys.
*p < .05; **p < .01

The NHES results indicate that enrollment declines with age, as would be expected. The findings also support the CPS finding that marriage inhibits enrollment for women, even when the marital role is not combined with the parental role. Married mothers are less likely to be enrolled than married women without children, and both are less likely to be enrolled than single childless women.

Several other results in the NHES data are not consistent with the CPS findings. The negative effect of being a single mother declined between 1995 and 1999 in the NHES data; the trend was sharply in the opposite direction for the CPS data. We place greater trust in the CPS findings on this particular point because the measure of parental status is not as precise in the NHES data.[15] There was no effect of being African American on enrollment for the NHES data in 2000 (there was a negative effect in 1995), but using the CPS data we found a consistently negative effect in both years. These inconsistencies remind us of the idiosyncrasies of survey findings and the need to bring as many different sources of data together as possible to support a particular conclusion. We repeated this NHES analysis for those younger than twenty-five and found the same patterns as those reported in table 3.4. In other words, the differences between the CPS and NHES results are not due to the restricted age group included in the CPS sample.[16]

FINDINGS FROM THE SURVEY OF INCOME AND PROGRAM PARTICIPATION (SIPP)

As noted above, the SIPP data have a large sample, and allow us to build on the CPS data in two ways: by distinguishing between part-time and full-time enrollment and by covering the full age range of enrollees. As we will see, the full-time distinction turns out to be an important one in revealing the nature of the recent trends.

Table 3.6 displays rates of postsecondary enrollment of welfare recipients for 1996 and 2001 based on SIPP data. We restricted the sample to those who have completed high school or an equivalent, so that it is clear that any enrollment will represent attendance at a postsecondary institution. Among those receiving welfare, the results show a decline in postsecondary enrollment from 21.0 percent in 1996 to 13.5 percent in 2001. The data further reveal that the declines were concentrated among those attending full-time. The full-time enrollment of welfare recipients declined by half, from 15.5 percent in 1996 to 7.2 percent in 2001. Part-time enrollment increased slightly, from 5.6 percent to 6.3 percent in 2001, but this change was too small to offset the declines in full-time enrollment.

Table 3.7 presents the results of regression results using the SIPP data for 1996 and 2001.

In 1996, the receipt of welfare had a positive effect on postsecondary enrollment; by 2001, it had a negative effect on enrollment. This finding is consistent with the NHES result that suggests that welfare reform reduced not only the number of welfare recipients attending college but also the chances of college attendance of those who remained on welfare.

The analysis also confirms the impact of policy variation on enrollment rates. Enrollment rates were higher in states with more inclusive policies re-

Table 3.6   Percentage of Female High School Graduates Enrolled in
Postsecondary Education, by Full-Time and Part-Time Status

	Total Students	Total Enrolled		Full-Time		Part-Time	
		N	Percentage	N	Percentage	N	Percentage
			1996				
Total high school grads	3,517	756	21.5***	560	15.92***	196	5.57***
White	1,987	437	22.00***	329	16.54***	109	5.46***
Black	1,378	283	20.57**	202	14.71***	81	5.86***
With children under eighteen	2,582	581	22.52***	437	16.95***	144	5.57***
Under twenty-five	932	336	36.03***	279	29.88***	57	6.15***
Over twenty-five	2,585	420	16.26***	282	10.89***	139	5.37***
			2001				
Total high school grads	2,109	295	14.00	152	7.20	143	6.80
White	1,357	167	12.32	100	7.38	67	4.94
Black	631	112	17.70	47	7.45	65	10.24
With children under eighteen	1,375	214	15.59	111	8.09	103	7.49
Under twenty-five	432	120	27.67	55	12.75	64	14.92
Over twenty-five	1,677	176	10.48	97	5.77	79	4.71

Source: 1996 and 2001 SIPP data.
*** p < .01; **p < .05

garding the college enrollment of welfare recipients. We collapsed the measures of state-level policy into a single dummy variable. As is consistent with the CPS findings reported in table 3.4, we were unable to statistically distinguish among the types of educational rules. In other words, states that did not authorize education as a work activity had lower enrollment rates than did other states, but we were not able to discern the impact of different types of education-friendly rules—which were most favorable. The educational time limits (results not shown) also did not end up being statistically significant, perhaps because in 2001 the time limits had not yet been reached.

We also examined the impact of other welfare-related state policies. We found that states with higher payments to welfare recipients had higher college enrollments, as did those states with a larger percentage of the population on the welfare rolls. Thus, welfare-specific policies affect enrollment rates even when other aspects of the state-level policy environment are taken into

Table 3.7   Weighted Logistic Regression of Female High School Graduate College Enrollment, 1996 and 2001

	Model 1		Model 1		Model 2	
	1996	Odds Ratio	2001	Odds Ratio	2001	Odds Ratio
Intercept	3.535** (.107)		3.238** (.080)		3.223** (.080)	
Welfare receipt	.174** (.045)	1.190	−0.234** (0.069)	.791	−.237** (0.069)	.789
Age	−.230** (.004)	.795	−.219** (.004)	.803	−.219** (.004)	.803
Age squared (× 10)	.017** (.001)	1.020	.015** .001	1.015	.015** .001	1.015
Children under eighteen at home	−.136** (.010)	.873	−.190** (.011)	.827	−.190** (.011)	.827
African American	.002 (.029)	1.001	.169** (.030)	1.184	.174** (.030)	1.190
Log of total benefits (1,000*)	.643** (.075)	1.902	0.659** (0.080)	1.932	.690** (0.080)	1.994
Welfare enrollment rate	.124** .070	1.132	.353** (.073)	1.423	.262** (.078)	1.300
Education as authorized work activity					.079** (.023)	.789
Pseudo R-squared	0.211		.232		0.232	

Source: 1996 and 2001 SIPP data.
*p < .05; **p < .01; **p < .001

account. The data are consistent with the view that national policy changes, as well as differences in approaches between the states, have a significant impact on the level of postsecondary enrollment of welfare recipients.

Several other coefficients in table 3.7 are of interest. Enrollment in postsecondary education declines with age, as one would expect. Women with children under eighteen are less likely to enroll than other women. However, there are several less-expected results. In 2001, African American women became more likely to enroll in college, all else being equal, than in 1996. This finding is part of a broader trend toward greater educational investments on the part of African American women.

ANALYSIS OF THE NATIONAL POSTSECONDARY STUDENT AID SURVEY (NPSAS)

One important limitation of the analyses we have presented thus far is that they did not allow us to identify the type of program in which students are enrolled. Interviews conducted with state-level welfare officials, community college leaders, welfare rights advocates, and others have indicated that welfare reform has increasingly shifted recipients toward shorter-term noncredit programs and away from curricula that lead to a degree (see chapter 4 for a more extended discussion of this point). To explore this issue further, we analyzed data on college students in 1996 and 2000 drawn from the NPSAS. As table 3.8 shows, in 1996 slightly less than 1 percent (0.9 percent) of students enrolled as undergraduates reported having received some financial support from welfare during the past year; by 2000 this fraction had declined to 0.6 percent. This one-third decline is very much in line with the data indicating a decline in financial aid applications noted earlier. Both of these sources suggest a more modest decline than that indicated by our calculations based on the Job Opportunities and Basic Skills data discussed previously.

The NPSAS data also allowed us to consider the type of program students are enrolled in. Between 1996 and 2000 there was a sharp increase in enrollment in short-term certificate programs. In 1996, 27.5 percent of welfare recipients were enrolled in certificate programs; by 2000, this figure had jumped to 43 percent of welfare recipients enrolled in postsecondary education. This change occurred despite no overall change in the incidence of enrollment in certificate programs. (In 2000, 12.1 percent of all postsecondary enrollment was in certificate programs versus 12.2 percent in 1996.)

This growth in enrollment in certificate programs was matched by a decline in the enrollment of welfare recipients in both associate's degree programs (a 7.0 percent decline) and bachelor's degree programs (a 6.7 percent decline). By 2000, welfare recipients were markedly overrepresented in certificate programs (welfare recipients were 3.6 times more likely to be enrolled in these programs than were other students); slightly overrepresented in associate's degree programs (1.06 times as likely to be enrolled); and markedly underrepresented in bachelor's degree programs (only 0.34 times as likely to be enrolled). The NPSAS data thus confirm what we have found in interviewing state welfare and community college officials: that TANF has not only reduced access to higher education but also shifted enrollment to short-term certificate programs and away from associate's degree and bachelor's degree programs. This trend is consistent with other studies that suggest a growing

Table 3.8   Female College and Certificate-Program Enrollment, by
             Welfare-Receipt Status

	1996	2000
Percentage of students receiving welfare	0.9	0.6
Percentage of these enrolled in certificate programs		
Who are welfare recipients	27.5	43.0
Who are nonrecipients	12.2	12.1

Source: National Postsecondary Student Aid Survey (NPSAS). National Center for Education Statistics (1996, 2001).

concentration of students with limited resources in the lower echelons of postsecondary education (Institute for Higher Education Policy 2003).

DRAWING CONCLUSIONS FROM THE QUANTITATIVE EVIDENCE

Our analysis of national quantitative data provides an unusually comprehensive investigation of existing evidence regarding the effects that welfare reform has had on access to postsecondary education. As we stated at the beginning of this chapter, welfare reform eliminated many of the reporting requirements that existed under AFDC; therefore, no single consistent source of postsecondary enrollment trends pre– and post–welfare reform exists. Although none of the four national databases that we analyzed are perfect, when taken together they provide us with a picture of important shifts in the amount and quality of education that is available to welfare recipients in the wake of welfare reform.

All of the data presented in this chapter indicate a decline in the number of welfare recipients attending institutions of higher learning in the United States in the period after the enactment of TANF. The number of welfare recipients enrolled in postsecondary education peaked two years before the enactment of welfare reform in 1996; but, as figure 3.1 indicated, the number dropped sharply after 1996. Other published analyses support this general finding. Much of this decline is due to the decline in the size of the welfare population, indicating that one aspect of welfare reform's work-first approach—namely, a reduction in the size of the welfare population—has successfully reduced the number of individuals accessing postsecondary education via welfare.

Has the rate of enrollment of those on welfare declined as well? The data on this point are not entirely consistent, but most of our analyses point to declines in enrollment rates, especially among those enrolled full-time and those in degree-granting programs. Analyses of one of the most powerful databases, SIPP, show large and consistent declines in enrollment rates over time. These results are broadly consistent with those of the Urban Institute study (Cox and Spriggs 2002) and the other available analyses of survey data (Peterson, Song, and Jones-DeWeever 2002). JOBS data also suggest that the decline in college enrollment exceeded the rate of decline in the welfare population, and the AFDC and NPSAS data indicate a decline as well, although smaller than that indicated by the JOBS and SIPP data.

The CPS data yield less clear results. According to our analysis of this database, the odds of welfare recipients younger than twenty-five being enrolled declined between 1995 and 2000, but this decline was not statistically significant. The NHES data, in contrast, do indicate a statistically significant decline in the enrollment of all ages of welfare recipients between 1995 and 1999.

Analyses of multiple and varied national databases would not be expected to display absolute consistency. Differences in sample size and type, variables, and time periods would naturally lead to some variation, and a comparison of our analyses of the four databases confirms this. However, when taken as a whole, our analyses clearly suggest that the rate of postsecondary education attendance has decreased in a moderate but significant way since the enactment of welfare reform, despite the fact that enrollment rates prior to welfare reform were never very high. Thus, we have reasonable evidence to suggest that the work-first philosophy guiding welfare reform functions to reduce the rate of college-going among the much smaller pool of welfare recipients that remain.

The NPSAS data make it clear that the enrollment of welfare recipients also shifted markedly from degree-based programs to short-term certificate programs. Welfare recipients are now substantially overrepresented among students in certificate programs. At the same time, their traditional overrepresentation in associate's degree programs is eroding, and their underrepresentation in bachelor's degree programs is growing. These findings are ominous, given recent research reviewed in chapter 1 which shows that short-term non-degree-granting education and training is less effective for lifting the poor out of poverty than more traditional postsecondary education. But they are not surprising, given that there are clear restrictions on both the amount of time an individual can receive welfare and the amount of time she is allowed to pursue postsecondary education and training. These findings confirm the recent analyses of administrative data in North Carolina and Missouri, which show that the median duration of postsecondary education among enrolled welfare recipients is about twenty weeks in Missouri, and only about fourteen in North Carolina (Dyke et al. 2005).

Not surprisingly, our data also indicate that those who do pursue postsecondary education after welfare reform are much more likely to enroll part-time rather than full-time. Analyses of SIPP data showed that the full-time enrollment of welfare recipients declined by half, while part-time enrollment increased. Part-time enrollment has been shown repeatedly in national analyses to increase the risk of dropping out and to decrease the chances of completing college (Hoachlander, Sikora, and Horn 2003; Horn and Berger 2004).

Finally, as we have seen, TANF is a decentralized system that allows for states to design their own systems, within certain restrictive constraints imposed by the federal government. Do formal differences in policies between states actually translate into differences in enrollments? Both the CPS and SIPP data provide support for the conclusion that state policies matter. States with the most restrictive policies regarding welfare recipients had lower enrollment rates than states with more expansive options. The data suggest that it is not time limits per se or the level of welfare funding that is most relevant, but rather policies regarding whether access to higher education is allowed as a stand-alone activity, is allowed combined with work, or is not allowed.

As illustrative as these data are, they provide only a partial picture of welfare reform and its effects on access to postsecondary education. Using a national lens, we know that welfare reform has reduced the number of individuals who access postsecondary education via welfare; we also know that the rates of postsecondary attendance have dropped in the wake of welfare reform. The quality of postsecondary education that is available has shifted as well, away from degree-granting programs toward short-term nondegree training. And increasingly, welfare recipients must attend college part-time rather than full-time.

Yet our quantitative analyses also suggest that access varies to some degree according to state-level policy. This finding raises an important set of questions: How powerful is the work-first message as the implementation of welfare reform rolls out across states? Where, how and why do formal policy and policy implementation diverge? What are the policy levers that affect the degree to which states reflect a work-first philosophy? Our analyses of state-level quantitative and case-study data in the next chapter clearly show that we must look more closely at how welfare reform is implemented "on the ground" in a variety of states to more fully understand the meaning and impact of welfare reform in a variety of contexts.

CHAPTER FOUR

THE IMPLEMENTATION OF WELFARE REFORM: CONSISTENCY AND CHANGE

THE MOVE to "end welfare as we know it" was an action formally initiated by the federal government and signed by President Bill Clinton over the objections of his two chief advisers, Mary Jo Bane and David Ellwood.[1] This new approach toward serving America's poor was intended to be enacted across the fifty states in a "devolved" yet consistent manner. And in fact, as we have discussed in previous chapters, we have observed some real differences in the ways that states have developed their formal policies regarding access to post-secondary education and training under welfare reform. While most states clearly embraced the work-first emphasis, at least on paper, other states attempted to retain at least some elements of the human-capital philosophy in their welfare policies. We specifically chose our sample of six states to reflect this variation.

Despite the variations, in practice welfare implementation in our six states looks strikingly similar. While some differences in educational participation do exist across states, there is less than the state-level variation in formal policy would predict. In other words, although states had some official leeway in how they implemented welfare reform, the overriding "work-first" message was clear—the poor would benefit the most from going straight to work, and all state policies should effectively send them there. In theory, "devolution" left many implementation decisions up to the states—seemingly opening the door to real differences in implementation outcomes—but in reality the work-first message was powerful and unambiguous, and as a result policy outcomes were far less diverse than differences in formal policy would suggest.

The distinction between variation in formal policy and variation in implementation is an important one, and is central to our analysis of how the work-first rhetoric operates at many levels to restrict approaches to poverty alleviation. In chapter 3 we presented analyses indicating that differences in formal state policies with regard to whether education is treated as a formal work activity resulted in variation in the proportion of welfare recipients in education across states. However, formal policy is rarely neatly translated into practice, and actual practices may be more similar than formal policies suggest. During the often messy process of implementation, state and local actors have the opportunity to exert their own influence on policy enactment, and thus on policy outcomes. As Stephen Maynard-Moody (2003) notes, in many ways, "a policy does not meaningfully exist until enacted; the act of interpreting and delivering the policy is the authoritative act that gives the policy validity and efficacy" (7). Therefore, a detailed understanding of how the formal work-first policy was interpreted, translated, and constructed by the policy actors themselves is essential to an assessment of how and why this policy has almost consistently narrowed access to postsecondary education for significant numbers of low-income women.

As described earlier, we undertook such an in-depth examination in six states—Florida, Illinois, Massachusetts, Pennsylvania, Rhode Island, and Washington. These case studies yielded both quantitative data on welfare caseloads and participation in college, as well as dozens of interview transcripts from conversations with state and local officials, caseworkers, college administrators, welfare program operators, and recipients themselves. By speaking with so many actors who were executing (and in some cases challenging) welfare policy at various levels of the implementation process, we were able to trace the rhetoric of the work-first idea and follow it as it was put into practice.

In this chapter we first use state-level official data to illustrate shifts in caseload size, and the overall number and rates of welfare recipients participating in postsecondary education and training. These data suggest that variation in access did occur, but the variation was quite modest. The overall number of participants in postsecondary education dropped precipitously in all six states, and the rates of participation were quite low in all of the states we studied.

We next use our interviews and other case-study data to further explore how the goals of work-first were so consistently achieved. Our analysis suggests that the work-first idea operates on two distinct levels: the policy-development level, and the policy-implementation level. We examine the interplay between them in case studies of two states, Washington and Illinois. These states provide an important contrast regarding the role that the work-first idea has played in welfare-reform implementation. Whereas Washington reflects a more consistently work-first approach in formal policy and policy implementation, the Illinois case illustrates how the work-first idea dominates welfare-reform implementation *despite* a state-level policy that includes several human-capital elements. In the end, the combination of our quantitative data indicating significantly less variation in postsecondary access than might have been anticipated under devolution, together with our qualitative data explaining the ways in which implementation processes actually converged rather than diverged in practice, illustrates the power of this new narrative in poverty policy.

The work-first ideology was especially powerful at the local level, even affecting the work of community colleges—the postsecondary institutions most closely connected to low-income communities. Thus we conclude the chapter with a discussion of the way in which implementation of welfare reform in our six states resulted in specific programmatic efforts at community colleges designed to preserve access to college for low-income adults. Many of these efforts failed, in spite of what formal policy allowed for, and we discuss the reasons why.

TRACKING ACCESS ACROSS SIX STATES

In an effort to assess the impact of welfare reform on postsecondary enrollment we contacted individuals at the appropriate state departments (usually human services or education) to obtain data on the number of welfare recipients enrolled in college before and after the passage of welfare reform.[2] This step was necessary because, as mentioned earlier, states are not required to report enrollment in postsecondary education to the federal government, since it does not fulfill the work requirement under the federal guidelines. However many states do collect data on the number of Temporary Assistance for Needy Families (TANF) recipients taking college course work, for a variety of reasons. In some cases (for example, Florida) the state offers some tuition assistance to current or former recipients enrolled in college. In other states (for example, Illinois) formal state policy allows recipients enrolled in specific college programs to be exempt from the work requirement or the time clock, or both. And even in states that do not allow much access to postsecondary education at all (for example, Massachusetts), the state continued to collect data on postsecondary enrollment under TANF because it did so for the AFDC-era JOBS program.

In order to examine the impact of TANF on welfare-recipient college enrollment, we requested that each state provide us with the number of AFDC recipients enrolled in a two- or four-year degree- or certificate-granting programs in 1995 or 1996 (whichever was available), representing the last years of AFDC, and similar numbers for TANF recipients in 2001 or 2002 (whichever was available), and then in 2003, 2004, or 2005 (again, whichever they could provide). In order to calculate a percentage enrolled, we also obtained a relevant denominator—usually the number of adults receiving welfare who were available to work.[3]

These data are not without flaws. First and foremost, states only record the postsecondary enrollment of recipients who make their caseworkers aware that they are enrolled. Depending on the state rules, recipients may be more or less likely to do that. For example, in states such as Florida, where recipients can receive tuition assistance, they may be likely to report enrollment, whereas in states such as Massachusetts and Pennsylvania, where no postsecondary education can be used to meet the work requirement, a recipient has little reason, or may even have a disincentive, to report enrollment, especially when not required to. Recent studies in California and Illinois indicate that recipients often enroll in college prior to notifying their caseworker (Jones-DeWeever 2005; Sosulski 2004). Thus, for the most part we can expect our numbers to be somewhat conservative estimates of enrollment. However, since recipients were also not required to report enrollment under AFDC, except through the JOBS program, we have reason to suspect that those numbers are also somewhat underreported (though possibly to a somewhat lesser extent). Therefore, our numbers in both cases may be underestimates of actual enrollment, but the change over time is likely a good reflection of the actual trend.[4]

It should also be noted that the official caseload data do not show the proportion of adults that are truly college-eligible by virtue of having completed a high school or GED degree. (We were able to restrict the analysis to the college-eligible in the analyses presented in chapter 3.) This means that the caseload data include high school dropouts who are not immediately eligible for college entrance. As a result, the enrollment rates calculated from caseload data will not match those calculated from national survey data presented in chapter 3. In particular, the former will be lower than the latter because a significant group with no immediate chance of attending college is included in the analysis. It also means that year-by-year and state-by-state comparisons will be imprecise, since there may be variation in the proportion eligible to enroll in college.

In analyzing this data we argue that it is helpful to focus on both raw numbers (how many recipients are in college) and percentages (what percent of recipients currently in the caseload are in college). Work-first affects college access in two ways—first, by promoting work above education, and second, by reducing the number of people receiving welfare. The former is hypothesized to affect the percentage enrolled in education, the latter to affect the number enrolled in education. Both, we contend, are very important indicators of college access. If a state has shifted to providing work instead of education to a greater proportion of recipients, that is noteworthy. But if they have instead concentrated on simply getting everyone off of welfare entirely that is also significant, since it means that fewer poor women have access to the supplementary income and benefits which they and their children might use to survive while the mother is enrolled in college. Analyses in chapter 3 revealed that poor women are especially unlikely to attend college at all—this is probably because college is not only expensive, but time-consuming. The likelihood that a poor woman has the luxury of attending college while also earning a living wage and raising children is quite low. Thus, by moving more poor women off of welfare, we argue that states effectively reduce their chances for attending college—at least in the short term.

REDUCING ACCESS TO COLLEGE

Six years after welfare reform was passed, there was a 67 percent decline in the number of adults receiving cash assistance (U.S. Department of Health and Human Services, Administration for Children and Families, Office of Planning 2002). Data collected from the six states in our study reflect this trend and provide additional detail of the scope of the reduction in caseloads. As table 4.1 shows, the reduction in monthly adult caseloads between 1996 and 2002 varied from a low of 37 percent in Rhode Island to a high of 85 percent in Florida and Illinois. The number of people affected by this reduction is in some cases quite striking—for example, the Illinois caseload dropped from nearly 200,000 adults to just under 30,000. In these six states alone, welfare reform reduced the caseloads by over a half million people (544,087).

Rates of participation provide a more equivocal picture. Data indicate that half of our states enroll a smaller percentage of welfare recipients in postsecondary education under welfare reform than they did prior to welfare reform. As table 4.2 and figure 4.1 show, even prior to welfare reform the percentage of recipients who were enrolled in postsecondary education was not high; none of our six states enrolled more than 10 percent of welfare recipients in postsecondary education. Yet after welfare reform was enacted, in three states these percentages dropped to even lower levels, with no state enrolling more than 7 percent of recipients, and several states enrolling under 5 percent. In Pennsylvania, less than 1 percent of TANF adults were enrolled in postsecondary education in the 2003-to-2004 academic year. In addition, there are some important trends in the three states where the percent of recipients in college is higher under TANF in recent years than it was under the last years of AFDC. In Illinois and Massachusetts, that percentage declined initially following implementation, and then several years later rebounded to a somewhat higher level than before, whereas in Florida, the percentage increased initially, and then declined. We do not want to make too much out of these changes since the percentages are so small to begin with, but we do think these trends are notable because they may represent fluctuation in the influence of the work-first idea—a hypothesis we discuss in more detail later in this chapter.

The raw numbers of recipients enrolled declined virtually uniformly across the six states (with the exception of Massachusetts). As figure 4.2 indicates, whereas many of our states had 6,000 to 8,000 recipients in college programs prior to welfare reform, following reform those numbers decreased to 2,000

Table 4.1   Trends in Welfare Adult Caseload Reduction from AFDC to TANF, by Monthly Averages

	AFDC, FY 1996, Number of Participants	TANF, FY 2002, Number of Participants	Caseload Change, from 1996 to 2002	
			Number of Participants	Percentage
U.S. Total	3,973,334	1,315,029	−2,658,305	−67
Florida	165,764	24,614	−141,150	−85
Illinois	199,805	29,486	−170,319	−85
Massachusetts	84,021	31,001	−53,020	−63
Pennsylvania	175,631	56,783	−118,848	−68
Rhode Island	19,376	12,138	−7,238	−37
Washington	96,935	43,423	−53,512	−55

Source: U.S Department of Health and Human Services, Administration for Children and Families, TANF Sixth Annual Report to Congress, "Proportion of Children and Adults in State AFDC/TANF Caseloads Fiscal Years 1996 and 2002," available at: http://www.acf.hhs.gov/programs/ofa/annualreport6/chapter01/0103chartdata.htm.

to 4,000. Pennsylvania's enrollment in two- and four-year degree-granting programs fell by 94 percent, Illinois by nearly 90 percent, and Rhode Island and Washington by over 70 percent. Most strikingly, between 5,500 and 7,000 fewer welfare recipients were in college in Pennsylvania and Washington after TANF, compared to under AFDC. In states where the percentage of welfare recipients who were furthering their education went up over time, the actual number of recipients often declined, because the overall caseload was reduced. For example, after TANF Florida increased the percentage of recipients in college from the AFDC figure, but meanwhile the number of recipients in college was cut in half.

In Massachusetts there was a different trend. Following the passage of welfare reform the number of welfare recipients enrolled in college dropped immediately, from just over 2,500 to just over 700, but then increased to a level higher than pre–welfare reform: 2,759. We attribute this change first and foremost to changes in both the caseload and the rate of participation in higher education. Much of the caseload in Massachusetts was exempted from work requirements early on during welfare reform, but as fewer exemptions were made, and as the state went through an economic recession, the caseload grew substantially between 2001 and 2004.[5] More recipients on the rolls meant more recipients eligible to be enrolled in college. At the same time, however, the post-reform caseload (2004) never exceeded the pre-reform caseload (1996), and yet the number in college was higher during the later time. This we attribute to shifts in the work-first philosophy driven by polit-

Table 4.2   Welfare-Recipient Enrollment in Postsecondary Education
Under: AFDC and TANF, by State

| State | Data Type[a] | Total Adults | AFDC, FY 1996 | | | TANF, FY 2001 | |
			Number in Postsecondary Education[b]	Percentage in Postsecondary Education	Adults	Number in Postsecondary Education[c]	Percentage in Postsecondary Education
Florida	Annual	383,016	8,361	2.18	109,417	3,044	2.78
Illinois	Monthly	199,805	8,674	4.34	39,739	1,204	3.03
Massachusetts	Monthly	84,021	2,558	3.04	28,864	703	2.44
Pennsylvania	Annual	196,417	6,714	3.42	63,093	377	0.60
Rhode Island	Annual	16,557	561	3.39	14,341	479	3.34
Washington[c]	Monthly	96,935	7,624	7.87	43,795	1,974	4.51

Source: Compiled by authors from data reported by states.

Note: Postsecondary education means two- or four-year degree-granting programs only.

[a] Florida, Pennsylvania, and Rhode Island are yearly public-service-employment totals, divided by yearly adult total caseload (states provided denominator). Other states are a monthly average in public-service employment divided by a monthly average adult caseload.

[b] FY 1996 for Illinois, Pennsylvania; fall 1995 for Washington; and May 1997 for Rhode Island.

[c] FY 2001 (July 2000 to June 2001) except for Massachusetts (January 2001) and Washington (fall 2000).

ical change and activism, which we discuss later. Massachusetts, then, serves as a prime example of the importance of examining multiple contributors to college access—the number eligible to participate, the rate of participation, and the actual number participating.

LESSONS FROM THE QUANTITATIVE EVIDENCE

The national-level quantitative data on postsecondary participation rates among welfare recipients and other poor women presented in chapter 3 indicate a significant drop in the rate of college-going among welfare recipients, and a more drastic drop in the number of individuals obtaining access to postsecondary education via welfare. The national data also suggest that variation in state policy had an effect on the degree to which welfare recipients received access to postsecondary education. However, looking more closely at access rates among our six states suggests that there was, in fact, only modest variation around a very low average, and caseloads dropped precipitously in all six of our states. The rate of participation dropped in half our states, or rose slightly, hovering around a low rate of enrollment that did not exceed 7

Table 4.2   (*continued*)

	TANF, Most Recent		Overall Caseload Change		Overall PSE Change	
Adults	Number in Post-secondary Education[d]	Percentage in Post-secondary Education	Number	Percent	Number	Percent
166,531	4,251	2.55	−273,599	−56.52	−4,110	−49.16
15,736	882	5.60	−160,066	−92.12	−7,792	−89.83
47,845	2,759	5.77	−55,157	−43.06	201	7.86
54,933	390	0.71	−133,324	−72.03	−6,324	−94.19
8,924	140	1.57	−2,216	−46.10	−421	−75.04
41,441	2,044	4.93	−53,140	−57.25	−5,580	−73.19

[d] Fall 2003 findings for Florida; July 2003 to June 2004 for Illinois; January 2005 for Massachusetts; February 2005 for Rhode Island; and fall 2003 for Washington.
[e] Note that in Washington, public-service employment is reported by the college system rather than by the Department of Human Services. Welfare recipients may attend college in all states without DHS knowing about it, which means that in the other states, these are likely underestimates. For example, of the 3,071 TANF public-service employment known to the college system in 2001 in Washington, 1,957 were known to DHS. We do not know analogous figures for AFDC clients in Washington.

percent. How are we to interpret these data? To address this question, we next draw on qualitative data from our case studies across our six states to examine two central mechanisms through which the work-first idea has exerted its considerable influence on welfare reform: formal policy formation, and policy implementation.

WELFARE REFORM "ON THE GROUND"

The work-first idea functioned at two separate levels in the wake of welfare reform. In the policy formation process, high-level policymakers sent powerful ideological signals indicating its ascendancy and institutionalized it through a set of incentives and laws that narrowed the range of action possible, reinforcing its dominance. The degree to which this occurred varies by state, but our analyses suggest that no state was left untouched by the power of the work-first rhetoric in the formation of state-level welfare-reform policy. At the implementation level, the work-first idea has perhaps an even more tenacious hold, as caseworkers appear to consistently embrace its message—most often in accordance to state-level policy, but sometimes in defiance of it as well.

In the next section we present two case studies that illustrate the interplay

Figure 4.1   Percentage of Welfare Recipients Enrolled in Postsecondary
              Education Under AFDC and TANF

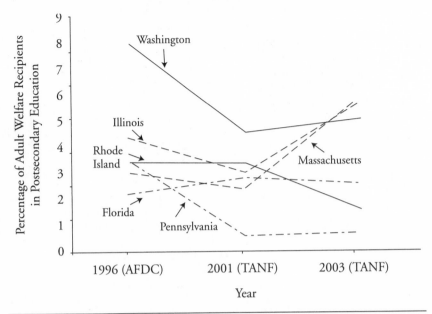

Sources: Caseload data—U.S. Department of Health and Human Services, Administration for Children and Families, *TANF 5th Annual Report to Congress*, "Proportion of Children and Adults in State AFDC/TANF Caseloads Fiscal Years 1996 and 2001," available at: http://www.acf.hhs.gov/programs/ofa/annualreport5/0203chartdata.htm#2001 (provided by state officials in Florida, Pennsylvania, and Rhode Island). Postsecondary enrollment data— provided by state officials directly to the authors.

between state-level policy and policy implementation. The two states we chose to highlight, Washington and Illinois, provide contrasting examples of how the work-first idea has come to dominate welfare reform. As we noted in chapter 1, Washington is included in our sample because its formal policy reflects a consistent work-first orientation. Not surprisingly, the implementation process has also been decidedly work-first, and has resulted in consistent declines in college access among welfare recipients. This case study provides us with a clear example of what happens when a state consistently adopts welfare policy and implementation practices that reduce access to postsecondary education.

In contrast, Illinois was included in our sample of states because it was a "high-access" state—that is, it enacted welfare-reform policy that contained several human-capital elements that preserved at least the possibility of college access for some welfare recipients. The college-going rate among welfare

Figure 4.2   Number of Welfare Recipients Enrolled in Postsecondary
              Education Under AFDC and TANF

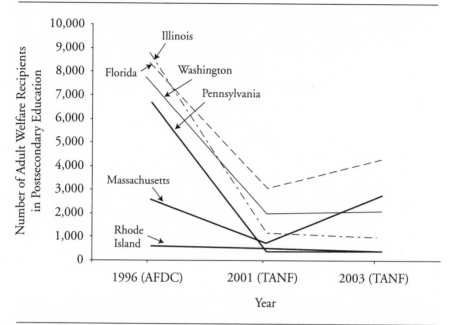

Sources: Caseload data—U.S. Department of Health and Human Services, Administration for Children and Families, *TANF 5th Annual Report to Congress*, "Proportion of Children and Adults in State AFDC/TANF Caseloads Fiscal Years 1996 and 2001," available at http://www.acf.hhs.gov/programs/ofa/annualreport5/0203chartdata.htm#2001 (provided by state officials in Florida, Pennsylvania, and Rhode Island). Postsecondary enrollment data—provided by state officials directly to the authors.
Data for "2003" is actually for the most recent year for which the state could provide data, ranging from 2003 to 2005; see notes to table 4.2.

recipients actually increased to some degree, after a slight drop early in the policy's implementation; but caseworker resistance to human-capital ideas has proved to be a consistent barrier to higher levels of college access. As a result, we see very little distinction in the end result of welfare reform in both states, despite clear differences in formal policy.

WASHINGTON: A CONSISTENTLY WORK-FIRST STATE

Washington's initial response to federal welfare-reform policy was decidedly work-first in orientation. Legislation for the state's WorkFirst program was passed by a Republican legislature and signed by Governor Gary Locke, a Democrat, in April 1997. It followed federal law in mandating a five-year lifetime limit on welfare benefits and requiring work as a condition of public assistance. There is near unanimous consensus that the initial law was "fairly narrow in terms of . . . work-first" and attempted to move away from previous welfare-to-work efforts in the state that focused greater attention on human-capital building and skill development. As one respondent put it, the governor's advisers "concluded that they had to put the labor market test first . . . that it had to be work-first. And they wanted to send that message very aggressively everywhere. To clients, income maintenance workers, social workers, CSOs, advocates and legislators, this is where we're going to go."[6]

The state was remarkably successful in communicating this message. To ensure implementation of the new welfare law, the governor created a Work-First subcabinet initially made up of representatives from his office, the Department of Social and Human Services (DSHS), the Employment Security Department, and the Office of Trade and Economic Development to work out the details. The initial implementation followed the tenor of the law. Clients would first go to a DSHS case manager, where they completed an "individual responsibility plan" that included a minimum work requirement of twenty hours per week. Then the client was placed in mandatory job search for up to twelve weeks. Under the initial interpretation of the law, only after twelve weeks of job search could clients enter postsecondary training of some sort. According to one welfare advocate, case managers were discouraged from even mentioning education options because clients would have an incentive to fail at job search if they were aware of alternatives.

The consensus among welfare advocates and others was that the state's new direction on welfare stemmed from the governor's own values and beliefs as well as the need to reduce public assistance caseloads. "I think he [the governor] believes in the work ethic strongly . . . and he believes that, by George, you ought to go to work," noted one advocate. Work First was also influenced by reactions to previous welfare policies in the state, most especially the Family Independence Program (FIP). FIP was an initiative of a former governor, Booth Gardner, that used an aggressive human-capital-building approach to getting clients off of welfare. The consensus among many policymakers in Washington—both Democrats and Republicans—was that FIP was a massive failure which raised caseloads, cost too much money, and created perverse "incentives that make welfare better than a job." This perception was shaped by a "devastating" Urban Institute evaluation of the program. "If you talk to a lot of the governor's advisers, they won't mention FIP necessarily, although they might, from time to time, but they'll say, we tried that in the old days, we tried education and training and it failed," noted one advocate.

Yet within the first few months of Work First there was a push from the governor's office to provide limited education and training opportunities within the framework of the law. How and why this happened is a matter of some dispute in the state. According to a representative from the governor's office, from the beginning his staff recognized that "there was no practical way to expect large numbers of poor families to be able to get ahead unless they were able to build skills." Some advocates recognize that "this may have been the vision" from the start, but that it was buried under the work-first rhetoric. As one advocate put it, "I think he [the governor] really believes in the theory . . . that once people make an effort, that we ought to help them with education and training and child care and so on." However, it is important to note that increased access was limited to short-term training only; degree-granting programs were deemed unnecessary for welfare recipients and were generally not available to welfare recipients.

To develop a means to provide some access to college for welfare recipients, the governor invited the State Board for Community and Technical Colleges (SBCTC) to sit on the subcabinet. Both the college-system office and Department of Social and Health Services (DSHS) were reticent at first, a reflection of the "clear difference in philosophy" between the two agencies regarding education access for welfare clients. Upon being included in our study, the SBCTC conducted some analyses of their data and realized that a significant number of its students—around 9 percent—were current or former welfare recipients. As one advocate tells it, "While colleges and the college system were initially resistant to short-term skills training, they eventually realized that Work First wasn't going away and the only way they could keep their students was to embrace these kinds of programs."

In August of 1997, the subcabinet unveiled a pre-employment training (PET) initiative in collaboration with employers in Seattle and Spokane. The vision of the governor's office and DSHS was that PET would provide short-term training in initial employment skills that would directly lead to employment. Though one senior DSHS staffer admits advocates and a high-tech business community concerned about skills shortages initially raised the training issue, DSHS fully supported the notion, as long as there were "assurances of a job at the end of training." In particular, they saw PET as a way for some of their higher-skilled clients, and former clients, to transition to better-paying jobs.

Under the program, the SBCTC awarded colleges competitive grants to develop twelve-week full-time pre-employment training modules. The DSHS model of a "guaranteed job" morphed into a sectoral strategy of industry-specific training, but this occurred only after much back-and-forth between advocates, employers groups, and the subcabinet. In practice, the local colleges run a "boutique" training operation for employers in key sectors experiencing job growth and skill shortages. Employers make no guarantee to hire PET graduates, which is still a bone of contention for DSHS since some regions have poor placement rates. In 2001, DSHS began to collect systematic data on PET placement rates, with a target goal of 50 percent successful placement (Washington Work First 2001).

PET was the centerpiece of a $30 million allocation to the SBCTC, which also included monies for colleges to redesign programs and services to make it easier for students to access college; provide tuition assistance to employed students; offer workplace and family literacy services; and provide evening and weekend child care for Work First participants attending colleges. Each of these programs was available broadly to low-wage workers who were at or under 175 percent of the poverty level. In the first two years of the program, 18,800 students received Work First training at the state's community colleges, of whom 3,170 were in PET programs specifically (State of Washington Board for Community and Technical Colleges 2001). In the summer of 2000, advocates and the SBCTC successfully lobbied to expand PET from twelve to twenty-two weeks. In 2000, a new "high-wage, high demand" PET program was created that allowed up to one year of education in informational technology.

Yet very few welfare recipients were referred to this program. As the governor's subcabinet and DSHS adjusted its message on education and training, they faced some daunting obstacles at the implementation level, particularly among the local welfare offices. In one sense, this was a predictable consequence of the strong work-first signal initially sent. As one advocate put it:

> They said okay, we have to change the culture of the welfare offices. We have to change this whole system from income maintenance to getting people into jobs. The only way we can do that is to send a very simple message: work-first. . . . [One of] the governor's advisers on Work First, he told me directly . . . he said this department DSHS is capable of doing one thing well, if that. We can't send out multiple messages. . . . We can't say but, you know, they have to go to work, but they also need soft skills or they need ESL, or they might need short-term training. That was not a message they felt they could impart to the field offices and have them carry that out.

This message was reinforced by the legislation itself, which mandates job search for all clients who cannot be placed in immediate employment. Even though DSHS now counts pre-employment training as the equivalent of job search, many case mangers require clients to go through twelve weeks of job search before promoting PET to the client. Taken together, these factors have led to an underutilization of pre-employment training, to the dismay of one senior DSHS staffer:

> Here's where our problem was. When the governor says that clients would take the first available job we knew that we were going to send every able-bodied client to job search. . . . We didn't want to say we will send everybody to job

search where they'll take the first available job, but for a small portion of people, determined by us somehow, we'll divert those folks to pre-employment training. What we thought was more equitable was to go to job search and then from job search every client will have the opportunities to go to pre-employment training. . . . Okay, what's wrong with this picture? When you send people to job search, the ones that are most likely to benefit from pre-employment training in the economy we've had for the last four years are also most likely to get placed in a job and exit. What is the job of the people running job search? It is to get people a job.

This unintended outcome has left PET both under-enrolled and serving a harder-to-serve clientele than was initially envisioned. To address the enrollment problem, DSHS is now keeping data on whether local offices (CSOs) are maximizing their available PET slots. Nevertheless the challenges in promoting education and training at the local offices are daunting. For one thing, case managers still spend around 60 to 75 percent of their time on eligibility determination, despite DSHS efforts to have staff do more client assessment and referrals to PET or other appropriate programs. DSHS staff repeatedly noted that few training opportunities were made available for case managers and there were extreme pressures from offices to reduce caseloads and raise placement rates. Many case managers themselves are not convinced of the merits of education for their clients. One observer expressed shock at the "harsh" treatment of clients by DSHS eligibility workers and case managers.

Barriers to education are also present once clients are sent to job search and the Employment Security Department (ESD) office. Specifically, caseworkers are lukewarm about referring clients to education and training. One job-service specialist at ESD reported that she referred "maybe one client every three months." The same employee noted there seem to be two kinds of case managers at ESD. "A certain group . . . they're of the philosophy that . . . we're not doing people any favors, to be slack on them as far as job search and let the months roll by. . . . They want them to prove they're going to get a job first." The other group of case managers "is more liberal and takes the approach that training is an investment in the future, that if you can upgrade somebody's skills, [and] you can help somebody get a better job . . . its worth the time and risk." Clearly, consensus regarding education and training does not exist among welfare caseworkers, and where resistance exists, it is quite difficult to erode. So difficult to erode, in fact, that access to college has continued to remain quite limited in the state compared to what it was before reform. In 2001 the legislature introduced a bill to stop the clock on time limits for recipients in approved postsecondary programs, but neither DSHS nor the governor's office supported the bill.[7]

The State of Washington provides a clear example of the ways political actors send powerful ideological "signals" about welfare (Gais et al. 2001, 9). These new signals stress the centrality of work to welfare, the personal responsibility of clients, and the time-limited nature of public assistance. In essence, the shorthand term "work-first" has become the guiding principle for state welfare policy and local implementation, and has become institutionalized through law and incentives. In some ways Washington is a victim of its own success. Although its state policy has been adjusted to allow for more access to education and training (albeit to short-term programs), the relative subtlety of this shift has not been embraced or acknowledged by those who implement the policy. As a result, implementation processes have remained steadfastly work-first in practice.

ILLINOIS: THE STRUGGLE TO PRESERVE ACCESS

Of our six states, Illinois appeared the most likely to make college attendance readily available to welfare recipients. Illinois's state-level policy encompasses several elements that are clearly intended to reflect a human-capital approach to welfare reform. Not only does the state allow postsecondary education to count toward the work requirement, but it also allows recipients' welfare time clocks to be stopped while they are attending college, as long as they are in degree-granting programs full-time and are maintaining at least a 2.5 (C+) grade-point average.

Recall from the introductory chapter that the time limits on welfare receipt exert significant pressure on recipients' lives, often affecting their decisions and structuring how they meet the work requirements. From these liberal formal provisions in Illinois, we might expect to see relatively high rates of college attendance among recipients. Moreover, given the rules of the stop-the-clock provision, it would be reasonable to find recipients in longer-term educational programs that are likely to yield higher earnings returns, and to see a relatively high caseload as well, since time limits are in essence suspended for those attending college.

One of these expected outcomes has in fact come to pass—after a period of declining college-enrollment rates shortly after welfare-reform implementation, the college-going rate of welfare recipients has increased slightly, from 4.34 percent in 1996 to 5.6 percent by 2003 (see table 4.2).[8] Yet a 1999-to-2000 survey of over one thousand Illinois welfare recipients, conducted as part of the Illinois Families Study, found that 84 percent of respondents reported that they "wanted to pursue education and training," and 40 percent of those respondents who were also college-eligible (meaning they had finished high school) specified that they would like to go to a two-year or four-year college (Sosulski 2004, 10). It is unlikely that such high demand waned so dramatically over the period of a few years in order to fully explain participation rates of only 4 to 5 percent in 2002 and 2003. Moreover, the Illinois welfare caseload has dropped steadily and precipitously, from nearly 200,000 just prior to welfare reform to less than 16,000 in 2003. Thus, some aspects of the work-first idea have not translated into outcomes and other aspects have. As a result, the profile of Illinois welfare recipients, although somewhat more positive when compared to that of other states, is still less positive than formal state-level policy would suggest. This paradox is rooted in a disconnect between formal "human capital" policy in Illinois and an implementation process that is largely work-first. Using detailed time-series data provided by the Illinois Department of Human Services we illustrate our story with depictions of changes in college access following welfare reform.

Prior to the 1996 federal reform and its attendant move to TANF, Illinois had several education programs for welfare recipients, including a JOBS program known as Project Chance that sent people primarily to adult education classes, and a community college–based case-management program called Opportunities. These programs were funded by the Illinois Department of Public Aid and did not require nor focus on specific, measured outcomes. AFDC recipients were allowed to receive their welfare check and participate or not participate in these programs, as they saw fit.[9] Community colleges were happy to participate in the program, since it increased their enrollment and funding slightly and also fulfilled part of their mission to serve the community by expanding access to higher education.

But Project Chance was reportedly somewhat less popular among welfare administrators. One welfare advocate said:

> The sense was it was almost meandering, there was a sense that people could go and stay for a while and there wasn't any real focus on outcomes. And I think welfare reform was in part a reaction to that type of program in which there was a lot of adult education done and very little of it focused on actual workforce outcomes.

As in Massachusetts, welfare administrators were dissatisfied with the policy that preceded welfare reform because it was seen as too disconnected with workforce participation.

Yet the advocacy community—that is, those people and organizations who worked to create more liberal welfare policy—in Illinois was successful in softening some of the work-first elements of the proposed legislation. When they became aware of the mandatory work requirements of the coming federal welfare reform, they lobbied for the inclusion of education and training as a work activity, and they were partially successful. Illinois has a sixty-month lifetime limit on benefits, but these months do not include time when the recipient is working at least thirty hours per week, the required work participation, but activities permitted to count as "work" include on-the-job training, up to twelve months of vocational education training, job skills training directly related to employment, and up to two years of adult basic education (ABE) or GED classes.

Moreover, as one of his last acts before leaving office, the Democratic governor, Jim Edgar, issued a decree requiring the time clock on benefits to be stopped for up to thirty-six months to allow for participation in postsecondary education. As a result, beginning in January 1999, the five-year clock was stopped for TANF recipients attending "an accredited post-secondary education program full-time" and earning a cumulative GPA of 2.5 or better. The recipient did not have to meet the work requirement in order to participate in postsecondary education.[10] Under this provision, one's clock can be stopped for up to a lifetime maximum of thirty-six months (Peters 1999).[11] This is among the most generous provisions for access to postsecondary education in the fifty states.

One advocate attributed this progressive move in part to the work of those who understood that the state wanted to maximize the federal dollars and worked with officials to develop a way to spend the maintenance-of-effort dollars in a way that would help prevent a return of people to the rolls. "I think DHS realized that they had the money to do some things that would help buffer them against people moving back onto the rolls. And they didn't want to see people moving back onto the rolls," she said. In other words, savvy advocates pitched college access to state officials as a form of insurance; an economically advantageous approach to keeping people off the rolls for much longer while people studied, or even permanently.

But not everyone agreed with this new provision, which seemed designed to allow education and training to occur prior to work. Despite the state's education-friendly legislation, leadership in the Illinois Department of Human Services (which administers TANF through a division currently called "Human Capital Development") fully embraced the work-first philosophy of the federal welfare reform in the early years of implementation. Within this department welfare reform was interpreted as strictly focused on immediate workforce attachment, in spite of the formal change in rules. One advocate reported that the director of the department "was single-mindedly driven by work-first and his whole thing was any job is better than no job, and that's what drove everyone there [at IDHS]." Said another advocate, "Although Illinois kept its plan the same plan on paper, what happened [was] that, essentially, very, very few people were allowed into education and training. . . . The prevailing philosophy was get a job, any job, and get it quick." Recipients got the message. A qualitative study of fifteen Illinois welfare recipients revealed that most had never heard of the "college option" nor had they been given information about it. One woman reported, "They'd rather for you to, uh, get a job than to go to school, you know what I'm sayin'?" (Sosulski 2004, 90).

As a result, the number of TANF adults enrolled in postsecondary educa-

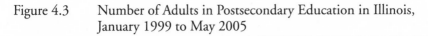

Figure 4.3   Number of Adults in Postsecondary Education in Illinois,
             January 1999 to May 2005

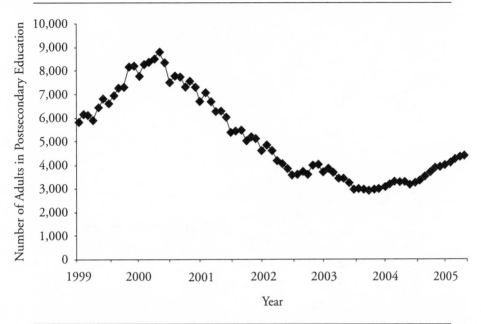

Source: Illinois Department of Human Services Bureau of Research and Analysis, "Employment and Training Numbers."

tion began to decline, albeit unsteadily. Between January 1999 and May 2000
the number of TANF adults attending any form of postsecondary education
rose from just under 6,000 to just under 9,000, but after this there was a
pattern of decline. By October 2003 the number fell to under 3,000, before
rebounding somewhat (see figure 4.3). Thus, the formal stop-the-clock provision failed to move more recipients into college, and perhaps more surprisingly, it actually stopped the clock of relatively few who did go. The percentage of TANF adults in college with their clocks stopped has never exceeded
20 percent (though this figure has increased somewhat over time [see figure
4.4]). In Illinois, liberal policy did not translate into liberal practice.

There are several reasons for these discrepancies. As noted earlier, one of
the most powerful ways in which work-first affects college access is by simply
moving more low-income women off of the welfare rolls. Although we are
not arguing that welfare ought to be the primary mechanism via which low-
income adults should access college, it is important to recognize that poor
women with young children require more than tuition support in order to attend college. By withdrawing their monthly check, health coverage, and often

Figure 4.4   Percentage of TANF Adults in Postsecondary Education
with Clock Stopped in Illinois, January 1999 to May 2005

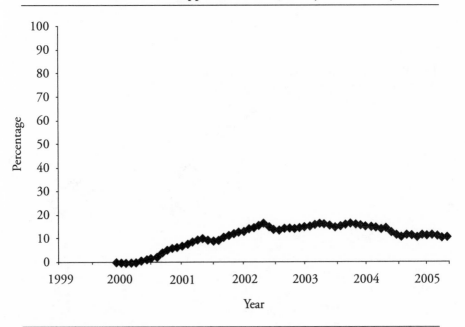

Source: Illinois Department of Human Services Bureau of Research and Analysis, "Employment and Training Numbers."

child-care subsidy, states make it increasingly unlikely that they will have the time to upgrade their skills in postsecondary education. The declining caseloads in Illinois directly contributed to the steep declines in the number of TANF women in college.

A second reason relates to the rules for stopping the clock. As noted earlier, in order for a recipient's aid clock to stop, she must be enrolled full-time in a degree-granting program and must have at least a C+ average (2.5 GPA). These rules raise several problems. First, although recipients are exempted from the work requirement while they attend college in Illinois, they are not exempted from caring for their children, nor are they often provided with child care. Thus, it is quite a struggle for them to enroll full-time in school. In interviews with fifteen Illinois welfare recipients, Marya Sosulski (2004) discovered their complicated attempts to combine school with work—one woman was taking morning courses and then working through the afternoon until 11 p.m. daily; another worked a full-time job and took self-study classes via the Internet. It is worth noting that part-time attendance is increasingly common not only among welfare recipients but among the general college population: two-thirds of community college students nationwide attend primarily part-time (Berkner, Horn, and Clune 2000; U.S. Department of Education 2003).

Second, there are significant social class differences in the academic preparation individuals receive throughout their lives, which results in a cumulative disadvantage among our poorest adults. Over 40 percent of the people who make up the TANF caseload in Illinois lack a high school diploma or GED (Chicago Jobs Council 2003a). This group of women, even those with a high school diploma or GED, are unlikely to be adequately prepared for college-level work, and thus less likely to perform well academically and maintain the requisite GPA during their initial years without significant academic and social support.

Finally, the requirement that recipients be in a degree-granting program in order to stop the welfare time clock disqualifies many recipients from receiving this benefit, because such programs require ABE or a GED or the work-first philosophy pushes recipients into shorter-term vocational training. Thus, it is not surprising to find that among TANF adults in Illinois, the greatest proportion (around 15 percent) are enrolled in non-degree-granting vocational programs and approximately 6 percent are in an ABE and GED programs, whereas less than 3 percent are in degree-granting academic or vocational programs (see figure 4.5). (It is worth noting again that although 40 percent of welfare recipients in Illinois lack a high school diploma, less than 10 percent are in ABE or GED programs.) In other words, taken together, very few welfare recipients in Illinois meet the qualifications to have their clocks stopped while attending college. As a result, barely one-fifth of TANF adults enrolled in college in Illinois take advantage of this provision.[12]

But there is another, more complex, reason that seemingly liberal changes in welfare policy in Illinois did not translate into practice, even after the conservative head of IDHS departed. While there were some small increases in college participation among TANF adults, and shallow increases in the percentage of adults in college with their clocks stopped, overall fewer and fewer low-income women who were welfare recipients were accessing college each year. This reason, we contend, is work-first—the message, the philosophy, and the implementation.

Policies cross multiple administrative levels during the implementation process, and during that process policy messages and ideas are particularly important. Work-first was a powerful message in Illinois, one that often transcended written policy. Work-first was promoted by administrators at the top of Illinois's welfare reform, and that message was clearly heard by the caseworkers meeting daily with clients across the state. The pro-education stop-the-clock provision was reportedly unpopular with some caseworkers and their supervisors, who failed to inform recipients of this new option. One welfare advocate said, "These caseworkers I think really embrace the notion of preaching about getting a job. . . . They did buy-in well ideologically speak-

Figure 4.5   Percentage of TANF Adults in Postsecondary Education in Illinois, by Program, January 1999 to May 2005

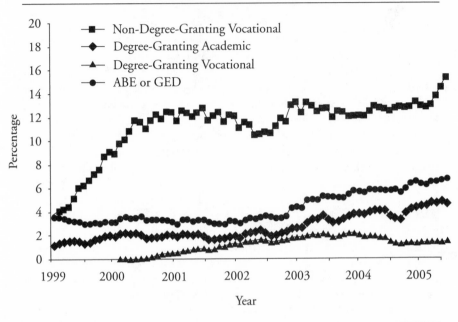

Source: Illinois Department of Human Services Bureau of Research and Analysis, "Employment and Training Numbers."

ing, they support the [work-first] philosophy." He added, "The consistent message they get is caseload reduction, enter employment, and everything else is bullshit. . . . There are a lot of cases of people who said, 'I want to go to college,' and their workers say, 'You can't, you need to go to work.' The overall message coming from the top was, get people off, get people off, and education didn't fit in." Again we see the power of the caseworkers in the implementation process, as well as a clear example of how informal communications regarding the work-first message trumped formal policy.

By 2003 and 2004, the welfare caseload in Illinois had declined dramatically, leaving on the rolls only those who had not managed to get work. These adults are known in Illinois as "harder to serve," and many recognize that moving them off welfare requires more than simply putting them to work. In 2001, when we spoke with the head of the Department of Human Services, she acknowledged that the state would have to move toward doing more education and training when the rolls got smaller. What the data show (see figure 4.5) is that the growth in postsecondary education during those later years was largely in short-term vocational programs, along with some growth in ABE or GED programs.

In November 2003, advocates presented IDHS with a proposal for a mixed-strategy service-delivery approach toward serving those remaining on the rolls. According to the Chicago Jobs Council (2003b), "A mixed strategy service delivery approach is employment focused, maximizing the use of a thorough individual assessment and a flexible menu of barrier remediation, job search, and education and training options to assist participants making the transition from welfare to work in their local labor markets" (1). Such an approach is similar to one taken in the Portland JOBS program, evaluated in the NEWWS study (see chapter 2 of this volume). In February 2004, IDHS responded to the Jobs Council proposal by issuing a request for proposals for employment services, with a particular interest in those using strategies combining education and training.

To date those contracted to provide the services have struggled with local actors still committed to work-first. Specifically, local caseworkers are still resistant to including educational activities on individual work plans.[13] One contractor reported to welfare advocates that she had to argue with local IDHS officers in order to place recipients in school (Chicago Jobs Council 2005a). Moreover, there is difficulty in finding tuition monies for the training, since the programs provide only $300 per recipient to cover all school-related expenses. Further, over 50 percent of TANF adults attending college are in short-term vocational programs (see figure 4.6), which does not make them eligible for financial aid. It does make them eligible for Workforce Investment Act (WIA) funds (see chapters 5 and 6 of this volume), but WIA contractors in Illinois "are hesitant to register these customers in their programs" (Chicago Jobs Council 2005b).

In Illinois, pressure from advocacy groups persuaded an already relatively liberal governor to include several policy provisions that were designed to retain elements of a human-capital approach to welfare reform. These aspects of the policy have had some effect on access to college, and college attendance among welfare recipients rose slightly by 2003, after taking a slight dip in 2001. The IDHS also created a pamphlet for caseworkers to distribute, called "Know Your Opportunities: Going to College" (Sosulski 2004, 248). Yet the proportion of those accessing college who have taken advantage of the stop-the-clock provision is still stubbornly low; most welfare recipients are enrolled in short-term noncredit programs that tend to produce lower income and poorer employment outcomes. And the welfare caseload has dropped so precipitously that the raw number of those obtaining access to college via welfare is less than 10 percent of what it was in 1996.

The work-first ideology has clearly played a role in these outcomes, most strikingly in the implementation process. Whereas the state of Washington

Figure 4.6   Percentage of TANF Adults in Postsecondary Education in
              Various Illinois Programs, January 1999 to May 2005

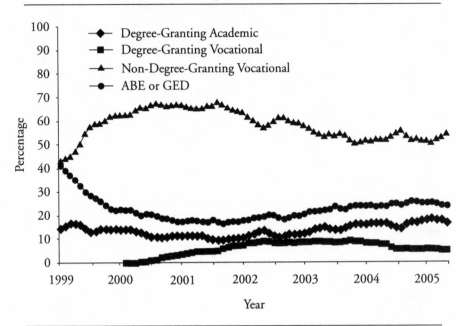

Source: Illinois Department of Human Services Bureau of Research and Analysis, "Employment and Training Numbers."

sent clear work-first policy signals that caseworkers embraced despite slight midcourse changes in formal policy, Illinois provides an example of how the work-first idea can trump official policy that contains relatively generous formal human-capital provisions. As our interviews clearly show, a relatively liberal welfare-reform policy was implemented in a decidedly work-first manner. As a result, despite the opportunity for welfare recipients to use degree-focused postsecondary education to count as a work requirement—and despite the fact that such enrollment would stop the welfare clock—few have taken advantage of these provisions.

FORMAL POLICY FORMATION: THE ROLE OF POLITICS IN WORK-FIRST PROGRAMS

The Washington and Illinois case studies illustrate the central role that the work-first idea played in the policy-formation process, and this phenomenon was evident across all of our states. However, the exact role of the work-first idea varied by context. For example, in Massachusetts and Florida, where state-level efforts to change welfare policy actually predated federal efforts, implementation was already occurring and the work-first rhetoric was firmly in place. In other cases, such as Washington and Illinois, reform really began with the passage of the Personal Responsibility and Work Opportunity Reconciliation Act (PRWORA) in 1996, and many battles over the work-first approach had yet to be fought. As a result, governors and department administrators, as well as advocates, had the opportunity to play key roles in deciding how "work-first" a state would become.

Take the case of Massachusetts. Despite its reputation for liberal social policies, in many ways Massachusetts' initial version of welfare reform was more conservative than the federal legislation. The state has a shorter time limit for welfare receipt (twenty-four months out of every sixty), and does not count postsecondary education toward the work requirement. Moreover, the state has been under Republican gubernatorial leadership since 1991—throughout the design and implementation of welfare reform.[14] Yet over time—particularly in the last several years—access to college has slightly increased, rather than decreased. These changes reflect the struggle between a set of powerful conservative governors and the efforts of an increasingly effective group of welfare advocates who challenge work-first policy.

During the early stages of welfare reform in Massachusetts, the Democratic legislature passed several relatively progressive welfare-reform laws, which were subsequently vetoed by Governor William Weld, a Republican. The governor then proposed his own more restrictive welfare-reform legislation, which was passed by the legislature in 1995 and was implemented beginning in December 1996 (Kirby et al. 1997). The legislation was strictly work-first, and reflected the thinking of not only the governor but other prominent leaders in the state, including the future governor Paul Cellucci, who "fired his entire board of welfare advisors when they suggested that hours spent in education should be counted toward satisfying workfare requirements" (Lafer 2002, 204). The rules held that education programs did not count toward fulfilling the work requirements. Initially, some recipients, including mothers of children under the age of six, were exempt from those requirements, but in the years immediately following federal welfare reform, Massachusetts tightened its rules, requiring mothers of children between the ages of two and six to work.

At that point, local advocates, especially the United Way and the Massachusetts Taxpayers Foundation, increased their efforts to liberalize access to education. In April 2001 they proposed a plan to increase the number of hours in the work requirement from twenty to thirty per week, but also to allow education and training to count as work. Furthermore, they conducted a study in April 2001 which showed that recipients with multiple barriers to employment needed training, and in 2003 used that evidence to lobby the state legislature on bill 4141, which was designed to allow education to count as a work activity for up to twelve months.[15] The proposal received some support from Governor Jane Swift near the conclusion of her term as governor, but when Mitt Romney took office in 2003, he vetoed the legislation. Remarkably, the state legislature overrode his veto, on July 17, 2003. Thus the work requirements in Massachusetts were changed: participation in an education or training activity now counts toward the work requirement for up to twelve months, and the months can be nonconsecutive. After twelve months a recipient may still be in education, but must also enroll in another activity to meet the work requirement. Moreover, a recipient may be in education past the twelve-month mark and have it count toward the work requirement if the program will end within three months of month 12 and the recipient has been "cooperative." The new rules applied to mothers of children under age six as of July 2003, and to everyone as of July 2004. Gradually, following these changes, a greater (though still quite small) percentage of welfare recipients in Massachusetts have begun to enroll in college. Yet the state climate continues to be unstable with regard to welfare reform. Since 2003, Governor Romney has continued to try to roll back the allowance of education as a work activity.[16] However, the state provides a clear example of how the advocacy community can achieve at least limited victories in the battle over ideas in state policy formation.

Advocates also played an important role in the political process in a neighboring state, Rhode Island. Eighteen months prior to the passage of TANF, an advocacy coalition was organized that included an unusually broad range of actors, ranging from church groups, the United Way, and child-advocacy organizations to straightforward research and policy advocacy groups such as the Rhode Island Poverty Institute, as well as groups that included solid business representation, most notably the Rhode Island Public Expenditure Council (RIPEC), which was crucial in building a welfare reform coalition that was perceived as bipartisan. RIPEC is a private, nonprofit, nonpartisan research organization funded by both private- and public-sector employers in the state, including businesses and educational institutions.

The coalition formed to influence the state's emerging welfare-reform legislation and drafted its own proposed legislation. This legislation was significantly more liberal than the proposal of Governor Bruce Sundlun, and included strong language in favor of access to education and training, a case-management approach to delivering welfare, an entitlement to child care and health care, and a stop-the-clock provision for those on welfare working more than thirty hours per week. According to a number of people interviewed at the state level, the welfare-reform advocacy group convinced a range of interest groups, including the business community, that a human-capital development approach to welfare reform would benefit them as well as welfare recipients. The group's effectiveness was due in large part to its broad membership base and to the ability of varied interest groups to perceive their common interests and to work together to develop a proposal that reflected these common interests. As a result, Rhode Island's formal welfare policy retains some elements of a human-capital philosophy.

The Massachusetts and Rhode Island examples illustrate a clear pattern in our findings: in all of our states, political actors sent powerful "signals" about welfare (Gais et al. 2001, 9). These new signals stressed the centrality of work to welfare, the personal responsibility of clients, and the time-limited nature of public assistance. Advocates had to do battle with these signals in order to try and create change in formal policy, and in some instances, they achieved modest success. Yet even if a state policy reflects some aspects of a human-capital approach, there is no guarantee that the policy will be implemented in this spirit.

IMPLEMENTING WELFARE REFORM:
THE POWER OF CASEWORKERS

Our case studies of Washington and Illinois illustrate that in addition to the role played by political actors and rhetorical signals in the policy formation process, caseworkers are street-level actors who are essential to the implementation of the policy, since to a large degree they decide whether or not a policy will actually go into effect. Caseworkers have embraced the time limits and work requirements of TANF in most of our states, arguing that such clear rules make their work easier by compelling recipients to work with them. They also expressed a belief that such rules push poor mothers to be better role models for their children. One caseworker from the Massachusetts Department of Transitional Assistance stated:

> The new requirements are breaking the cycle of generations of dependency that I've seen over the past three decades. Time limits are a good thing for the recipients' children—they get to see their mothers go out to work. It's one thing for mothers who have private financial support to stay home. But those who don't [have enough resources to stay home] ought to go to work in order to be role models for children.

Welfare researchers have concluded, similarly, that "frontline workers generally believe welfare recipients should work" as a precondition for receiving public assistance (Lurie 2001, 2).

It is not uncommon for caseworkers in states where some forms of postsecondary education are allowable under specific circumstances (for example, Massachusetts, Illinois, Rhode Island, Washington) simply not to mention that option to recipients. In one case, advocates reported that the caseworkers were never trained in a comprehensive way to know all of the rules. In other cases, the disconnect between rules and the actual practice of caseworkers is attributed not only to a lack of training but also to the education and background of the caseworkers themselves. In the words of one community college administrator who had attempted to work with caseworkers to bring welfare recipients to her campus, "The welfare caseworkers aren't educated themselves. So they resent welfare recipients because they think they can get school for free. It's no mystery to me why they aren't referring them [to my college]. All in all, I haven't found them to be very cooperative."

Thus, the beliefs and values of frontline workers can stand as a barrier to educational access for their clients. Caseworkers operate in an environment characterized by limited opportunities to build their own professional capacities and strong pressures to reduce caseloads and get clients into the workforce as a measure of their job performance (Lurie 2001). Efforts to "change the culture of the welfare office" have only added to the responsibilities of frontline workers without reducing client loads or subtracting responsibilities such as eligibility determination. Few frontline workers have the skills and formal credentials to engage clients about their lives, problems, and the barriers they experience to work or career advancement (see also Lurie 2001; Meyers, Riccucci, and Lurie 2001), making real "case management" little more than the wishful thinking of welfare policymakers. In short, regardless of specific elements of formal welfare policy, caseworkers' tendency to fully embrace the work-first philosophy can greatly reduce the ability of recipients to obtain access to postsecondary education.

COMMUNITY COLLEGE RESPONSE TO WELFARE REFORM

Community colleges are the institutions that are most likely to provide access to whatever postsecondary education is afforded to welfare recipients; as such they both receive and respond to welfare-reform policy, and the implementation of this policy has the ability to impact the actual workings of these schools. As we noted in chapter 1, community colleges are being pushed by a variety of economic and political forces to move away from serving the most disadvantaged adults, and we argue that welfare reform provides yet another incentive to do so. The sheer reduction in caseloads and the corresponding drop in the number of welfare recipients accessing college reduces the demand on the institution to continue to serve the unique needs of this increasingly small college-going population. Moreover, restrictions on both the type and the duration of education allowed under the welfare-reform laws of many states and the increasing emphasis on short-term training conflicts with community college conceptions of high-quality education and thus erects further barriers to welfare recipients' attending community colleges.

For example, the Massachusetts Department of Transitional Assistance (DTA) developed a program called Education That Works, designed to provide for the delivery of "intensive, high caliber, short-term academic skills training and employment services [so that] recipients can access employment opportunities that enable them to transition from welfare to successful employment." Education That Works provided tuition assistance for noncredit course work, and community colleges that participated in this program were subject to explicit job-placement outcome measures. The program required job placement within four months, and paid colleges for enrollment, job placement, and retention in the job for ninety days.

Most of Massachusetts' community colleges chose not to participate in Education That Works.[17] Some argued that the rates DTA was willing to pay were not high enough to operate quality training programs. Others objected on principle. Various individuals at several Massachusetts community colleges, when interviewed, pointed to the job-placement outcomes requirements attached to this funding as the key reason for their nonparticipation. One community college administrator stated, "We're not an employment service. We're an educational institution. I don't think it's appropriate for the state to be subjecting us to such measures." Thus, many Massachusetts community colleges essentially gave up on efforts to participate in training welfare recipients through this program, either because it did not provide enough resources to deliver high-quality training or because the emphasis on job placement was perceived to conflict with the educational mission of their institutions.

The state of Illinois developed a program designed to deliver education to welfare recipients that was in many ways quite similar to that of Massachusetts. During the initial implementation of welfare reform, Illinois operated a welfare-to-work program based at community colleges, known as the Advancing Opportunities (AO) program. AO was a collaborative effort of the Illinois Community College Board (ICCB) and the Illinois Department of Human Services (IDHS). Prior to welfare reform, the focus of this program was on providing AFDC recipients with "comprehensive education, training and counseling" (Illinois Community College Board n.d.). In response to welfare reform, the program emphasis was shifted to include a focus on "post-employment support and job upgrading" (Illinois Community College Board n.d.). Although AO retained its case-management model, the training offered was shifted to short-term, and was most often occupational or vocational in nature. In addition, funding for AO was based on performance outcomes, so completion and placement became more important to program directors.

In contrast to the low levels of participation among community colleges in Massachusetts, thirty-six of the forty-eight Illinois community colleges participated in AO from 1998 and 2001, and served nearly 4,000 current and former TANF recipients. Yet in the spring of 2001, Governor George Ryan, a Democrat, sacrificed the $3.4 million program to budget cuts. According to a letter from the heads of IDHS and the ICCB in 2001 (Baker and Cipfl 2001), the reduction in TANF caseloads was the cause. According to one advocate, the Advancing Opportunities program existed as a way to draw additional federal matching dollars available under AFDC, and when TANF took over, those matching dollars disappeared and the motivation to maintain the program declined. "The Department of Human Services understood that and made noises from the beginning about pulling [AO] and the community colleges had gotten used to a pot of money and were pretty good at lobbying" and thus the program persisted for a while longer, he said. "But I think the department started to take the attitude that they're not going to pay for education anymore to the extent they ever were. They're not going to pay for hard skills training and education, but they will pay for supports for people to be involved with that."

The demise of the AO program is another example of the disconnect between formal welfare policy and its implementation that exists in so many states. As we have discussed, Illinois welfare policy had retained some human-capital elements, and the AO program was in keeping with this philosophy, providing avenues to obtain education and training for welfare recipients. In fact, while AO was in operation, community college administrators reported that they felt that "the staff at DHS really [had] an understanding of the value of education. . . . While they had a work-first policy to implement, they were committed to education and training." But the demise of the AO program was a signal to community colleges that the IDHS administration had succumbed to work-first pressures. "As educators we truly believe that in order for people to get to their full potential they need skills training and education, not to just be put out in a job. . . . And we see our role as really fundamental to those kinds of improvements in people's lives. And welfare has taken a work-first philosophy that is just devastating to those outcomes for individuals," noted a staffer at the ICCB. Illinois welfare policy essentially eliminated the one avenue for real community college participation in the training of welfare recipients.

When community colleges do continue to provide access to education and training to welfare recipients, our analyses suggest that it is most often because committed individuals identify ways to overcome existing barriers, rather than because formal policy provides viable opportunities to do so. A Rhode Island community college provides an example of this phenomenon. Its REACH program (Realizing Education and Career Hopes) is remarkably effective in serving the educational needs of the state's welfare population, despite the fact that the actual numbers served are quite small. Because of those small numbers, the college can afford to devote relatively few resources to serving this population; the program does not garner the same scope of resources that a larger population of low-income students might demand or require. Instead, the success of the program is due to the enormous dedication of a relatively few individuals who succeed in serving low-income students without the benefits of broad institutional support.

Multiple interviews and visits to the college consistently suggested that the program attempts to mitigate the structural barriers to postsecondary education for welfare recipients by working closely with the state's Department of Human Services; and it strives to remove the more emotional barriers to educational success by creating a culture of respect within the program itself. For example, to mitigate what she sees as the potential for discouragement among some DHS welfare caseworkers, the director of REACH has sought to take on more of the tasks of intake and eligibility screening of welfare recipients interested in postsecondary education. For a period of time the REACH staff was empowered by DHS to certify funding for school and for child care as well. In response to a question regarding the child-care needs of a new welfare recipient interested in enrolling in college, REACH's director said:

We can assist them. We have all the paper work; we have all the child-care forms that DHS would normally hand out. We show them how to fill out the forms. . . . We provide the paperwork process and sometimes the instruction.

Q: And they can also get this information from their caseworker?

REACH director: Yes. But they often choose us. . . . Sometimes we are the first person, or the second person that they see. If they call DHS and say "I want to go to school," sometimes the response is "call REACH." So we are sometimes the first person that they meet.

This example is instructive because it illustrates the degree to which the REACH program acts to remove the structural barriers that often prevent many welfare recipients from pursuing postsecondary education. Clearly, the availability of child care as an entitlement to welfare recipients is a result of the state welfare-reform legislation. But REACH program staff work to ensure that recipients actually receive what they are entitled to. In doing so, they remove what is generally regarded as the most significant barrier to the pursuit of postsecondary education among welfare recipients—the lack of child care—when access to postsecondary education is available.

REACH is able to perform such activities in large part because of the interpersonal skills of the director, who has worked diligently to create and sustain productive relationships with DHS staff. She communicates with people in DHS regularly and at all levels—with caseworkers as well as with DHS administrative personnel. She sits on many committees and uses these contacts to advance her program. As a result of this consistent and close contact, there is ample evidence that DHS staff trust the REACH office to perform an unusually wide array of functions that are directly related to the welfare office. For example, REACH was not required to report to DHS whether REACH participants were complying with welfare regulations. Instead, the director asserted, "DHS allows us the flexibility of documenting [compliance] monthly for ourselves and if the person is not compliant for the semester then we would inform the social caseworkers. We keep them informed." She went on to say that her office worked so closely with DHS that "we have some social caseworkers that did not know we were not their coworkers. They thought that we were actually social caseworkers." Relations with caseworkers are not uniformly positive, however, and recent grievances filed by the caseworkers' unions have reduced the ability of REACH staff to perform a number of functions, such as formally activating child care. Yet REACH continues to assist and facilitate the process of enrolling welfare recipients in the services to which they are entitled by filling out application paperwork and simply faxing it over to the DHS caseworkers, who then activate the funding.

Clearly, this community college has found an effective way to meet the needs of its welfare clientele. The success of the program is built on the hard work and commitment of its staff—not on a large pool of resources or vast amounts of institutional support. With very few resources, an enormously dedicated staff is able to maintain access to college for welfare recipients. The very success of CCRI's REACH program provides a compelling example of just how much work a community college must do to continue to serve a relatively small pool of low-income students.

Sadly, community college efforts to maintain access for low-income adults in the face of welfare reform were often frustrated. In some cases, community college officials objected to the work-first message because they did not want to comply with the demands of short-term training. In other situations, promising programs were developed and then sacrificed in the name of belt-tightening. Only where charismatic individuals worked in unique small settings with specific social ties to social workers did they succeed in preserving even a modicum of access to education. Overall, even at educational institutions where one would have expected the work-first message to fail, it triumphed in creating a move toward closing doors,.

ASSESSING THE EFFECTS OF WELFARE REFORM ON COLLEGE ACCESS

What can be learned about the effects of welfare reform on access to postsecondary education from the quantitative and qualitative data we present here and in chapter 3? What does each type of analysis contribute, and, more important, what does the process of combining both types of analyses provide us that looking at each type of data individually does not?

The quantitative analyses presented in chapter 3 provide a critical piece of the puzzle. College attendance among welfare recipients has dropped significantly since welfare reform was enacted in 1996. Moreover, welfare recipients are less likely to enroll than women with similar demographic characteristics. And finally, the quality and type of education that is available to welfare recipients in general has decreased since 1996 as well, with recipients far more likely to enroll only part-time and in occupational programs. Thus, at the aggregate level, the quantitative analyses presented here provide clear and convincing evidence of the significant negative impact that welfare reform has had on college attendance.

Yet when we look at welfare policy at the state level, the picture becomes significantly more complex. We do see some variation in access to postsecondary education across states, as would be expected given the significant variations in state-level welfare reform policy. As our case studies illustrate, the strong work-first emphasis seen in both the policy and implementation aspects of Washington's welfare reform policy has, not surprisingly, resulted in a significant reduction in access to postsecondary education. In contrast, Illinois, which has retained the possibility of access, has seen its college-going rate grow to some degree among welfare recipients, although its caseload has plummeted and the quality of education that is available has dropped as well. Yet we see less variation in outcomes than might be suggested by formal policy differences across the states. Caseloads have dropped precipitously in all six states as the vast majority of welfare recipients have rapidly been moved off the rolls; and no state enrolls more than 6 percent of recipients in any form of postsecondary education.

As our qualitative case-study data clearly illustrate, the road from formal policy to actual implementation is not short, straightforward, nor necessarily predictable. Access to postsecondary education for welfare recipients is a far more complicated issue than an analysis of "official" policy would suggest. National policy frames—that is, the ideas that drove welfare reform at the federal level—have proved to be tenacious, and the "work-first" ideology that characterizes federal welfare reform is enacted at the local level among caseworkers, even when state policy allows significant access to postsecondary education. For example, in both Illinois and Washington, groups or individuals favoring relatively generous access to postsecondary education attempted to influence the policymaking process to preserve at least some educational access. However, other actors or factors—state human service agencies, and caseworkers in particular—created an on-the-ground policy that is consistently work-first, despite variations in formal policy. Thus, our study suggests that even when states have adopted a more human-capital-based approach to education for welfare recipients, it is difficult for states to achieve such a goal. In short, the power and simplicity of the work-first message trumped other more complicated and less compelling messages. A true commitment to access to education for welfare recipients will require sustained attention from all relevant sectors to the complexities of policy implementation in order for access to be achieved.

CHAPTER FIVE

THE WORKFORCE INVESTMENT ACT: INVESTMENT OR DISINVESTMENT?

THE WORKFORCE Investment Act (WIA) of 1998 and the 1996 welfare-reform legislation (the Personal Responsibility and Work Opportunity Reconciliation Act) are inextricably linked by an endorsement of the "work-first" ideology and a rejection of the human-capital narrative. As such, the full impact of the work-first idea on access to education and training can only be discerned by means of an examination of the implementation and impact of both policies. This and the next chapter focus specifically on WIA.

Where welfare reform embodied one primary idea—that ending the entitlement to services and requiring work most benefits the poor—WIA was driven by two. In addition to the work-first philosophy, WIA also embodies a market-based philosophy focusing on outcomes and accountability measures designed to better address the needs of WIA clients, as well as their potential employers. This second notion is an attempt to rectify the flaws of WIA's predecessor, the Job Training Partnership Act (JTPA), which was roundly considered to be an incomprehensible assortment of training programs and policies guided by few requirements and producing little in the way of meaningful results (Lafer 2002). In reaction to this assessment, a single piece of legislation, WIA, was crafted to reflect both a market-approach to service provision and a work-first approach to determining who qualifies for services.

The presence of these often-competing ideas poses a unique set of challenges for the implementation of WIA. Most important for the purposes of our analysis, these ideas—viewed separately and together—have a distinctly negative effect on whether and how individual WIA clients gain access to education and training.[1] In this chapter we provide a basis for understanding both the philosophical underpinnings of WIA and their practical implications in terms of the policy's effect on access to education and training.

WIA'S PREDECESSORS

As discussed in chapter 2, federal workforce policy over the last thirty years has followed a clear trajectory away from federal guarantees of outcomes (through job creation and placement in public-service jobs), toward providing an opportunity to find a job. This movement occurred as welfare and workforce policy became increasingly intertwined. Whereas earlier iterations of welfare and workforce development policies had distinctly different goals, over time their goals and practices began to merge. Table 5.1 shows that workforce policy, like welfare policy, has moved from a focus on governmental responsibility to individual responsibility, and moved from explicit efforts to reduce poverty toward efforts at promoting "self-sufficiency." As a result, workforce programs, like welfare, have moved away from an emphasis on education and training altogether (Lafer 2002). Chapter 2 traced the emergence of the work-first ideology, primarily as reflected in federal welfare policy. Those changes effectively paved the way for parallel changes in workforce policy, resulting in a "work-first" Workforce Investment Act.

The Comprehensive Employment Training Act of 1973 (CETA) was an attempt to alleviate poverty directly by creating public-service jobs and providing the training necessary for unemployed workers to succeed in them. At its height, in the early 1980s, the program enjoyed a $6.1 billion budget (Reville and Klerman 1996). CETA was designed to concentrate control of the program at the local or municipal level; states were generally not involved in CETA's administration, and local entities reported directly to federal officials. In addition, the program was characterized by the heavy involvement of community-based organizations and other local entities for the development and provision of training programs. These organizations were often aligned with the interests of the poor rather than with the needs of the employment sector (Lafer 2002). Local business entities and the private sector in general did not play a significant part in the administration or oversight of CETA. Moreover, the program was subject to a relatively lax accountability structure, which focused only on the number of individuals served rather than on measures of employment or earnings outcomes.

Hundreds of thousands of jobs were created under CETA's auspices (Grubb and Lazerson 2004), and CETA was clearly effective in decreasing unemployment, especially among women. Its training programs also resulted in significant increases in earnings among disadvantaged women, but not for men (Bassi and Ashenfelter 1986). Yet these successes were generally ignored by mainstream policymakers; criticisms of CETA were abundant. A chorus of conservative critics argued that CETA's jobs-creation component was actually

Table 5.1   Comparison of WIA to Two Predecessor Programs

	CETA (1973)	JTPA (1982)	WIA (1998)
Target population	Disadvantaged adults and youth	Economically disadvantaged adults and youth (90 percent of adults had to pass means test)	Universal access (but youth services targeted at low-income youth) No means test
Goal	Job creation and training	Short-term training for poor	Job placement
Eligibility requirements for training providers	Subcontracted by nonprofits or local agencies	Accredited institution	Certification of institution by governor Eligibility of individual programs based on employment and earnings outcomes
Accountability measures	Number served	Data collected via follow-up with job seekers; focus on input and process measures: numbers served, number of days in training, number of credentials granted	Numerous outcomes, including: Entered-employment rate Employment-retention rate Average-earnings change Entered-employment and credential rate Customer satisfaction for employers Customer satisfaction for clients
Governance structure	Community-based organizations	Private industry councils	Private industry councils
Funding mechanism	Operated primarily at the municipal (city) level	Operated primarily by governors	Operated primarily by state and local Workforce Investment Boards
Funding attached to performance	None	Most stringent sanction not money but reorganization of local service-delivery organization	Incentive funds available to states ranging from $750,000 to $3 million annually Failure to meet performance requirements for two years results in 5 percent reduction in WIA grant

Source: U.S. Government Accountability Office (2002a); Lafer (2002).

detrimental to the poor because it shielded them from the harsh realities of the employment market (Grubb and Lazerson 2004). In addition, the program was chronically under attack by those who made allegations of fraud and a fundamental disconnect between training and local employment needs (Lafer 2002). An analysis of eleven evaluations of CETA concluded that, on average, participation in the program led to annual increases in income of between two hundred and six hundred dollars (Barnow 1989), although estimates of earnings gains varied widely across studies.

The findings on CETA were far from consistently negative, but they provided Ronald Reagan with more than enough ammunition to replace the program in 1982 with a new policy that addressed the concerns of conservative critics unhappy with the notion of government-sponsored job creation. The Job Training Partnership Act (JTPA) differed from CETA in several important ways. First, it eliminated the job creation component that was so central to CETA; thus JTPA shifted the focus away from directly alleviating poverty and unemployment toward providing the means through which individuals could rise out of poverty—hence the emphasis on job training rather than job creation. Second, to appease governors, who at that time were more likely to be Republican than the local or municipal government entities that controlled CETA, primary budgetary authority was given to the states. Third, for the first time private industry councils (PICs), rather than community-based entities, were directly responsible for the development of local job-training programs. In other words, the emphasis shifted toward the needs of local employers.

JTPA also marked a movement toward greater accountability. In response to criticism regarding a lack of performance measures in CETA, 6 percent of JTPA funds were allocated to provide incentives to meet performance standards designed by the secretary of labor: short-term job placement and weekly earnings three months after placement. Although limited in scope, these standards nevertheless sent a new message to job-training programs that emphasized program outcomes rather than program implementation (Reville and Klerman 1996).

Thus, JTPA was a significant break from CETA. Although it still focused on disadvantaged adults, the program's approach to addressing the issue of poverty now focused almost exclusively on training rather than job creation. Without a doubt, the program was hugely successful in providing training for low-income adults. In the last year of its operation, fully 91 percent of adult JTPA clients received some form of training (Social Policy Research Associates 1999; see also table 5.3). Because the program targeted low-income populations, this training was delivered to those who were most in need of it.

But like CETA, JTPA was vulnerable to attack. Despite supportive rhetoric from President George H. W. Bush as late as 1989, reports issued by the U.S.

Government Accountability Office indicate that by the late 1980s JTPA programs were generally perceived to be mismanaged and poorly coordinated, and often inaccessible to their intended participants (Holzer and Waller 2003). The results of large-scale evaluations were also adding fuel to the fire, as only modest levels of effectiveness were reported; in particular, the small increases in earnings for those who obtained training were noted (Lafer 2002).

THE EMERGENCE OF WIA

Even in light of the lukewarm evaluations of JTPA, the rapid erosion of the widespread and bipartisan support enjoyed by the program during its early years is nevertheless remarkable. Instead of addressing the problems identified in the evaluations by increasing the program's efficiency or improving the quality of the training provided, congressional leaders framed JTPA as irretrievably broken. When the Workforce Investment Act emerged in 1998 it was billed as an antidote to what Bill Clinton (1992) as a candidate had termed a "confusing array of publicly funded training programs."

But the changes inherent in WIA are far more profound than simply creating a more efficient service-delivery model. Unlike CETA and JTPA, WIA is not aimed at delivering its services exclusively to the poor. Rather, it is built upon the more politically palatable principle of universal access, so that any individual, from the poorest janitor to the wealthiest CEO, can utilize the services that it provides. Moreover, despite the promise implied by its name, the Workforce Investment Act took much of the training out of the program. Billed as a workforce development program that invests resources to improve the quality of the workforce, in fact it does the exact opposite: it provides superficial résumé-building and job-search services rather than access to high-quality training and postsecondary education. Its passage signaled a remarkable abandonment of federal investment in education and training as a means to promote workforce development. Indeed, this work-first emphasis renders it an imposter of sorts. It effectively reframed the mismatch that existed between the labor market and potential employees as one that could be remedied simply by rapid job placement. Job training was deemed a luxury that few—both employees and employers—would need.

In addition, WIA's reliance on a complex accountability system and the ideals of "consumer choice" has narrowed not only the pipeline to training but also the actual pool of training providers, thereby contributing to the work-first goal of rapid employment and reduced access to education and training. As a result, community colleges, once actively involved in JTPA, are much less involved in WIA. In short, this federal policy—seemingly central

101

to "workforce development" efforts—in fact does little to develop American workers.

THE DOMINANCE OF THE WORK-FIRST IDEA IN FORMAL WIA POLICY

As noted, the goals of federal workforce and welfare policies are becoming increasingly similar. We can clearly see the linkages between welfare reform and WIA in the statements issued by the Department of Labor in response to welfare reform. A memo on WIA from the Department of Labor's Employment and Training Administration (ETA) stated the following:

> This legislation provides ETA and its grantees with new and expanded opportunities and challenges to ensure that welfare recipients receive training and employment services to help them make the transition to jobs. . . . Immediate job placement, or "Work First," is the central focus of the welfare reform legislation. . . . This approach, however, may not be suitable for welfare recipients who need additional information and guidance to decide their employment direction or who need basic skills. For such individuals, the "Work First" approach should include work coupled with training and related services to form a career path or ladder.

At the time this statement was issued JTPA was still in existence, and this fact explains the emphasis on job training in the memo. But the notion that the work-first approach to welfare reform could somehow link with a federal job-training program is quite obvious.

And in fact, formal linkages between the two policies are becoming more common as time goes on. In debates over the reauthorization of both acts, discussions about the connections between WIA and welfare reform have been common. The access point for WIA services are one-step career centers, which are run by local Workforce Investment Boards (WIBs). Yet they can also serve as job placement centers for welfare recipients. In remarks made by Assistant Secretary for Employment and Training Emily Stover DeRocco to the American Public Human Services Association on July 22, 2002, she stated, "We are fully behind the concept of one-stop career centers being a community access point for an integrated employment and training service delivery system. . . . The Department of Labor has worked closely with the Department of Health and Human Services to assure that the TANF legislation has the appropriate links to the One-Stop system and the flexibility to combine and coordinate the economic and workforce development underpinnings of WIA and the assistance to low-income individuals and family building underpinnings of TANF" (3). This is a clear example of the philosophical link between the two programs.

There is some evidence that states are taking advantage of the opportunity to link WIA and welfare reform. In a summary of states' WIA Strategic Plans in September 2001, the National Governors Association reports that nineteen states formally include TANF in their WIA plans (National Governors Association Center for Best Practices 2002). However, the report points out that states that have submitted strategic plans after the year 2000 are far more likely to include TANF in their unified plans than were states whose plans were submitted prior to July 1, 2000. Sixty-six percent of unified plans in the latter group included WIA, whereas only 12.5 percent of the earlier group did so (National Governors Association Center for Best Practices 2002, 3).

At least at the rhetorical level the Department of Labor advocates for the combination of education and job training. It could be said that the linkages made between WIA and welfare reform create the appearance that neither policy is work-first and that, rather, they constitute a highly coordinated system designed to provide low-income welfare recipients with access to the education and training they need via WIA. In fact, welfare recipients referred to the WIA system seldom obtain education and training (a point to be discussed in more detail later).

WHAT MAKES WIA WORK-FIRST

WIA, like nearly all federal policies, is a complex piece of legislation. In the next section we explore the aspects of the policy that relate most directly to its dual focus on work-first ideas and market-focused service-delivery and accountability systems.

WIA employs a number of mechanisms whose end result is a decrease in access to training. The most important of these is the idea of the one-stop career center. These centers were designed to provide a single point of access to employment-related services and thus to become more efficient deliverers of service and to foster a system of "universal access" to training and employment. According to the federal regulations, four major federal agencies—the Department of Labor, the Department of Education, the Department of Health and Human Services, and Housing and Urban Development—are required to offer a broad range of employment-related programs at the one stops, such as employment and training for migrant and seasonal farm workers, dislocated-workers programs, unemployment insurance, and welfare-to-work.[2] The one-stops also have the flexibility to include other partners, such as the welfare department (U.S. Government Accountability Office 2003).

Yet as the access point for WIA services, one-stop career centers do not provide equal access to all types of services offered. Rather, they employ a three-tiered, hierarchical delivery of services that essentially operationalizes the work-first idea. The specific services one has access to are hardly universally available; rather, they are determined via a system of "sequential eligibility." Under this system, the broadest access is provided to "core" services, which are superficial at best; an example is unassisted access to the Internet for job searching.[3] Those who do not obtain employment via these "core" services are then referred to "intensive" services, which are slightly more substantial, for example, assistance with preparing a résumé.[4] The third level, education and training, typically is available only to individuals who cannot obtain employment via the first two levels of services. Available training services must be "directly linked to job opportunities in [the] local area" (U.S. Department of Labor 2003, 5) and may include occupational skills training and adult education and literacy activities in conjunction with other training.

Training funds are usually distributed to eligible clients via Individualized Training Accounts (ITAs), which are similar to educational vouchers that clients can use to purchase training at approved training providers.[5] In areas where funds are limited, one-stop centers are supposed to give priority to low-income and public-assistance individuals. However, the federal government does not specify what proportion of services should be targeted at these populations, nor do they provide clear definitions of these terms, leaving this task instead to state and local entities (Lafer 2002, 14).

In sum, core services are available to "adults with no eligibility requirements"; intensive services are available to "unemployed individuals who are not able to find jobs through core services alone"; and training services are available only to "qualified customers . . . who are still not able to find jobs" (U.S. Department of Labor, Employment and Training Administration (DOLETA) 2003, 5). Thus, the tiers of service are more accurately described as a pyramid, whose pinnacle, which is education and training, very few WIA clients are likely to reach.

Even though these tiers of service clearly exist (and were discussed and present at all one-stop centers we visited), the Department of Labor claims that it does not mandate that access to education and training must be granted only after a client passes through the first two tiers of services. In a 2002 Training and Employment Notice, the Department of Labor states, "it is feasible for [access to training] to occur in one visit to the One-Stop Career Center" (U.S. Department of Labor, Employment and Training Administration (DOLETA) 2002). Yet according to the *Code of Federal Regulations*, regulation 20CFR663.160, individuals must receive services in a sequential order.[6] Thus:

At a minimum, an individual must receive at least one core service, such as an initial assessment or job search and placement assistance, before receiving intensive services. The initial assessment determines the individual's skill levels, aptitudes, and supportive services needs. The job search and placement assistance helps the individual determine whether he or she is unable to obtain employment, and thus requires more intensive services to obtain employment. The decision on which core services to provide, and the timing of their delivery, may be made on a case-by-case basis at the local level depending upon the needs of the participant.

In addition, according to regulation 20CFR663.240, individuals must receive intensive services before receiving training:

> At a minimum, an individual must receive at least one intensive service, such as development of an individual employment plan with a case manager or individual counseling and career planning, before the individual may receive training services.

But the law does not mandate the amount of time core and intensive services must last before training may be accessed: "There is no Federally-required minimum time period for participation in intensive services before receiving training services (regulation 20CFR663.250)."

Despite the fine-tuning and slight changes in language, it is quite clear that formal federal WIA legislation does require a work-first approach to the delivery of services, even if the amount of time an individual has to spend in those services is not specified. The law explicitly creates a hierarchy of services that must be accessed in the proper order, beginning with "job search." In essence, such an approach operationalizes the work-first philosophy, despite the nuances in policy articulated by the Department of Labor. As a result, 70 to 80 percent of Workforce Investment Boards require participants to do job search, research on occupations, or skills assessment, or all three, before they can receive an ITA for training (U.S. Government Accountability Office 2005).[7]

WIA AS A MARKET-BASED REFORM

WIA is driven by two major elements—the work-first philosophy described above, derived largely from its increasing proximity to welfare reform; and a market-based model for delivering services that is designed to address the critiques of JTPA that focused on efficiency and responsiveness to the labor market.

When it comes to training under WIA, the vendor who actually delivers the training is not the central element in the equation; instead, the needs and desires of two sets of customers, the business sector and the WIA clients who become students, drive the model. The Department of Labor states, "The most important aspect of the Act is its focus on meeting the needs of businesses for skilled workers *and* the training, education and employment needs of individuals" (U.S. Department of Labor 1998, 4, emphasis in original). Notably absent from this statement is any mention of the system that will deliver the needed educational and training services.

WIA operationalizes its customer-driven orientation via the use of two tools: a voucher-like Individualized Training Account (ITA) and a performance-accountability system. Under JTPA, community colleges and other educational institutions competed for federal dollars distributed by local entities via training contracts. For example, upon receiving a contract to provide a training program for office assistants, the community college would develop the program, staff it, advertise the program, and recruit to fill its classes. Thus, while there was an element of competition for these dollars, on receiving the contract, community colleges could be sure that they would receive a sizable fee for developing and staffing such programs if they could fill these classes.

Under WIA, the use of ITAs essentially ensures that the available training dollars will be distributed so broadly across eligible training providers that the total amount of funding per institution will most often be negligible. Clients are able to choose among any existing program for which a community college or other educational organization submits the requisite accountability information. Thus, community colleges are not competing for contracts to develop programs; they are competing for individual students. In much the same way that K through 12 school-voucher program models provide parents with the opportunity to shop for the best existing school, ITAs explicitly treat students as consumers and education as an open market (Chubb and Moe 1987). Fewer dollars overall, coupled with the fact that the dollars that do exist are not delivered up-front, combine to create a markedly less appealing climate for training providers interested in federal workforce-development funds (Patel and Strawn 2003, 4).

The ITA is only one aspect of WIA's broader "customer satisfaction"–oriented approach to service delivery, which is gauged by a relatively extensive series of customer-satisfaction and job-placement measures, including employment, retention and credential rates, changes in earnings, and customer-satisfaction ratings for both participants and employers (U.S. Department of Labor 2002). These complex performance measures obscure the interface between the policy and training providers such as the community college, shifting the relationship between the federal government, training providers, and WIA customers in a number of ways. The system is designed so that clients examine available outcome data on service providers and choose the highest-quality program when they "cash in" their ITAs. To remain eligible, service providers must meet or exceed minimum levels of performance established by states and localities and collect evidence of customer satisfaction for both participants and employers as well. These outcome measures are then fed back to the one-stop career centers, where WIA clients approved for training can examine them and make an "informed" choice regarding which program is most likely to help them achieve their educational and employment goals.

With the adaptation of both ITAs and performance measures, WIA in theory embraces a market-driven model for the delivery of education and training. These aspects of WIA are designed to increase customer autonomy and choice. As Burt S. Barnow and Christopher King (2001) point out, "WIA is quite clear about providing accurate, up-to-date performance information on providers to support informed consumer choice, an essential element in fostering reliance on market mechanisms" (7–8). They go on to say, "It is no longer unusual to see proposals and provisions referring to both participants and employers as 'customers' of workforce services and viewing service providers (such as state and local agencies, community colleges, and community-based organizations) as entities addressing their needs" (8).

Materials from the U.S. Department of Labor (2001) use similar language to describe WIA:

> Provisions of the Act promote individual responsibility and personal decision-making through the use of "Individual Training Accounts" which allow adult customers to "purchase" the training they determine best for them. This market-driven system will enable customers to get the skills and credentials they need to succeed in their local labor markets.

Yet it is questionable whether this market orientation is effective, especially in the case of clients with low levels of formal education who are unfamiliar with education and training generally, and unused to interpreting quantitative outcome measures (see Grubb and Lazerson 2004 for a more extensive discussion of this point). The increased emphasis on "individual responsibility" allows for a corresponding decrease in collective responsibility among WIA caseworkers and others charged with service delivery.

MARKET REFORMS IN AN EDUCATIONAL CONTEXT

The market-based elements of WIA are consistent with the increasingly common market-based reform efforts that exist in schools (Chubb and Moe 1987; Gross, Shaw, and Shapiro 2003; Levin 2001). This type of reform is driven by a free-market approach that is often associated with the University of Chicago economist Milton Friedman and more recently with the ideas of

Chester Finn, Bruno Manno, and Diane Ravitch. The market approach to education places schools in the same category as other institutions in our economy—that is, organizations that must compete for customers who theoretically enjoy free choice.

Market-based reform has been present in the elementary and secondary educational sectors for some time, and in recent years these principles have become increasingly common in efforts to reform postsecondary education as well (Levin 2001). Tennessee was a pioneer in this movement, instituting performance-based incentive funding and accountability measures for its colleges and universities as early as 1978 (Tennessee Higher Education Commission 2004). Indeed, the move toward accountability appears to stem from "several major trends and stakeholders of higher education, including government, the private sector, and citizens" (Choitz and Bosworth 2002, 2). Its advocates work from the premises that taxpayers demand that the government justify spending public dollars on education, employers expect educational institutions to produce skilled workers, and consumers of higher education need and expect more services than ever (Choitz and Bosworth 2002).

As a result of the successful dissemination of these ideas, accountability and other market-based, competitive principles have increasingly guided higher-education institutions and systems across many states to varying degrees. A recent "report card" on higher education revealed that states are increasingly subject to comparison on such measures of success as preparation, participation, affordability, and completion (National Center for Public Policy and Higher Education 2004), and the number of states implementing accountability plans doubled between 1994 and 1997 (State Higher Education Executive Officers 1998). Performance reporting, budgeting, and financing have all become commonplace in state systems of higher education. The bulk of financing for all colleges and universities continues to be based on fixed costs such as faculty salaries and enrollment, but "the increased use of performance budgeting and funding does indicate the growing belief in state capitals—but not on public campuses—that performance should somehow count in state budgeting for higher education" (Burke and Minassians 2001, 5).

These elements of a market-based system could mitigate the negative effect of the work-first elements of the policy by providing incentives for one-stop career centers to provide high-quality services, and for training providers to deliver quality training. Unfortunately, however, the data presented in the next section of this chapter suggest that WIA has had a consistently negative impact on access to education and training by diverting clients into relatively superficial, ineffective services. In fact, our analysis of how WIA has been implemented (see chapter 6) suggests that it is precisely the market-based aspects of the policy that serve actually to further reduce access to high-quality training, in particular by erecting barriers to the delivery of training among community colleges. In the next section we set forth our analyses of national and state-level data on access to education and training, and focus specifically on whether this policy has had a disproportionate effect on disadvantaged populations.

EARLY-ACCESS OUTCOMES

Our analysis of the development of the WIA philosophy and the context in which it is implemented raises very basic questions: How has WIA affected access to education and training? How many individuals are participating in WIA? What proportion of them are receiving education and training? How do these numbers compare to those under the final year of JTPA? We explore each of the questions.

We begin by analyzing federal-level data derived from the WIA reporting system, known as WIA Standardized Record Data, or WIASRD.[8] Table 5.2, comparing demographic characteristics of clients under JTPA and WIA, shows that levels of funding remained relatively stable during the transition from JTPA to WIA, from $892 million in the last year of JTPA to $900 million in WIA funds in 2003 (U.S. Government Accountability Office 2002a, 2003).[9]

A comparison of the percentage of funds spent on training for clients under WIA and JTPA, respectively, is especially relevant to this analysis. However, states are not required to disaggregate annual expenditures with regard to the proportion of funding spent on each of the three tiers of service, so we do not know exactly how much of that nearly $1 billion was spent on training each year.[10] According to a recent report by the U.S. Government Accountability Office (2005), in program year 2003 approximately 40 percent of the $2.4 billion in WIA funds received by local boards to serve adult participants was spent on or earmarked for training, but the same report states that the Department of Labor's estimate of that percentage is lower.

DISADVANTAGED CLIENTS AND WIA

JTPA was a job training program directly targeted at low-income adults, whereas WIA is designed to provide universal access to services. Thus, we would expect that disadvantaged groups would be a smaller proportion of the total WIA population than was the case under JTPA. Existing data support this expectation and reveal a trend away from serving disadvantaged clients. As can be seen in table 5.2, in 1997, 98 percent of the adult population served by JTPA was economically disadvantaged, and 31 percent received cash welfare (AFDC or TANF) (Social Policy Research Associates 1999); 78 percent of the adults lacked a high school diploma.[11] In 2003, 68 percent of WIA

Table 5.2 Characteristics of and Services Received by Adult Exiters under JTPA and WIA

	1997, JTPA	2003, WIA
Funding allocated to serve adults	$892,627,443[b]	$900,000,000
Adult exiters by race		
Percentage white (not Hispanic)	44	46
Percentage black (not Hispanic)	35	31
Percentage Hispanic	17	18
Percentage other	4	5
Adult exiters receiving intensive or training services[a]		
Percentage low-income	98	68
Percentage receiving cash welfare (AFDC or TANF)	31	8
Adult exiters' highest grade completed:		
Percentage less than high school diploma	22	18
Percentage high school diploma or equivalency	57	54
Percentage post high school	21	28

Sources: U.S. Department of Labor 2004; Social Policy Research Associates 1999.

[a] Types of training services do not add to 100 because clients could receive more than one type.

[b] 1997 JTPA dollars are not adjusted for inflation. Adjusted, the figure would be approx $1 billion.

adult "exiters," or those adults who received WIA services were low-income, and only 8 percent received TANF (U.S. Department of Labor 2003).[12] Notably, the percentage of the WIA caseload in poverty and receiving welfare declined steadily between 2001 and 2003. Further, a larger proportion of the WIA clientele were high school graduates; 28 percent had received some education beyond high school.

The racial and ethnic composition of the adult clientele also shifted under WIA. The representation of whites and Latinos increased slightly, and there was a small decline in black participation, from 35 percent under JTPA to 31 percent under WIA in 2003. In short, our data suggest a movement away from serving the most disadvantaged adults. WIA is a much narrower path to

Table 5.3   Adult Caseloads from JTPA to WIA, Nationally and Six States, Between 1997 and 2003

	JTPA Caseload, July 1997 to June 1998	WIA Caseload, October 2002 to September 2003	Caseload Change	Percent of Change
U.S Total	147,717	253,053	105,336	+71
Florida	6,746	11,395	4,649	+69
Illinois	6,241	6,454	213	+3
Massachusetts	2,626	1,727	−899	−34
Pennsylvania	9,663	4,405	−5,258	−54
Rhode Island	495	627	132	+27
Washington	3,618	3,958	340	+9

Sources: U.S. Department of Labor, 2004, *WIA Performance Measures by State*, available at: http://www.doleta.gov/performance/results/WIASRD/PY2003/State_WIA_Performance_Measures_Adult_2003.pdf; Social Policy Research Associates 1999.
Figures in this chart are for adults only; dislocated workers are excluded.
Title III is excluded in PY 1997 (PY 1997 includes title II-A only; WIA included adults only).

training for welfare recipients, African Americans, and other low-income and undereducated populations than was its predecessor.

CROSS-STATE VARIATION

As noted earlier, devolution led to much more state control over the implementation of WIA than had been the case with JTPA. Therefore, it is important to explore the extent to which access to training under WIA varies among states. An examination of data culled from annual WIA reports submitted to the U.S. Department of Labor by each of our six states sheds light on the variation in access to training among those states. Table 5.3 shows that overall, the trends in these states are generally consistent with the national trend of an increasing caseload under WIA. In four of the six states, caseloads increased, although the degree to which they did so differed substantially. Florida saw a dramatic increase in its caseload, while Illinois, Rhode Island, and Washington experienced more moderate gains. In Massachusetts and Pennsylvania. however, the caseloads were reduced by one-third to over one-half between 1997 and 2003. In 2003, Pennsylvania served nearly 5,300 fewer adults under WIA than it did in 1997 under JTPA.

While the caseloads generally increased, the proportion of adult WIA clients who received education and training declined significantly in all six states, as was the case nationally. Table 5.4 shows that in 1997 the majority of

Table 5.4   Percentage of Adult Exiters Who Received Services Beyond Objective Assessment Receiving Training in Six States and Nationally

	JTPA, July 1997 to June 1998			WIA, October 2002 to September 2003			Change from 1997 to 2003			
	Adults	Number Trained	Percentage Trained	Adults	Number Trained	Percentage Trained	Adults	Number Trained	Percentage Trained	Percentage Reduction in Number Trained
U.S Total	147,717	134,422	91	253,053	102,950	56	105,336	−31,472	−35	−23
Florida	6,746	5,060	75	11,395	6,836	60	4,649	1,777	−15	35
Illinois	6,241	5,617	90	6,454	3,219	50	213	−2,398	−40	−43
Massachusetts	2,626	2,442	93	1,727	993	57	−899	−1,449	−36	−59
Pennsylvania	9,663	8,987	93	4,405	3,056	69	−5,258	−5,931	−24	−66
Rhode Island	495	470	95	627	356	57	132	−114	−38	−24
Washington	3,618	3,401	94	3,958	2,165	55	340	−1,236	−39	−36

Sources: States' PY 2003 number trained—state annual WIA reports, available at: http://www.doleta.gov/performance/results/AnnualReports/annual-report-03.cfm. States' PY 2003 number of adults—U.S. Department of Labor, WIA performance measures by states, available at: http://www.doleta.gov/performance/results/WIASRD/PY2003/State_WIA_Performance_Measures_Adult_2003.pdf. States' PY 1997—Social Policy Research Associates 1999. National PY 2003—U.S. Department of Labor, http://www.doleta.gov/performances/results/WIASRD/PY2003/WIA_Summary_03_adult.pdf. National PY 1997—Social Policy Research Associates 1999.

Figures are for adults only; dislocated workers are excluded; Title III is excluded in PY 1997 (PY 1997 includes title II-A only; PY 2001 included adults only).

Number Trained for PY 2003 comes from Table B, Employment and Credential denominator. Table B comes from the 2003 annual WIA reports from the states.

Number Trained for PY 1997: Raw numbers were calculated from the percentages provided.

Figure 5.1   Percentage of JTPA and WIA Exiters Receiving Training

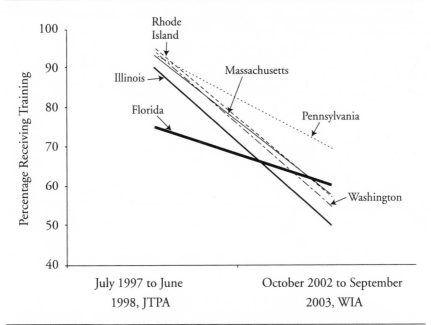

Sources: States' PY 2003 number trained—state annual WIA reports, available at: http://www.doleta.gov/performance/results/AnnualReports/annual-report-03.cfm. States' PY 2003 number of adults—U.S. Department of Labor, WIA performance measures by states, available at: http://www.doleta.gov/performance/results/WIASRD/PY2003/State_WIA_Performance_Measures_Adult_2003.pdf. States' PY 1997—Social Policy Research Associates 1999. National PY 2003—U.S. Department of Labor, http://www.doleta.gov/performances/results/WIASRD/PY2003/WIA_Summary_03_adult.pdf. National PY 1997—Social Policy Research Associates 1999.
Figures are for adults only; dislocated workers are excluded; Title III is excluded in PY 1997 (PY 1997 includes title II-A only; PY 2001 included adults only).
Number Trained for PY 2003 comes from Table B, Employment and Credential denominator. Table B comes from the 2003 annual WIA reports from the states.
Number Trained for PY 1997: Raw numbers were calculated from the percentages provided.

our states provided education and training to over 90 percent of JTPA clients (Florida was the exception, providing education and training to 75 percent of its JTPA client base). But by 2003, all six states provided education and training to a far smaller percentage of their client base than in 1997. As can be seen in figure 5.1, rates of access to education and training across the states ranged from a high of 69 percent in Pennsylvania to a low of 50 percent in Illinois in 2003, representing reductions of 15 to 40 percent among the six states.

The decline in the percentage of clients trained was so steep that the raw number of individuals receiving training under WIA also dropped, despite

Figure 5.2   Number of JTPA and WIA Exiters Receiving Training

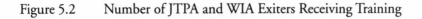

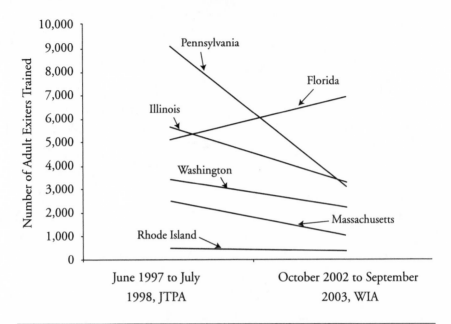

Sources: States' PY 2003 number trained—state annual WIA reports, available at: http://www.doleta.gov/performance/results/AnnualReports/annual-report-03.cfm. States' PY 2003 number of adults—U.S. Department of Labor, WIA performance measures by states, available at: http://www.doleta.gov/performance/results/WIASRD/PY2003/State_WIA_Performance_Measures_Adult_2003.pdf. States' PY 1997—Social Policy Research Associates 1999. National PY 2003—U.S. Department of Labor, http://www.doleta.gov/performances/results/WIASRD/PY2003/WIA_Summary_03_adult.pdf. National PY 1997—Social Policy Research Associates 1999.
Figures are for adults only; dislocated workers are excluded; Title III is excluded in PY 1997 (PY 1997 includes title II-A only; PY 2001 included adults only).
Number Trained for PY 2003 comes from Table B, Employment and Credential denominator. Table B comes from the 2003 annual WIA reports from the states.
Number Trained for PY 1997: Raw numbers were calculated from the percentages provided.

the significant increases in overall caseload. As table 5.4 and figure 5.2 show, the absolute numbers trained under WIA dropped precipitously in five of the six states (Florida was the exception). In the most extreme example of this phenomenon, in 2003 the state of Pennsylvania provided training for 3,056 clients under WIA, a mere 34 percent of the 8,987 who received training during the last year of JTPA.

These data demonstrate an unmistakable reduction in access to education and training under WIA. Yes, WIA is serving a larger number of clients overall when compared with JTPA in 1997. But even within that larger pool of clients, WIA is providing education and training to a significantly smaller percentage of clients than was the case under JTPA, as well as a smaller absolute number, despite the increase in number of clients. This is problematic since training provides a larger earnings boost than either core or intensive services. A year after exiting WIA, clients who received only core services increased their earnings by $2,315, whereas those who received training increased their earnings by $3,445. The middle level of services, résumé-building services labeled "intensive," appear to result in no more gains than the "core" services of job search (Social Policy Research Associates 2005, 66).

TRACING CLIENTS THROUGH SEQUENTIAL SERVICES

As noted earlier, one mechanism whereby access to education and training has been reduced under WIA is through the sequential provision of services, which means that usually a client has to pass through "core" (job-search) and "intensive" (résumé-building) services before receiving "training." Examining the flow of clients through one-stop services allows us to understand the extent to which this mechanism has been implemented and limits the number of clients receiving training. An analysis of WIASRD data conducted for the Department of Labor by the Jacob France Institute provides a detailed picture of one-stop client flows in three of our states: Florida, Illinois, and Washington (Stevens 2003a, 2003b).[13] The data describe the services adult exiters received during program year 2000 (July 2000 to June 2001) and program year 2001 (July 2001 to June 2002).[14] (These data are from different time periods than the data on training presented in table 5.3, and should not be directly compared.) Researchers assigned each WIA adult exiter a single code indicating the highest level of service received.

The data presented in table 5.5 allow several comparisons. First, we can compare the proportion of adults receiving core, intensive, and training services within each state, and across the three states for which we have data. Second, we can look at any change over time within WIA's implementation period, in order to assess the effects of implementation, both within and across states.

Overall, the number of individuals receiving some kind of service through WIA increased in Florida, Illinois, and Washington between July 2000 and June 2002 (although the numbers served remained smaller than under JTPA). Indeed, Washington served nearly twice as many adults using WIA dollars during program year 2001 as it did during program year 2000, and Illinois and Florida increased their WIA caseloads by about one-third.[15] However, during the same time period, the percent of WIA clients receiving training declined in all three states, even as the absolute numbers trained grew. The client-flow data show that whereas Florida, Illinois, and Washington provided training to 51, 59, and 73 percent, respectively, of all clients, in

Table 5.5   WIA Adult Client Flow in Florida, Illinois, and Washington

Time Frame	Total Participants	Core[a]	Core, Percentage	Intensive[b]	Intensive, Percentage	Training[c]	Training, Percentage
Florida							
PY 2000[d]	10,821	2,792	26	2,497	23	5,532	51
PY 2001[e]	15,143	4,345	29	3,724	25	7,074	47
Illinois							
PY 2000	2,742	610	22	521	19	1,611	59
PY 2001	3,490	718	21	1,126	32	1,646	47
Washington							
PY 2000	1,248	72	6	260	21	916	73
PY 2001	2,225	184	8	793	36	1,248	56

Source: Stevens (2003a).
[a] Core = Those receiving core services only.
[b] Intensive = Those who advanced from core services to intensive services only.
[c] Training = Those who progressed from core services through intensive services to training services.
[d] PY 2000 = July 2000 to June 2001.
[e] PY 2001 = July 2001 to June 2002.

Program Year 2000, by program year 2001 the proportions had all dropped, to 47 percent in Florida, 47 percent in Illinois, and 56 percent in Washington.[16] This change reflects a growing tendency for WIA clients to receive only core and intensive services—little more than basic job-search and résumé-building assistance. Access to training has become increasingly rare, a fact that strongly suggests that the work-first ideology is becoming increasingly pervasive as WIA is implemented over time.

If WIA clients did not receive training in these three states, what services were they most likely to receive? Comparing the states, we see that in program year 2001 Florida clients had about an equal probability of receiving both core and intensive and receiving core service only, whereas in Illinois and Washington the probability was greater that a client would receive both core and intensive rather than just core services. This may mean that Florida caseworkers were more able than were other states' caseworkers to successfully place clients in jobs at the core stage. But in any case it reflects less access to higher levels of services. Access to the higher tiers of services, including training, is clearly greatest in Washington in program years 2000 and 2001, but we note a precipitous decline over time in the percentage trained.

Overall, the case-flow data presented in table 5.5 demonstrate the existence of the sequential provision of services under WIA, and do indeed indicate a reduction in access to training under WIA. Although a portion of WIA clients in these three states do proceed through the tiers to eventually access training, the number of WIA clients who have access to education and training is limited by the sequential nature of the system.

ACCESS FOR THE MOST DISADVANTAGED

As we noted earlier, because of limitations in reporting requirements, we are not able to know at the federal level how many low-income adults receive training under WIA. However, the Jacob France Institute's analysis of the WIASRD data does provide information on the extent to which access to WIA services is evenly distributed across a range of demographic categories in Florida, Illinois, and Washington.

TANF RECIPIENTS

Table 5.6 indicates that TANF recipients are not well served by WIA. First, it is clear that in Illinois and Washington, less than one-fifth of the WIA adult clients served in program years 2000 and 2001 were TANF recipients. In sharp contrast, more than two-thirds (69 percent) of the WIA adults served in Florida in program year 2000 were TANF recipients. And yet, by program year 2001, that proportion dropped substantially, to just over one-third (35 percent). Thus, in all three states, TANF recipients represent a minority of WIA clients, and WIA clients are a small proportion of TANF recipients (see the last two columns in table 5.5). Indeed, in Illinois and Washington, less than 1 percent of all TANF adult recipients are also WIA clients. In Florida, about one-fifth of TANF clients are also served with WIA dollars. This state variation is likely the result of the extent to which TANF and WIA are coordinated at the state and local levels. But overall, it is clear that few welfare recipients receive WIA services, and they represent a small proportion of adults served by WIA.

Next, we examine the proportion of TANF adults receiving training within each state. Illinois and Washington, which both serve small WIA TANF adult populations, greatly reduced the proportion of those adults receiving training between program year 2000 and program year 2001 (from 74 to 61 percent in Washington, and from 73 to 38 percent in Illinois). The major shift in both states appears to have been from "training" to "intensive" services; in other words, in program year 2001 the majority of TANF recipients received core (job-search) and intensive (résumé-building) services, but not training services. In Florida, by contrast, though the proportion of WIA adults that were TANF recipients in Florida declined over time, the propor-

Table 5.6   WIA and TANF Adult Client Flow in Florida, Illinois, and Washington

Time Frame	Total Participants	Percentage of Total	Core[a]	Core, Percentage	Intensive[b]	Intensive, Percentage	Training[c]	Training, Percentage	TANF Caseload	Percentage of TANF Caseload Served by WIA
Florida										
PY 2000[d]	7,497	69	1,128	15	1,636	22	4,733	63	32,164	23.31
PY 2001[e]	5,239	35	798	15	1,101	21	3,340	64	25,604	20.46
Illinois										
PY 2000	282	10	40	14	37	13	205	73	66,143	0.43
PY 2001	325	9	58	18	145	45	122	38	25,353	1.28
Washington										
PY 2000	189	15	10	5	39	21	140	74	48,307	0.39
PY 2001	305	14	9	3	109	36	187	61	42,022	0.73

Sources: Stevens 2003b. *TANF Adult Caseload Numbers:* U.S. Department of Health and Human Services, 2004, *TANF Sixth Annual Report to Congress,* Table 3:4:a, http://www.acf.hhs.gov/programs/ofa/annualreport6/chapter03/0304a.htm; U.S. Department of Health and Human Services, 2002, *TANF Fourth Annual Report to Congress,* Table 3:4:a, http://www.acf.dhhs.gov/programs/opre/ar2001/0304at.htm
[a] Core = Those receiving only core-assisted services.
[b] Intensive = Those who progressed from core services only to intensive services.
[c] Training = Those who progressed from core services through intensive services to training services.
[d] PY 2000 = July 2000 to June 2001.
[e] PY 2001 = July 2001 to June 2002.

tion receiving training remained stable: nearly two-thirds in both program year 2000 (63 percent) and program year 2001 (64 percent). Comparing our three states, it is evident that Florida's WIA program both serves a greater proportion of TANF recipients and provides greater access to training than either Illinois or Washington. This may be explained by the fact that Florida's WIA and TANF programs are better integrated than they are in the other two states. Of the three states, Illinois experienced the greatest decline in access to training under WIA. These results confirm the data presented in table 5.4, and also tell us that the trends in access to education and training for TANF adults and for the overall WIA adult population are similar.

The small proportion of TANF recipients served by WIA leads us to ask: To what extent does WIA serve other groups of disadvantaged adults? Table 5.7 breaks down WIA clients by several demographic categories (income, race and ethnicity, English proficiency, and income), and the proportion of each group that receives access to training in Florida, Illinois, and Washington, using the WIASRD data provided by the Jacob France Institute (Stevens 2003a, 2003b).

LOW-INCOME CLIENTS

First, we examine the broadest category of disadvantage, those clients designated "low-income," to gain a general sense of whether WIA clients are being disproportionately turned away from training by virtue of their financial status. This measure (table 5.7) appears to indicate that WIA serves substantial numbers of low-income adults, even if the number of these receiving cash welfare is quite small. Across the three states, low-income adults make up the majority (70 to 87 percent) of WIA clients. In addition, these low-income adults enjoy approximately the same access to training as the overall WIA adult population in each of the three states.[17] Thus, when WIA clients are categorized according to income alone, we do not see a reduction in access to training.

RACIAL AND ETHNIC MINORITIES

The picture looks quite different when we examine WIA clients according to their racial and ethnic backgrounds (table 5.6). Black and Hispanic adults make up 72 percent of the Florida WIA clientele, 50 percent of the Illinois WIA clients, and 14 percent of Washington WIA clients—differences that are partly explained by overall state demographics. We can see that access to training across racial groups is not distributed evenly. In Florida, Illinois, and Washington, 65 percent, 63 percent, and 59 percent, respectively, of white WIA clients received training. The percentage of blacks and Hispanics receiv-

Table 5.7   Demographic Characteristics of WIA Adult Client Flow in Florida, Illinois, and Washington, Between July 2001 and June 2002

	Total Participants	Percentage of Total	Core and Intensive Services		Training Services	
			Participants	Percentage	Participants	Percentage
Florida						
Race						
Latino	4,152	27	3,022	73	1,130	27
White	3,975	26	1,382	35	2,593	65
Black	6,838	45	3,589	52	3,249	48
Asian	92	1	31	34	61	66
Other	86	1	45	52	41	48
Low income	10,532	70	5,066	48	5,466	52
Limited English proficiency	1,475	10	1,093	74	382	26
Total	15,143	100	8,069	53	7,074	47
Illinois						
Race						
Latino	274	8	176	64	98	36
White	1,604	46	594	37	1,010	63

Black	1,463	42	974	67	489	33
Asian	118	3	83	70	35	30
Other	31	1	17	55	14	45
Low income	3,028	87	1,540	51	1,488	49
Limited English proficiency	243	7	178	73	65	27
Total	3,490	100	1,844	53	1,646	47
Washington						
Race						
Latino	187	8	87	47	100	53
White	1,648	74	669	41	979	59
Black	136	6	71	52	65	48
Asian	59	3	24	41	35	59
Other	195	9	126	65	69	35
Low income	1,925	87	807	42	1,118	58
Limited English proficiency	174	8	98	56	76	44
Total	2,225	100	977	44	1,248	56

Source: Stevens (2003b).

ing training was significantly lower in all three states: only 48 percent of black WIA clients in Florida and Washington, and only 33 percent in Illinois. For Hispanics, the training-access figure is below both that for whites and the overall average in all three states: 27 percent in Florida, 36 percent in Illinois, and 53 percent in Washington. Although the degree of these inequities in delivery of services across the three states varies, the overall trend is clear. White WIA clients are disproportionately more likely to receive access to training than are their black and Hispanic counterparts (see also Goldrick-Rab and Shaw 2005).

THOSE WITH LIMITED ENGLISH PROFICIENCY

Another way to examine disadvantage is to discern the degree to which WIA clients with Limited English Proficiency (LEP), who represent 10 percent or less of the total WIA clientele across these three states, receive access to training through WIA. Table 5.7 shows that their rates of training are less than half those for the overall WIA population. In the state of Florida, 47 percent of the overall WIA clientele but only 26 percent of LEP clients receive access to training. The patterns are similar in both Illinois and Washington—47 versus 27 percent in Illinois, and 56 versus 44 percent in Washington. This finding is particularly troubling in light of the fact that these adults may well require additional English skills before they can obtain a job that ensures self-sufficiency.

SOME CONCLUSIONS

Clearly, WIA makes a much smaller investment than JTPA in America's unemployed and underemployed workers. The data presented indicate a rather drastic drop in participation in education and training under WIA. Although more people receive some type of services under WIA, a growing percentage receive only superficial and rather ineffective services of job search and résumé-building assistance. A far smaller percentage of clients receive access to training under WIA than under JTPA, and as WIA moves toward full implementation, the trend is toward even less access to training. Disadvantaged clients, particularly TANF clients, nonwhites, and those with limited English proficiency, receive consistently lower-than-average access to training. This is ironic, since WIA data clearly indicate that low-income and TANF clients who receive training services accrue larger earnings gains than other clients (Social Policy Research Associates 2005, 62). Worse, in the three states in which we could conduct a finer-grained analysis, we see that WIA has essentially been eliminated as an avenue toward training for most welfare clients.

These policy outcomes are startling, given that President Bill Clinton (1998), speaking in the Rose Garden the day he signed the bill, stated that the WIA was intended to "giv[e] all Americans the tools they need to learn for a lifetime." Unfortunately, these tools have become increasingly inaccessible to WIA clients in general, and in particular to those with the most barriers to employment success. Despite the customer-friendly rhetoric, it is clear that when Congress rechristened the Job Training Partnership Act, its employment and training program, as the Workforce Investment Act, it eliminated in both name and practice much of the training available to disadvantaged adults.

Yet even these data do not tell the whole story of how and why WIA has so greatly reduced access. As noted earlier, WIA is guided both by the work-first philosophy and by an emphasis on increased efficiency and accountability. An examination of the implementation of this policy in the next chapter illustrates how these two guiding philosophies work to reduce access to education and training.

CHAPTER SIX

THE IMPLEMENTATION OF WIA:
DOES THE RHETORIC MATCH THE REALITY?

PUBLIC POLICIES are driven by political ideas, goals, and rhetoric, and the Workforce Investment Act is no exception. As explained in the last chapter, WIA contains two major philosophies: a work-first approach, which is designed to foster immediate attachment to the labor market without much concern about investment in education and skills; and a market-based approach to the delivery of training that utilizes accountability and customer satisfaction as means to improve both choice and quality of training. These two philosophies are in many ways contradictory: work-first is based on the premise that rapid workforce attachment is a "one-size-fits-all" solution, whereas the market aspects of WIA are designed to increase the ability of clients to develop individualized solutions to their employment problems. In spite of this contradiction, we argue, the market-oriented aspects of WIA actually reinforce the goals of work-first by contributing to the reduction in access to education and training, especially for disadvantaged adults. As a result, the goals of the work-first philosophy dominate WIA.

Quantitative evidence strongly indicates that access to education and training has been greatly reduced under WIA, particularly for disadvantaged groups such as TANF recipients and nonwhite WIA clients. How did this happen? How were the dominant philosophies in this policy put into practice? How were they enacted at the ground level? In this chapter we trace the effects of WIA from formal policy to implementation, using qualitative data from multiple state case studies. First we examine how a central aspect of WIA—its three tiers of services—functions to reduce access to training for WIA clients. Next, we examine how WIA accountability measures provide strong incentives for one-stop career centers to direct their limited training dollars toward assisting relatively advantaged WIA clients, while diverting those with more extensive training needs. We further trace the implementation of WIA to the community colleges, illustrating how stringent reporting requirements combine with the overall reduction in the number of WIA clients to discourage community colleges from participating in the training of WIA clients. Their reluctance to participate is exacerbated by what the colleges perceive to be a clash between their traditional academic mission and an increasingly aggressive push toward workforce development. These factors combine to marginalize the role of community colleges in the delivery of training to WIA clients.

Finally, we explore the complexity and effects of WIA implementation in detail by examining the case of Florida.

SEQUENTIAL ELIGIBILITY: CLOSING THE PIPELINE TO TRAINING

Chapter 5 describes how WIA's model of sequential eligibility creates a hierarchy of services that restricts access to training. Effects of this restriction in the pipeline from local WIA offices to contracted training providers were felt acutely at the community colleges that we studied. Most reported a significant decrease in the number of WIA clients enrolled at their colleges than under JTPA. For example, in Illinois the ideology of rapid labor-force attachment was so clearly embraced by caseworkers at one-stop career centers that very few individuals received the vouchers—Individual Training Accounts, or ITAs—needed to access training during the initial years of implementation. According to a director of a program for truck-driver training (a short-term training program appropriate for many WIA clients) at an Illinois community college, the college experienced a large decline in the number of clients served when the transition from JTPA to WIA occurred. He said, "We had a very small number of folks that came through WIA. We had a great pool of people that *should* have been coming through WIA; I was interviewing people every day that were qualified. But they would not send them; they would not fund them."

A one-stop career center employee in the college's local area confirmed his impression, saying:

> You have to go through core and intensive services before you ever get to training services. I've been in meetings where it has actually been stated that nobody is ever going to get to training because everybody is going to get a job in core or intensive. Our clients that are going to be left as we get to the bottom of the caseload are people who have a lot of barriers they have to overcome before they can even get training. So at this point, the ITAs really aren't an option for that group of people.

It was not until the federal government began talking about rescinding unspent WIA dollars that the state began to issue more ITAs. But even then, as discussed in chapter 5, access to training in this state remained low. As of 2004 to 2005, local advocates were still citing difficulties in getting local WIA offices to issue ITAs for training (Chicago Jobs Council 2005a, 2005b).

Pennsylvania provides an example of the particular difficulties faced by low-income WIA clients seeking training. The state has developed a job-training program for welfare recipients, using WIA funds. This program is designed to "provide job readiness preparation and job placement services for welfare clients" by providing eight weeks of job-readiness training for at-risk clients (Pennsylvania Department of Public Welfare 2004). Very few low-income WIA clients or welfare recipients are referred to this program. As a one-stop career counselor stated, "The focus is getting these clients working." Even those who manage to enter this program designed for particularly disadvantaged clients receive little more than job-search assistance. As the career counselor noted, the program "wants to get them to work." Actual job-skills training is absent from the program.

The abrupt closure of the training pipeline via WIA has had a direct effect on the ability of community colleges to provide education and training to disadvantaged populations. A Pennsylvania community college administrator details the effect of the shift from human-capital to work-first philosophies on her college's ability to train low-income adults. With the enactment of welfare reform and WIA, she said,

> We've kind of transitioned into new and different things. . . . Not by choice so much as by we had to. . . . Money wasn't there any more to support the programs. . . . As a matter of fact, there was a year or two where we weren't even allowed to do job training. There was not money, and it was all get a job, get a job. Then in the last three years they've kind of mixed the program a little bit but the focus is on getting a job and retaining a job. Work-first—that's the buzzword. The training has been kind of left in the dust.

These interview excerpts are typical of those we conducted across our states. As they clearly suggest, the power of the work-first philosophy is substantial at the local level. Sequential eligibility has taken firm hold on one-stop career centers, and the subsequent reduction in those eligible for training has greatly reduced the number of students supported by WIA in community colleges. As a result, as WIA is implemented, the dominance of work-first in both formal policy and in the interpretation of this policy by state officials and caseworkers prevents many WIA clients from ever setting foot on a college campus.

DEVOLUTION IN PRACTICE: LESS
FUNDING FOR WIA SERVICES

WIA's governance structure places increased responsibility for coordination and implementation on state and local Workforce Investment Boards (WIBs). States are required to develop and maintain a system of service delivery that reduces many of the barriers that existed to services in the past, such as having to travel to multiple offices to obtain services, and they are required to provide universal access to services. WIA has, in essence, required states to develop a new system of service delivery.

However, funds were not earmarked for this purpose, and so they had to be drawn from the general WIA fund that each state and locality received; and states and localities were also required to provide the resources needed to collect and report on outcome measures (U.S. Government Accountability Office 2002). As a result, a significant proportion of state and local WIA funds have been allocated for building an infrastructure of one-stop career centers and collecting data, rather than for direct services. Thus, because local career centers are mandated to provide "universal access" to their services, their limited funding and the need to funnel a portion of that funding to the operation of one-stop career centers further reduces their ability to provide training, their most expensive service. WIBs have responded to these restrictions; 85 percent of them limit the amount of money participants can spend on training using ITAs (the limit is generally $3,000 to 5,000), and two-thirds limit the amount of time participants may be enrolled in training, usually two years (U.S. Government Accountability Office 2005). One Florida WIB director described the dilemma in this way:

> When WIA came into being we had to start improving our core and intensive services, because less dollars are available for training. . . . We have had to put a cap on our number of ITAs so we could serve a broader number of people. . . . We tried for as long as we could to not put a cap because it creates issues for individuals trying to get to school; we didn't want to put another barrier in place. . . . But it was the only way we could continue to serve . . . a wide variety and number of people.

As this example illustrates, the increased autonomy afforded to states via devolution comes with a substantial price tag. The costs of implementing the one-stop career-center service-delivery model has decreased overall funding for direct services, and this has served to limit rather than expand educational opportunities for WIA clients. Simply put, when less funding is available for education and training, less education and training occurs.

127

EFFECTS ON THE ONE-STOP CAREER CENTERS: ACCOUNTABILITY MEASURES AND CREAMING

WIA's accountability system is a feature central to its market-oriented service-delivery model. One-stop career centers and training providers are required to provide data on an array of outcome measures, including job placement and earnings, client satisfaction, and employer satisfaction. These reporting requirements were designed to improve quality and to provide clients with the tools to make informed decisions regarding training, but in practice they often send conflicting signals to WIA caseworkers regarding which services, if any, are most appropriate for clients. Moreover, our interviews with caseworkers revealed that they consistently interpreted WIA reporting requirements in ways that made it more difficult for disadvantaged clients to receive training.

For example, strictly enforced outcome measures in the form of job placement rates and customer satisfaction measures encourage one-stop centers to provide services only to clients who are most likely to produce successful outcomes. Some outcome measures are designed to encourage caseworkers to address the needs of disadvantaged clients, but others discourage them from doing so. And in many cases, even measures intended to promote assistance to the most disadvantaged, such as earnings gains, fail to fulfill their purpose because their construction is so complex that even administrators and caseworkers misunderstand them. In other words, some states fail to serve disadvantaged adults and simultaneously fail to perform well on outcome measures simply because caseworkers and WIA administrators do not understand how to best meet those measures, or choose to ignore them.

Our interviews with caseworkers clearly suggest that their decisions regarding which type of WIA outcome measures to focus on disproportionately hurt the most disadvantaged clients. The result is a phenomenon referred to as "creaming." Creaming is "the practice of selecting people [to participate in a program] who are most likely to succeed" (U.S. Department of Labor, n.d.). In this case, creaming occurs when caseworkers pick clients for services on the basis of their perceived ability to complete those services and find work, rather than on their need for increased skills or education. This goal leads caseworkers to select the seemingly "better-off" clients and advance them, leaving individuals with greater perceived barriers (and perhaps greater need) behind. A caseworker who enrolls only the clients who are most likely to get a job quickly, or who only refers those clients to training, may well meet his job placement target, but in so doing he may fail to pass the earnings measure.

This creaming phenomenon occurs despite the fact that creaming in one area, job placement, often leads to poor results in another, earnings gains. To see why this is so, one must understand how earnings gains are measured. In order to meet the target for the earnings measure, a client must not only get a job but earn a certain amount more than she did at a previous job. Thus, if the required earnings increase is $8 per hour, caseworkers must place clients in jobs where they earn $8 per hour more than they did at their last job. Therefore, caseworkers will more easily meet the measure by finding a job that pays $8 per hour for a previous unemployed client, whose last earnings were $0 per hour, than by finding a job for a previously employed minimum-wage worker ($5.15 per hour) that pays $13.15 per hour. So although it may be easier to place a client with some previous employment, the caseworker is less likely to meet his earnings measure that way—especially if he does not refer that client to training first. Thus, opting for easy placements in order to meet the job-placement measures may simultaneously result in a failure to meet the earnings measure.[1] Yet, caseworkers often fail to comprehend the complexity of this set of measures, and simply choose to focus on placing those they perceive as the "easiest" clients—those who are already well trained and educated—although enrolling disadvantaged clients and providing them training before sending them into the labor market is more likely to meet both the job placement *and* the earnings measures. Perhaps most important, the complexity of the policy itself provides caseworkers will little explicit incentive not to cream.

Caseworkers can and do decide which types of potential clients they will serve, as a conversation with an employee in a Rhode Island one-stop career center reveals. This caseworker described a steady pressure to meet performance targets for job placements, asserting that "the fewer of those [low-literacy] people I have to deal with, the more I am ensuring that my performance will be in the higher level, the more acceptable level." When asked, "So there's more outreach to [high-skilled workers]?" he answered, "Yes."

The strategy the caseworker uses is clearly intended to meet the job-placement targets by enrolling only the more-advantaged customers and making quick job placements rather than sending them to training. This career-center worker went on to detail the differences between what he sees as a desirable client and an undesirable one. Of the undesirable client he said, "The person says, 'Yeah, I can collect for twenty-six weeks; I'll worry about it on the twenty-fourth week and go out and get a job.' That's not a motivated client." A desirable client is one who is highly motivated to get a job: "Somebody comes in and says, 'I don't want to be here, I want to be working.' . . . We're going to enroll you in WIA, yes. Because what do I have? I have a motivated client for which I can get an outcome. . . . Now if that sounds like creaming, it might be, to an extent." In this way, career-center workers make strategic decisions in response to their often incomplete understanding of the job-placement requirement of the outcomes-oriented funding formula.[2]

This situation is exacerbated by the fact that many WIA caseworkers seem to be unaware of the incentive embedded in WIA to serve low-income clients. Even though caseworkers can meet their measures by enrolling disadvantaged clients, since it is relatively easy to achieve a dramatic increase in earnings for a previous unemployed individuals with relatively modest employment, caseworkers are often unaware of this provision. A career-center director in Rhode Island reported,

> There is no regression model under these performance standards like there was under JTPA. Under JTPA, the more of the hard-to-serve that you served, the lower your standard of placement . . . and you looked at wages. Female was a criteria, because women get paid less. So the more females you serve, the outcome is probably going to be lower wages. So the more women you served, they gave you credit for that.

Clearly, this caseworker perceives a significant shift between JTPA and WIA policy, and he sees WIA as a hostile environment for individuals who are unlikely to obtain high wage employment.[3] In examining WIA's implementation, then, we see that WIA is in practice unreceptive to low-income clients in part because its accountability measures are interpreted as such by caseworkers, leading to practices that effectively result in work-first practices. This analysis is supported by the quantitative data reported in chapter 5, which clearly showed lower training participation among a range of disadvantaged clients.

We found additional evidence of creaming in Florida that resulted from the ways caseworkers interpreted accountability measures. Florida's twenty-four regional WIBs are rated on their one-stop career-center wage and placement rates in a document known as the "Red and Green Report," which places each region in a positive (green) or negative (red) performance category. This report is quite controversial throughout the state. Especially in urban areas, WIBs struggle to maintain good performance indicators while serving the state's most disadvantaged populations. Caseworkers are so wary of clients who may be bad bets for long-term employment that they often will not provide them with services of any kind.

In one Florida region, the local WIB felt intense pressure from the state to improve performance and in turn pressured the local one-stop career centers to improve their outcomes. The result was that many local one-stop workers, including those at community college one-stop locations, felt the need to cream clients, which they did by excluding from the record-keeping system those who were at high risk for failure, as a dialogue with a one-stop career center caseworker revealed:

> Caseworker: The emphasis is placement, and we are supposed to register in the database only those people who are looking for work. Only serious job seekers, and they [the State Department of Labor] are looking more for quality, not quantity.
>
> Question: You are only supposed to register in the database serious job seekers?
>
> Caseworker: Yes, serious job seekers. Meaning that we have students because of where we're located [at a community college] that either don't have to work or they're working at a job but they just come in here to look to see if there's something better.
>
> Question: But they [Workforce Florida, Inc.] don't want those people to be entered into the system in the first place?
>
> Caseworker: No, because we're supposed to place one out of three people.
>
> Question: Oh, right, it's for statistical purposes obviously.
>
> Caseworker: Yes.
>
> Question: So if you're entering too many into the system and you don't place all of them . . . your numbers don't look great.
>
> Caseworker: Yes.
>
> Question: But it's a little bit of "number-playing" then?
>
> Caseworker: Oh well, you know, we just have to be careful who we enter because we need to be successful.

The manipulation of the numbers used to report outcomes has many obvious consequences, but perhaps the most significant of these is that it affects the ability of some individuals to access WIA funds for training, because individuals who have never been enrolled in the reporting system are not eligible for training vouchers. Thus, the way WIA is actually implemented means that the accountability mechanisms inherent in the policy result in fewer services for harder-to-serve clients such as those without strong work histories or educational backgrounds. In some instances, those who are not readily employable are refused service. In this way, the accountability measures reinforce a work-first approach to WIA that erects, rather than dismantles, barriers to education and training for low-income clients.

ACCOUNTABILITY MEASURES: DISINCENTIVES FOR COMMUNITY COLLEGES

Under WIA, training providers are required to report an array of outcome measures, which in theory allows clients with ITAs to choose the highest-quality training available. Our case studies reveal, however, that measures of training-provider performance are perceived by many community colleges to be so onerous that they reduce the ability or willingness of many colleges to function as training providers for WIA. This element of WIA does provide WIA clients with more information about training delivered by providers that choose to participate. However, the reporting requirements also reduce the number of choices available by erecting barriers to community college participation in WIA-funded education and training.

For example, "customer satisfaction" is a core element of WIA, and training providers are required to deliver satisfactory service, both to the state and the individual client. Provider performance is assessed with a plethora of measures. First, data must be collected on program completion rates, percentage of participants obtaining unsubsidized employment, and wages at placement for *all* participants in programs in which even one WIA client is enrolled. Second, for all WIA participants in all programs, training providers must report the percentage who complete training and are placed in unsubsidized employment; the six-month employment-retention rate for those who are employed; the six-month wage rate for those who are employed; and rates of licensure, degree attainment, or certification (U.S. Department of Labor 1998).

As a result, colleges that participate tend to offer programs that are likely to produce the best outcome measures, and these tend to be short-term programs that lead to immediate employment. The director of the office of research at an Illinois community college described the challenges of providing data demanded under WIA:

> Some of them [local WIA administrators] are on my back. Some of them want a copy of your catalogue, you know, pull together a copy of this and a copy of that. And you know, in the past you've been recognized, you've been allowed to operate in Illinois for a long time, and now [for the first time] they want to see all of your paperwork. And because we didn't have a data collection office until recently, some of our data is pretty bad. And I know that next year we'll be required to produce certain rates, certain placement and completion rates. And

we'll probably have to drop some of our programs. But we're hoping that we'll at least get those programs on there initially, since we're a community college and all.

In this college, as in many others, the infrastructure needed to provide accurate and timely outcome data to WIA is simply not present. As a result, many community colleges no longer participate in WIA.

The U.S. Government Accountability Office has confirmed in several reports (2001, 2005) that there are significant disincentives to community college participation in WIA, including excessive data-reporting requirements, outcome measures that many providers believe are unfair, and a drastic reduction in the number of potential students who might enroll in these institutions via WIA. In its 2001 report the GAO stated, "WIA data collection coupled with the few job seekers sent to training has, to date, resulted in training providers reducing the number of programs they offer" (U.S. Government Accountability Office 2001, 11). In some states, the number of providers has been reduced by nearly half; only 35 percent of ITAs issued by local workforce Investment Boards are used at community colleges (U.S. Government Accountability Office 2005). Thus, training choices have actually been reduced, rather than expanded, under WIA.

An Illinois one-stop worker confirmed this statement saying,

There aren't a lot of providers on the list [of approved vendors]. That's the complaint we hear a lot. And community colleges aren't putting all of their programs on; they're just putting a few of their programs on. And I think the reason for that is because . . . if somebody enrolls in, say, a nursing program, then the performance of everybody that's in that program will be measured because the whole ITA system is going to be judged by their performance. It's not just the employment outcomes of the [WIA] student. It's the employment outcomes of everybody that was in that program. And, you know, a lot of those people take those classes or are in particular programs for different reasons. They may not all be taking them so they can get a job.

As this respondent suggests, the WIA reporting requirements conflict with the broader community college mission to provide access to education for a wide array of students; and they can also conflict with the real economic needs of these colleges to enroll large numbers of students. Our interviews with community college administrators suggest that if community colleges are asked to choose between maintaining the ability to enroll the few WIA clients who actually receive ITAs, and continuing to enroll a wide array of students in a wide array of programs, they will choose the latter. In part, this

133

is because WIA provides very little additional money to colleges, but imposes extensive additional administrative obligations. Consequently, some colleges choose to focus their energies in other areas, where they can both serve a greater variety of students and generate additional funds. The director of workforce development at one community college asserted, "The amount of money and personnel resources that we would have to devote to be active participants in WIA are better spent developing programs that serve a greater range of students. It's just a simple economic calculus."

"WE'RE NOT A JOB PLACEMENT FACTORY": PHILOSOPHICAL CONFLICT AT THE COMMUNITY COLLEGE

Economic and personnel concerns are not the only barriers to community college participation in WIA. For some colleges, WIA outcome measures present a philosophical barrier as well. In the training-employment equation, community colleges (like most four-year colleges) have traditionally seen their mission as providing a combination of excellent education and student services to enable students to achieve their educational goals. These institutions may place significant resources into helping students find employment via such mechanisms as a career counseling center or career days, but they have not been held accountable—nor have they viewed themselves as accountable—for the successful employment of their graduates. Those responsibilities have fallen squarely on the shoulders of students themselves or, secondarily, the local or regional employment sector.

Yet WIA holds training providers responsible for long-term employment and earnings, and in the eyes of many, these requirements conflict with the educational mission and identity of the community college. A career counselor at a Massachusetts community college who is engaged in multiple activities to infuse career issues into classrooms, the advising process, and the college environment more generally makes a critical distinction between what she does and what WIA would require her to do:

> In my little world, workforce development is really done in educational terms. We are not in the business of job placement. . . . We work with students around assisting them to figure out how to go and find a job. But it's very educational in nature. . . . If you were now in the business of placing everybody, and that becomes a requirement of your job, you're not doing the other part of your job. . . . I want to be accountable for how I choose to work with students and the quality of the services that I offer, the amount of outreach that I do, the way I try and attract students, and the follow-through I offer individuals, students,

and faculty. I don't want to be accountable for placing bodies in jobs. We're not a job placement factory.

Clearly, the outcome measures that training providers are required to collect are seen by some community colleges as a direct challenge to their educational mission. Resistance to the WIA philosophy, as expressed by the career counselor above, is another unintended result of implementation that can reduce community college participation. In the end, the reluctance of community colleges to participate in WIA, whether for practical or philosophical reasons, results in limited educational options available to WIA clients.

WIA in Action: The Case of Florida

Yet a lack of participation among community colleges does not characterize every state. In Florida, community colleges play an important role in the implementation of WIA, and the sector as a whole has adopted a workforce-development orientation that fits well with WIA's approach to training. Nevertheless, access to training continues to be restricted in this state, and the type of training available is increasingly short-term and targeted at high-skill, high-wage portions of the employment sector—a focus that effectively closes off access to training for WIA clients with low levels of formal education.

Because it was an early-implementation state for both welfare reform and WIA, Florida provides us with an unusually clear picture of how work-first policy operates on the ground. Florida's Workforce Innovation Act of 2000, which followed the passage of the federal Workforce Investment Act, merged state welfare-to-work and workforce-development agencies and services. As a result, Florida's workforce-development system is among the most integrated in the nation. Currently, both welfare reform and WIA are administered by one agency, Workforce Florida Incorporated. This move to integrate agencies and streamline the provision of services is clearly in line with the spirit of federal WIA legislation, which called for the creation of one-stop career centers to reduce administrative hassles and implement a single access point for services. In addition, Florida has been testing and refining its accountability systems, including those affecting the higher-education system, for some time. Thus, notions of accountability and a fight for funding are not new to the community colleges in Florida, which recognize, as one state senator put it, that Florida is in the "business" of education.

Florida does not provide an unfettered market in which these educational "businesses" compete. The market does not determine which types of education will flourish under WIA—the state does. WIA clients cannot access training at a community college unless their chosen work is on a regional "targeted occupations" list. These lists—there are twenty-four regions—are based on employer survey data on wages and openings that were developed by the labor-market statistics unit of the Agency for Workforce Innovation. The lists are created by calculating such factors as employment rates, job openings, program placement, and earnings data to determine a ranking of high-wage, high-demand occupations for each of the regions so that education and training can meet those needs. The lists are used to help identify vocational programs eligible for the state's performance-based funding, and these occupations are targeted for training by community colleges and local workforce investment boards. Therefore, if the regional labor market does not require workers for a specific job, or if available jobs do not pay a sufficiently high wage, individuals do not receive WIA dollars to train for that job, and colleges are not funded for student completion and placement in that job.[4]

This approach to funding education and training makes sense from an economic perspective, and is certainly in keeping with WIA's emphasis on targeted training. According to the Department of Labor, "Training services must be directly linked to occupations in demand in the local area or in another area to which the participant is willing to move." In other words, WIA clients may only choose among training programs and providers that will prepare them for jobs currently available. The state of Florida's implementation of its Workforce Innovation Act embodies this philosophy to a remarkable degree. According to a former Florida congressional legislative aide, the purpose of targeted-occupations lists is to ensure that state and federal money is spent in ways that benefit the state economy:

> The Workforce Investment Act said, "You will have the right to choose." You can make some decisions about the career you want to get into. . . . The WIA choice issue [means] you have to fix your cost. . . . You get to decide what you want to be, say you want to be an airline pilot. . . . We don't know where you're going to get a job, and we're certainly not going to pay $25,000 to have you not get a job. The targeted occupations mean our money is being put into your hands to be spent, and so we're going to put a condition on it—the condition is our workforce needs someone with those skills.[5]

The focus on targeted occupations for WIA training is also consistent with the state's increased emphasis on workforce education at community colleges in general. A recent report by the Florida legislature's Office of Program Policy Analysis and Government Accountability (State of Florida, Office of Program Policy Analysis for Government Accountability [OPPAGA] 2001) revealed that since 1997, when workforce education legislation was passed that tied funding to high-wage/high-skill training at community colleges, employment rates and wages for program completers are up. According to the report,

"Performance improvements have resulted from actions taken by community colleges and school districts in response to legislative initiatives linking performance to funding" (State of Florida, Office of Program Policy Analysis for Government Accountability [OPPAGA] 2001, iii). A dean of workforce development at one Florida community college, when asked whether there has been an increase in activity around workforce education at her school, said, "Yes, since the state decided to fund us for those activities in a very focused way with the performance state funding. All of the new academic programs we've developed have in mind that kind of high-demand, high-wage focus."

In fact, the new programs developed by the community colleges in response to the targeted-occupations lists and the 1997 workforce legislation respond specifically to the needs of companies in the high-tech industry such as Cisco Systems and Lucent Technology. Often the training offered is short-term, non-degree-bearing, and highly job-specific. Research clearly shows higher economic returns for degree- and certificate-granting programs (Kane and Rouse 1999), so a policy of restricting training to short-term programs that are designed to fill very specific industry needs generally does not serve the long-term interests of students themselves, despite the occasional exception to this general rule. Stanley Aronowitz (2000) explains:

> Ironically, the more specialized the knowledge, the more vulnerable is its bearer to the vicissitudes of the job market. At a time of rapid shifts in the job scene, high-level general education—arguably the best preparation for the new types of knowledge work dominating the upper and middle ends of the occupational structure—is declining, not only in the community colleges but in many four-year schools as well. Undergraduates are choosing accountancy, business administration, medical technology, computer science, and technology, even as those fields undergo profound changes that render some skills obsolete and require of labor more versatility than at any time in recent memory (112).

Marya Sosulski (2004), in a study of Illinois welfare recipients, found that low-income women often encounter caseworkers who deny their interest in nonoccupational education. One woman she interviewed reported having an interest in taking sociology course work, but was rebuffed. The caseworker reportedly said, "That's stupid. . . . It's just a general degree and you can't do anything with that degree. . . . Sociology ain't gonna get you nowhere, so I'm not going to approve that we do anything for you." The recipient responded being "just . . . devastated. And then I got angry . . . and then very calm. This guy had a sociology degree and he was trying to tell me about my sociology degree" (114–15).

By emphasizing short-term training for high-wage jobs, Florida may be effectively closing out low-income, low-skilled workers from training altogether. Fewer programs are created to train people for entry-level and less technical jobs, because those jobs are not on the targeted-occupations list. For example, many regions in Florida have a sustained demand for certified nursing assistants, but those jobs do not pay high wages and so they do not appear on many targeted-occupations lists. Since they are not on the targeted list, community colleges do not receive extra funding to train people for them. Some people may view these as dead-end, low-paying jobs, but the reality is that becoming a certified nursing assistant can function as the first step in a nursing-focused career ladder (Jenkins 2004), and it may be the only way that low-skilled adults can enter into a career path that will, with additional training and education, eventually lead to a well-paying job. High-wage jobs generally require high skill levels, and individuals with little formal education generally require far more education than short-term programs will provide. The data presented in table 5.5 (and national data presented in table 5.2), showing that WIA participation rates in training for low-income, limited English proficiency, and nonwhite individuals in Florida are lower than that of the general population, would seem to support this concern. Thus, the use of targeted-occupations lists short-circuits the "customer choice" notion that is a hallmark of WIA's market-driven educational model.

Outcome data for Florida's WIA adult clients who exited during the period from July 2001 to March 2002 reveal exactly which kinds of credentials adults who do access training receive. Among exiters who received training, 2 percent earned their high school equivalency, and nearly 5 percent obtained either a two- or four-year college degree. But the vast majority, 70 percent, obtained a credential that was relevant to a very narrow slice of the occupational structure. Fifty-two percent of exiters who received training earned an occupational skills license, credential, or certificate (U.S. Department of Labor 2003). Clearly, Florida's example suggests that as WIA moves toward full implementation, training funded under WIA is increasingly inaccessible to the most vulnerable populations, and what training there is leads to narrowly focused credentials that are unlikely to be transferable.

THE WORKFORCE DISINVESTMENT ACT?

On paper WIA appears to be both work-first *and* market-driven; and the latter feature is supposed to incorporate accountability and customer satisfaction as means to improve both choice and quality of training. While it might be expected that the emphasis on the "customer" would modify the work-first effect to some extent, our data suggests that it reinforces the work-first goals. Access is particularly restricted for disadvantaged populations—low-income, limited English proficiency, non-white, and TANF recipients (as was shown in chapter 5).

In this chapter we have shown how the WIA implementation process combines with formal WIA policy to produce these results. Reduced access to education and training results from a number of different factors, which together systematically winnow access to training, particularly for disadvantaged populations. Access is first curtailed by the sequential-eligibility process created by the three tiers of services delivered by WIA. As the most clearly work-first element of WIA, the tiers of service delivery explicitly limit access to training for most WIA clients, and instead encourages them to obtain employment quickly via the use of job-search materials.

Access is further narrowed by the fact that there are fewer dollars available for direct services under WIA. The requirement to create and staff one-stop career centers means that a significant portion of WIA dollars that might have been available for WIA services are instead being used for administrative purposes. This fact, coupled with the requirement that access to WIA services be universal, forces many one-stop career centers to provide superficial (and less effective) services to more clients, rather than using their funding to provide training for fewer clients.

Extensive accountability measures and reporting requirements create disincentives that act as another set of barriers to training. Some WIA outcome measures—earnings gains, in particular—could in theory reward caseworkers for encouraging wide access to training for even the most disadvantaged clients, who can show dramatic gains in earnings by placement in even moderate-pay jobs. But as our interviews with caseworkers clearly illustrate, the outcome measures that they most consistently emphasize are those having to do with job placement. Caseworkers frequently "cream" the most promising WIA clients and provide them with access to higher-level WIA services because they believe that these clients will produce the best measurable outcomes. Not surprisingly, access to training is further curtailed for the most disadvantaged WIA clients.

The small remaining pool of WIA clients who obtain access to training encounter a limited set of choices. Community colleges see little incentive to participate as training providers, because the detailed reporting requirements are beyond the existing capacity of many community colleges to meet, and it is not worth it for the few WIA clients that exist. Choices available to WIA clients are further narrowed because community colleges that do participate offer very few programs, as a result of a need to limit the amount of data they must collect and of restrictions placed on them by targeted-occupation lists. Some community colleges forgo participation altogether because of either a lack of resources or a perceived culture clash between the workforce orientation of WIA and the traditional academic mission of the community college.

Even in Florida—whose workforce development emphasis, impressive data collection system, and coordination of services make it the most hospitable of states—the implementation of WIA tells a cautionary tale. Access to training is not significantly greater in Florida than it is in other, less "advanced" states; its emphasis on placement in high-wage jobs may be closing out low-skilled workers from training options; and those who do receive access are directed toward short-term training that may assist them in obtaining a job in the near future, but could well prove to be useless in the long term as the local economy changes.

The end result of this complex set of accountability measures, reporting requirements, and service delivery models is a discouraging one. Far fewer WIA clients are receiving access to training than was the case before the Act was passed, and the hardest group of constituents to serve—those with low literacy rates, spotty employment histories, women (especially those with young children), and those with limited English proficiency—are getting the most restricted access. The type of education available to WIA clients is shifting as well. There is nothing inherently wrong with developing education and training programs designed to address the needs of the labor market; community colleges have been doing so for years and in fact have prided themselves on their developing connections to the business world. However, when the *only* education available to WIA clients is that which suits the needs of local employers, student choice is severely constricted. And again, it is important to note that this lack of flexibility has the most serious ramifications for the students who most need flexibility—students with young children, transportation barriers, or remedial educational needs. Once again, and through a variety of complex mechanisms, the goals of work-first triumph.

CHAPTER SEVEN

THE POWER OF WORK-FIRST: IMPLICATIONS AND FUTURE TRENDS

JULIE IS A twenty-year-old single white mother—demographically speaking, a typical welfare recipient.[1] She has a daughter just under two years old. In addition to working fifteen hours a week, she is enrolled in the local community college where she is pursuing an associate's degree in education. Julie is able to do this because she lives in Illinois, a state with relatively liberal welfare policies that allows welfare recipients to pursue a limited amount of postsecondary education while receiving welfare benefits. As she talks, it becomes clear that Julie has little doubt that college is her route out of poverty. Although she has worked since she was sixteen, she's never held a job that paid more than the minimum wage. Having dropped out of high school in the ninth grade, she knows that her prospects of obtaining living-wage employment without further education are slim. Asked why she is enrolled in college, Julie said, "In order to give [my daughter] the best possible life. I'm not going to just fall into a job that pays twenty or thirty thousand dollars a year if I'm uneducated."

She perceives that the current welfare system is making it very difficult for her to achieve her goal of becoming financially independent. Despite the fact that she lives in Illinois, a state where formal welfare policy allows relatively generous access to education and training, her experience in the welfare system tells her that it is hostile to the pursuit of postsecondary education. She reports seeing a sign in one welfare office that proudly advertised a drastic drop in the welfare rolls. "They are eager to push the people on welfare to get them a job, maybe at Burger King, making minimum wage or maybe a little above that, with no benefits." She goes on to critique the system, asking, "Is there an incentive program for [caseworkers] to get people off of welfare? Do they get cash benefits for throwing these people off of it because it's kind of their goal?" Denying access to college is, in her opinion, "irresponsible, and it's pushing the problem off to something that's going to grow even larger later." If parents don't have an education, "it's the kids that end up suffering. It's the kids who end up living in poverty and it's the kids who don't have good health coverage."

Without a doubt, Julie has a clear understanding of the benefits of education that accrue at many levels.[2] So, too, does the American public. There is broad agreement and strong evidence to support the contention that education is the surest and most consistent route to self-sufficiency that exists in American society today. Unemployment rates decrease, and median annual earnings increase, as a function of educational attainment; and welfare recipients in particular experience significant gains in income and employment when they receive quality education combined with job training (National Center for Education Statistics 2002). In fact, the education system in the United States has expanded at all levels for much of the last century, as the working class has steadily increased its average level of education from completion of grammar school at the beginning of the century to the completion of high school by mid-century and, in the postwar period, to a substantial increase in the percentages of high school graduates attending and completing college. Factors promoting access such as Pell grants, open admissions, and indeed the expansion of the community college system itself—all point to and reinforce one central tenet of American ideology: education is the best and surest way to climb up the social ladder and achieve some semblance of the American Dream. What the sociologist Randall Collins asserted in 1979 is still true today: "Education is the most important determinant yet discovered of how far one will go in today's world" (Collins 1979, 3).

But Julie's experience also illustrates a curious and disturbing paradox that has emerged in American thinking about the value of education. Despite the indisputable benefits of investing in human capital through education, somehow the American public has accepted the notion that the poorest amongst us do not deserve the same access to college as other Americans. Instead, the work-first idea has come to dominate recent federal policy regarding college access for our poorest citizens. In very concrete ways, welfare reform and the Workforce Investment Act represent a sea change in this country's beliefs about the role that education and training should play in providing opportunities for social mobility for our most disadvantaged populations. Driven by the idea of work-first, these policies directly contradict a fundamental tenet of contemporary American society: the centrality of education to individual and social betterment. Instead of giving the poor the opportunity to become self-sufficient by obtaining the training and education they need to lift themselves out of poverty, poor adults now need to enter the world of work as quickly as possible, regardless of pay, benefits, or the stability of the job. In short, higher education is not for all.

As advanced education becomes more essential than ever in this postindustrial economy, the story of how doors to college were closed to our poorest citizens is an important one. Our findings demonstrate that access to postsecondary education and training has decreased as a result of welfare reform and WIA, particularly for nonwhites and immigrants, and that the type of education available to those who do receive it most often is short-term and does not lead to a degree or college credit of any kind. The work-first notion has taken hold of federal workforce and welfare policy directed at the poor, and there is little indication that it is likely to lose influence anytime soon.

How and why did most states consistently adopt a work-first approach in the implementation of both welfare reform and WIA? Under what circumstances did they adopt approaches to mitigate this overall trend? And how did community colleges—the institutions at the front line of providing access to college for our most disadvantaged students—respond? The answers to these questions are complex and multifaceted. Traditional policy analysis tends to ignore the role that ideas can play in the formation of public policy, or assume that the relationship between ideas and policy implementation is relatively straightforward. Our study employed a different approach: we examine how the work-first idea took hold and played out in the implementation of welfare reform and WIA at multiple levels—federal, state, local, and institutional. By drawing on a combination of quantitative and qualitative data, we demonstrate how the work-first idea gained traction, and explain why the work-first approach to economic self-sufficiency for the poor has been so consistently adopted during the last ten years, despite a general policy environment that allowed states considerable autonomy in implementing work-first legislation. As a result of its staying power, the work-first idea has quite effectively worked to constrict the educational pipeline leading to college for our most vulnerable citizens.

The previous chapters of our book address in some detail the impact of welfare reform and work-first individually—welfare reform in chapters 3 and 4, and WIA in chapters 5 and 6. But to assess the full impact of the work-first idea, we need to examine how both policies work together to affect the postsecondary educational landscape for our poorest citizens. We provide such a synthesis of our findings here by examining the combined impact of welfare reform and WIA at multiple levels: national, state, local, and institutional, in the community college setting.

NATIONAL TRENDS

When taken as a whole, our analyses of several large national databases clearly indicate that both welfare reform and WIA have reduced access to postsecondary education for welfare recipients and low-income adults more generally. Analyses of imperfect but nevertheless illustrative national databases indicate that access to postsecondary education for welfare recipients has been reduced in several ways (see chapter 3 of this volume). First, the overall case-load of welfare recipients dropped by 65 percent between 1996 and 2001. This decline was expected, since there are a variety of aspects in the federal-level policy, such as time limits, sanctions, and the work-first provision that would combine to produce a reduction of this magnitude. Due in large part to this decline in sheer numbers, the number of welfare recipients enrolled in postsecondary education has dropped since 1996. Thus, one central goal of the work-first mechanism, drastic reduction of caseloads, has succeeded. Analyses also point to a reduction in the proportion of welfare recipients who attend college since the passage of welfare reform. Estimates of the extent of this decline vary from data set to data set, but the weight of the evidence clearly suggests that postsecondary enrollment of TANF recipients is lower than that of AFDC recipients. Despite their limitations, these national datasets are the only source of information on the college-eligible population. The estimates of postsecondary-enrollment declines obtained from the SIPP (Survey of Income and Program Participation), CPS (Current Population Survey), and other data sources are restricted to those with a high school or GED degree, and thus the analysis can isolate the effect of policy changes on the population most directly affected by these changes.

Equally disturbing is a shift in the *type* of postsecondary education that is accessible to welfare recipients away from degree- or certificate-granting pro-grams to short-term, non-degree-granting programs, as well as the fact that welfare recipients are enrolled in education for shorter periods of time than was the case prior to welfare reform. It can be hypothesized that lower levels of educational and economic attainment among those recipients are likely to result from these changes, although analyses have yet to be conducted to con-firm this hypothesis. In addition, the intersection of race and poverty appears to have affected access to education, with Hispanic and African American welfare recipients less likely to be enrolled than their white counterparts.

Analyses of national WIA data point to a much sharper decline in both the overall number and the percentage of WIA clients that receive training. By 2003, under WIA more adults were enrolled than under JTPA in 1997, its last year. However, 91 percent of JTPA clients received some sort of training, whereas the percentage of WIA clients who receive some training has hovered around 56 percent for the last several years. Thus, the proportion of WIA clients receiving training is about 38 percent less than the proportion of JTPA clients.

When we focus on the most disadvantaged populations, we see an even greater reduction in access to training under WIA. To a certain extent this re-sult is intentional, for WIA is designed to serve as a universal-access program and is not targeted at low-income populations as was JTPA. Nevertheless na-tional data documenting this shift are sobering. Whereas nearly all (98 percent) of the adult JTPA population that received training was economically disadvantaged, by 2003 only 68 percent of the WIA clientele enrolled in training was economically disadvantaged. Other indicators of disadvantage—receipt of welfare, or level of formal education—also suggest that the WIA population referred to training is more advantaged. There is little doubt that WIA is much less of a sure path to training for needy populations than was its predecessor.

Taken together, analyses of national-level data regarding welfare reform and WIA suggest that the work-first idea is alive and well in both program areas, but is manifested differently in each. Data on the effect of welfare reform show that not only has the rate of access to postsecondary education among welfare recipients clearly dropped, but also, and perhaps more significant, the overall number of participants is drastically lower and the quality and quantity of education that is available to them has declined as well. The effect of WIA is even more clear-cut: both the overall number and the proportion of WIA clients participating in training have declined significantly, and this is particularly true for low-income populations and nonwhite populations. In short, our analyses of national data force us to conclude that work-first has made it far less likely that low-income adults will receive access to high-quality higher education.

STATE AND LOCAL TRENDS

There is a lengthy distance between policy that emerges at the federal level and its eventual implementation at the state and local level. Especially within the context of devolution, it is particularly important to analyze how state and local actors interpreted and responded to welfare reform and WIA. The picture at the local level is more complex than that seen at the federal level, and it is also more nuanced, and sheds more light on the mechanisms through which work-first translates from an idea to a set of specific policies and practices.

As described in chapter 1, we chose our sample of six states in large part because they differed in the degree to which their formal welfare policies allowed college attendance. Analyses of two national databases suggest that variations in state-level welfare policy do have some effect on college-going rates among welfare recipients, but they are not as large as we would expect, given that some states have wholeheartedly embraced work-first, while others have retained elements of a human-capital approach to their welfare policies.

Our more fine-grained analyses of state-level outcomes and implementation data suggest that the work-first idea was so powerful in the implementation process that variation in formal policy mattered relatively little. In all six of our states, noticeably fewer individuals received welfare after the 1996 reform; caseload reductions were dramatic across the states. The percentage of welfare recipients who were enrolled in postsecondary education varied to some degree, dropping in three states and rising slightly in three—but they hover around a low average, with no state enrolling even 6 percent of recipients in postsecondary education. Thus, as the national databases suggested, the decrease in access to postsecondary education in these states was due to two separate but related mechanisms: an overall reduction in the number of individuals receiving welfare, and the rate of entry into college.

Our analyses of WIA data at the state level both reinforce our findings at the national level and reveal patterns that are not discernible using the limited national data that exist on this policy. The number of individuals accessing WIA has risen nationally, a trend echoed in four of our six states. However, consistent with our analyses of national outcomes data, the proportion of adult WIA clients that receive education and training has dropped to a significant degree in all six states. Taken together, our states reflect what we see nationally: far fewer individuals are receiving training via WIA than received training under JTPA. Moreover, more in-depth analyses of the types of services clients received in Florida, Illinois, and Washington reveal a trend away from providing training to WIA clients in favor of providing other services designed to facilitate rapid employment. Thus, the work-first ideology appears to be increasingly potent as WIA is implemented over time.

Although detailed demographic data for WIA are not available at the national level, we were able to collect such data for three of our states. Our analyses reveal a distinct bias against providing education and training for an array of disadvantaged individuals. In all three states, welfare recipients who are also WIA clients are less likely to receive access to training than non-welfare recipients; whites were more likely to receive training than were Latinos or African Americans; and those with limited English proficiency were less likely than the overall population to receive training as well. These analyses are consistent with our findings regarding national-level welfare outcomes, which also suggest that nonwhite or otherwise particularly disadvantaged recipients were less likely to receive access to education and training than were their white counterparts. Work-first seems to disproportionately penalize minorities and the desperately poor.

Analyses of our state-level implementation data provide us with a series of clear illustrations of how powerfully the work-first idea has taken hold in the implementation of both welfare reform and WIA. As our case studies of welfare policy implementation in Washington and Illinois illustrate, states do indeed differ in the degree to which they embraced work-first in their formal policy. However, despite variation in formal policy, implementation in both states reflected a decidedly work-first philosophy, as state bureaucrats and caseworkers embraced the spirit of work-first, regardless of whether it was formalized in actual policy provisions.

In our analyses of the state-level implementation of WIA in chapter 6, we did not find the degree of variation in formal policy that we found with regard to welfare reform. Most states have interpreted WIA as decidedly work-first, and the reduction in access to postsecondary education and training has, for the most part, been profound. Analyses of our states also revealed that the work-first philosophy coalesces with another important element of the policy—its market-oriented focus on outcomes, accountability, and customer satisfaction. This aspect of the policy might reasonably be seen as a lever to increase access, but in reality it further reduces access by saddling community colleges with burdensome reporting requirements.

Finally, frontline workers such as caseworkers in one-stop career centers and community colleges themselves have very little incentive to provide WIA clients with access to training and education, particularly those at risk of not completing a course of training or obtaining adequate employment. Thus, despite the fact that WIA is nominally a job-training program, in practice it is providing markedly little training. It is difficult to characterize WIA as a customer-driven policy, despite rhetoric to the contrary. Once again, work-first trumps other, competing, philosophies.

IMPACT ON THE COMMUNITY COLLEGE

In the end, however, a full understanding of the impact of welfare reform and WIA on college access cannot be achieved without examining how those policies play out at the community college. Our analyses reveal that the changes that we have documented in both WIA and welfare reform are conspiring to move these institutions away from their historic mission of providing access to college for the disadvantaged. As a result of the barriers erected by these policies, community colleges appear to be less likely than ever to actively seek out and support low-income or high-risk students.

The mechanisms resulting in this effect are complex. On the one hand, community colleges are far from passive recipients of these policies; as is true during the implementation of all policy, they are capable of embracing, resisting, or adjusting to the policy to some degree. Even so, powerful external forces that were in place prior to welfare reform and WIA restricted their range of response. Factors such as diminishing budgets and increased calls for accountability created an environment that greatly reduced the incentive for community colleges to actively fight to maintain their service to low-income students in general, since they are both expensive to educate and unlikely to produce the positive outcomes that state policymakers are increasingly calling for.

But the policies themselves have also had direct effects. Several specific aspects of TANF and WIA policy reinforce the colleges' movement away from serving low-income students, and send clear policy signals and incentives that restrict their ability and desire to continue to serve these populations. First, there are the numbers. Simply put, welfare reform and WIA have drastically reduced the number of clients who are eligible to obtain postsecondary education or training. In the case of welfare reform, the emphasis on reducing caseloads has resulted in the most dramatic reduction in the number of welfare recipients referred to education and training; the severe drop in the proportion of WIA clients who are referred for training has produced similar results. Without a critical mass of welfare or WIA students, many community colleges find it unnecessary or needlessly expensive to mount programs to address the unique needs of the small number of this shrinking population who do pursue postsecondary education or training.

Second, community colleges that continue to enroll WIA and welfare recipients have had to adjust their curricula to offer more short-term training, thereby reducing the possibility that welfare and WIA clients will obtain an associate's or a bachelor's degree. Furthermore, the Individualized Training Account created by WIA has shifted the funding mechanism for training in a way that makes it difficult for community colleges to develop programs for WIA recipients.

The ways in which accountability frameworks impact community colleges are less direct than the funding frameworks. As described in great detail in chapters 5 and 6, WIA contains a laundry list of outcome measures, many required of the educational institutions registered as training providers. But additional funding to supplement reporting data for those measures has not been provided. At the most basic level, colleges are being asked to track and collect outcome data on students who are receiving welfare or WIA, but only one-third of colleges have the data capability to identify whether a student is on welfare (Kienzl 1999), according to a survey by the American Association of Community Colleges. This lack of analytical capacity is due in large part to the fact that community colleges have been chronically underfunded at both the local and state levels, and the reporting requirements place a burden on community college staff and administrators that many are unwilling or unable to absorb. Community colleges often opt out of programs with accountability requirements because they can't afford them; as a result, they are far less engaged in training clients of workforce development programs than they had been prior to WIA.

Accountability frameworks deter community colleges from serving disadvantaged students in yet another way. Accountability outcomes tend to focus on increases in degree-completion rates, earnings, and job placements. Under WIA, the latter two measures are a centerpiece of the accountability framework. It is easier for community colleges to "meet their measures" if they enroll and track students with greater preexisting skills and aptitude, or at least those they perceive have such advantages, than with less well-prepared students. Thus, success appears to be contingent at least in part on "creaming"— serving students who are most likely to succeed.

Community colleges are thus faced with two sets of disincentives to serve poor adults contained in both welfare reform and WIA. Fewer low-income students exist to be served in the first place, and to serve them, community colleges must adjust their curricula and comply with burdensome reporting requirements. In institutions with an already strong push toward workforce development and other business-oriented practices, the barriers raised by both WIA and welfare reform provide yet another reason to continue to move away from serving high-risk students, and focus instead on more lucrative short-term training programs designed to suit the needs of local businesses, rather than the more extensive education and training needs of low-income populations (Dougherty 2000b; Grubb 1996). Clearly, work-first and accountability can be demoralizing to community colleges. They compound the difficulties inherent in serving low-income populations, rather than ameliorating them.

IMPLICATIONS FOR COLLEGE ACCESS

Viewed in a broader context, welfare reform and the Workforce Investment Act signal a shift in the role that the federal government is willing to play to ensure that low-income Americans will continue to have access to college. The rhetoric that frames discussions regarding access to higher education in general remains firmly attached to the human-capital idea, but emerging policies paint a more complex picture. Federal aid is increasingly distributed in the form of loans rather than grants, and states are increasingly focusing their financial aid programs on "merit" rather than "need" (Heller 2002). At the same time, large-scale reductions in funding for postsecondary education across many states have resulted in higher tuition, and an increasing number of state higher education systems are removing remedial education from four-year institutions altogether, thereby further reducing access to four-year institutions for high-risk students. All of these factors reduce the ability of low-income adults to enroll in postsecondary education and persist to obtain a degree, and they send a signal to the American public that ensuring equal access to college across income groups is not a high priority (National Center for Public Policy and Higher Education 2004).

Given this context, the work-first idea is particularly potent, because it reinforces and expands upon the policy signals that already exist regarding access to college for the poor. The notion of "work-first" is so simple and intuitive, and the policies send such clear signals and incentives, that avenues that once existed to provide a pathway to college for some of our most disadvantaged citizens have essentially been eliminated. When work-first policy is implemented within community colleges, whose decreased budgets and increased accountability pressures are powerful incentives to chart a course away from low-income adults, its ability to influence practice at the institutional level is particularly strong.

The analyses presented in this book are also part of a larger debate regarding the role of community colleges in American society. Do community colleges promote social mobility or simply provide the illusion of mobility, thereby perpetuating inequality? This question has been debated for nearly as long as the institutions themselves have existed, and the emergence of the work-first policy only serves to reinforce its importance. Critics of the community college ask whether these two-year schools are succeeding in providing a less expensive route to a bachelor's degree or instead are diverting ambitious lower-class students away from four-year schools, channeling them instead into lower-status vocational occupations (Brint and Karabel 1989; Clark 1960; Nora 1993; Rhoads and Valadez 1996; Zwerling 1976, 1992). Two such critics characterize community colleges as the "lowest rung in post-secondary education, both in terms of student composition and student life chances" (Brint 2003, 17).

Empirical findings support many of these claims. For instance, research clearly demonstrates that the traditional transfer function of the community college as a bridge from the two- to four-year school has declined. In the late 1960s, the majority of community college students transferred to four-year institutions (Dougherty 1994), but in recent years the percentage of students who transfer has been diminishing, and it has been estimated that about 20 to 40 percent ever transfer (Grubb 1996). Of the students beginning at two-year institutions in 1995 to 1996 who declared upon entry that they intended to complete a bachelor's degree, just over half (51 percent) transferred to a four-year institution so that they could do so, and 44 percent of those students completed a bachelor's degree by June 2001, for an overall graduation rate of 22 percent. The same study revealed that 63 percent of students who began their postsecondary education at a four-year institution completed a bachelor's degree by June 2001 (National Center for Education Statistics 2003).[3]

Overall, community college students earn fewer bachelor's degrees, persist fewer years, and end up in less lucrative jobs than do comparable students who begin their education at four-year institutions (Berkner, Horn, and Clune 2000; Grubb 1996; Grubb et al. 1997; Kane and Rouse 1995). Several institutional factors (poor social and academic integration; insufficient transfer policies; lack of financial aid) and individual factors (poorer social and academic preparation) help to explain some of the differences between two- and four-year-school outcomes (Dougherty 1994).

Still, the returns to an associate's degree, or even to one or two semesters of community college, are still substantially more than those of obtaining a high school diploma (Kane and Rouse 1995; Rouse 1998). Further insight is provided by the open-admissions experiment at the City College of New York (CUNY) in the 1970s, which greatly widened access to New York's two- and four-year colleges; studies reveal not only that the move led to an increase in the number of minorities in New York City who received educational credentials and jobs, but also that these attainments "helped to ensure more advantaged prospects for the children of many former students. Open admissions helped to raise the odds that the advantages to its immediate beneficiaries would be transmitted across generations," even for individuals who did not complete a degree (Attewell and Lavin 2003; Lavin and Hyllegard 1996, 198).

Steven Brint, a critic of community colleges, contradicts this conclusion. In revisiting his original position, which emphasizes the diversionary role of community colleges (see Brint and Karabel 1989), he still contends that although "the consensus among researchers today is that most students attending community colleges would not otherwise attend any postsecondary institution . . . most students who are the beneficiaries of this democratization effect of community colleges do not complete many units and, consequently, show only very small or negligible improvements in their job prospects" (Brint 2003, 27).

Clearly, work-first policies such as welfare reform and WIA create circumstances that serve to reinforce and support the arguments of Brint and other community college critics. Regardless of whether individual community colleges wish to sustain a commitment to low-income individuals, their efforts to do so are constricted by work-first policies, and the education that they are able to offer is increasingly short-term—which only serves to further identify community colleges as the sector of postsecondary education that provides low-quality, short-term education. In other words, work-first serves to reinforce social inequality first by restricting access to community colleges, and second by pushing these institutions to further differentiate the type of education made available to low-income adults.

It is also difficult to be optimistic about the impact of work-first on the educational success of recipients who do manage to enroll. The data we were able to obtain from these six states did not allow for such analyses, since they did not include individual-level data. However, results from several new studies have produced cause for concern. In separate examinations of data from the pre-welfare reform National Longitudinal Survey of Youth, both Sarah Simmons (2005) and Rebecca London (2004) found that welfare recipients enrolled in college were substantially less likely than nonrecipients to complete additional years of schooling or earn a degree. Further, the trend toward shuttling recipients towards shorter-term courses does not appear likely to result in higher levels of educational attainment. A study of data from Washington State found that less than one-third of community college students in adult basic education (ABE) programs made the transition to college-level courses, and only 4 to 6 percent earned a credential or degree within five years of matriculation (Prince and Jenkins 2005). But those who did persist at least a year in ABE realized an earnings gain of $8,500. Perhaps the most important finding was that students who knew from the start that they would be enrolled in college for a year or longer were more likely to persist. This finding suggests that the harsh restrictions of the work-first message serve only to diminish the expectations and, ultimately, the college performance of those welfare and WIA recipients who do obtain access to college.

THE FUTURE OF WORK-FIRST

The degree to which work-first policies will continue to dominate federal welfare and workforce policy remains to be seen. Emerging research suggests that work-first does not result in economic self-sufficiency as it purports to. National data continue to show a strong correlation between education and earnings, at the same time that labor-market research increasingly demonstrates the importance of skills and continuing skill development to success in higher-wage, higher-demand employment. Research examining the results of training programs has shown that even in an expanding economy, a large percentage of the people placed in entry-level jobs earned wages at or below the poverty level. Nationally, the mean yearly earnings of employed welfare leavers was around $10,400 in 2001 (Acs and Loprest 2001). In Florida, individuals placed in jobs shortly after the 1996 welfare reform implementation were earning an average of only $13,812 a year in 2001, well below the poverty line for a family of four (Workforce Florida Inc. 2001). More recent data suggest that employment rates and earnings of welfare leavers have *decreased* significantly since 2002, as the economy has cooled and overall unemployment has increased (Loprest 2003).

In addition, states and communities increasingly face challenges in producing an adequate supply of skilled workers. According to the Bureau of Labor Statistics, in 2000 only 40 percent of the 110.5 million of U.S. working adults between the ages of twenty-five and sixty-five had a postsecondary degree (associate's or higher) despite estimates that between 60 to 85 percent of jobs currently require, or will require in the immediate future, some education beyond high school. By 2020, there will be a net gain of 15 million new jobs requiring some postsecondary education, while only 3 million new adults will enter the workforce with such credentials, leaving a deficit of 12 million skilled workers (National Governors Association Center for Best Practices 2002; Carnevale and Desrochers 2004). Specific industries that are critical to our economic growth, including health care, information technology, and education, will continue to suffer disproportionately large skills shortages, with unfilled job openings numbering in the hundreds of thousands. Because of these changes, states are now realizing they need to raise the academic skills of their labor forces, labor forces whose demographics are shifting rapidly as a result of increased immigration and greater participation by women, ethnic and cultural minorities, and individuals with disabilities

(Aspen Institute 2002b; Wrigley et al. 2003). In November 2005, the National Center for Public Policy in Higher Education issued a policy alert warning of declines in the proportion of Americans with a college degree over the next fifteen years if trends do not reverse and access to education is not equalized across racial and class groups.

One byproduct of this renewed attention to the value of postsecondary education is a range of new state and national efforts to expand adult postsecondary access, although the extent to which degree-focused education is being pushed is negligible. Efforts to develop career pathways that allow students to receive college credit for incremental course work (see, for example, Jenkins 2002) are becoming more popular in many states, as are dual admissions programs and efforts to provide financial aid to students who are pursuing postsecondary education part-time. Supporting and sustaining this work are private foundations such as the Bill and Melinda Gates Foundation, the Ford Foundation, and the Lumina Foundation for Education, as well as the activities of influential policy organizations such as the National Governors Association, the Education Commission of the States, the Southern Regional Education Board, and the American Council of Education (Cook and King 2004).[4] These efforts have been further buttressed via a series of highly visible biennial reports, titled *Measuring Up*, by the National Center for Public Policy and Higher Education that grade the fifty states on their success at providing access and promoting postsecondary participation among the state's populace (National Center for Public Policy and Higher Education 2000, 2002, 2004; Karen Arenson, "National Study Shows Colleges in Need of Help, *New York Times*, September 15, 2004).

Whether this research, analysis, and advocacy will eventually influence federal and state policy remains to be seen. The work-first idea retains a powerful hold on welfare and workforce policy implementation at the state level by means of two main mechanisms: the rules and incentives built into the law that promote workforce attachment, and its power to signal to implementers that work, not education, is the best strategy to assist economically disadvantaged adults. The power of work-first ideology is such that even if changes in federal and state policy occur, they may not lead to enhancements in postsecondary access for the adults served by these programs. Our findings suggest two interrelated actions are necessary to move policy away from work-first.

First, laws and incentives must change so that states and local implementers are rewarded—or at least not punished—for promoting postsecondary access. A large part of the power of work-first is embodied in the force of legal sanctions; altering these, through changes in federal policy, will go a long way toward undermining the rationale for work-first.

Secondly, there must be an intentional effort to change the signal sent by work-first that postsecondary education is not a viable option for our most disadvantaged adults. The ascendance of work-first cemented a growing belief that education is not the preferred means of advancement for the poor. Throughout this book we have seen many individuals across a range of positions giving voice to the idea that work, not education, is the path for those on welfare or unemployed. Clearly, the work-first message has taken hold: education and work are no longer considered a "both-and" option for pulling the poor out of poverty; rather, they are seen as a dichotomous "either-or" choice, and work has trumped education. To change these signals will require an alternative set of powerful ideas that embrace work *and* education as the most appropriate pathway for the poor. In order to be effective, these ideas must be communicated in simple straightforward terms and a powerful message so all can understand and act upon it.

We began this book by quoting President Bill Clinton, who signed both welfare reform and WIA into law. His comments in 1996 reflected both a double standard and a profound contradiction: postsecondary education is the "key to a successful future" for all Americans, but the poorest amongst us do not deserve the same access as do more fortunate Americans. For this population there was no mention of education: "We expect work."

Ten years after President Clinton made these statements, the inherent contradiction contained within them is alive and well. In speaking to pupils at the Griegos Elementary School in Albuquerque, New Mexico, President George W. Bush said: "The question I like to ask every child I visit in the classroom is, are you going to college? In this great country, we expect every child, regardless of how he or she is raised, to go to college." Yet less than one month before speaking with this group of young Hispanic students, he made a contradictory statement. In arguing for even stricter work requirements in welfare reauthorization, the President stated, "Some people could spend their entire five years—there's a five-year work requirement—on welfare, going to college. Now, that's not my view of helping people become independent. And it's certainly not my view of understanding the importance of work and helping people achieve the dignity necessary so they can live a free life, free from government control."[5] Again, although higher education is framed in general as a universal good, when we speak about our most disadvantaged citizens, work at the expense of education is framed as the only viable—and indeed, the only moral—solution to the problem of poverty. The fact that two presidents of opposing political parties and vastly different ideological inclinations share an enthusiasm for the work-first idea is testimony to the extraordinary staying power of this concept.

The irony of this scenario is impossible to ignore. Despite President Bush's words of optimism, the children of Griegos Elementary School may well find themselves in an impossible bind. Many of them will be too poor to attend college, given rising costs and the growing scarcity of adequate financial aid; and as a result, they will enter the workforce directly from high school, without the education and training needed to obtain the kinds of jobs that will allow them to become economically self-sufficient. Welfare may become a last resort for some of them, and if this policy and its companion, the Workforce Investment Act, continue to deny access to postsecondary education for them, they are unlikely to ever find their way out of poverty.

The intellectual consensus around college-for-all must be made to include the most disadvantaged members of society. Work-first has moved the country away from this goal, effectively influencing policy development and implementation in ways that erect real and lasting barriers to postsecondary education for low-income adults. The lives of the poor are complex and varied, and effective policy must include multiple options for addressing and overcoming the underlying causes of poverty. The work-first idea effectively closes off this possibility, creating instead a deceptively simple one-size-fits-all solution to what is, in fact, an enormous and complicated problem. Until we challenge the rhetoric of work-first and replace it with a policy framework that makes higher education a truly viable opportunity for everyone, work-first will continue to narrow the choices of less-advantaged Americans.

CHAPTER 1

1. A transcript of Clinton's speech can be found at http://www.pbs.org/newshour/bb/election/june96/clinton_6-4.html.
2. A transcript of this speech is available at http://www.clintonfoundation.org/legacy/082296-speech-by-president-at-welfare-bill-signing.htm.
3. In that study, "intensive" training included work experience, basic education, and vocational and technical training or postsecondary education. The latter category was the most common activity of those listed in this category.
4. Under this new distribution of funds, declining caseloads left states "rolling in dough," since that decline was not accompanied by a reduction in federal dollars. As welfare rolls got smaller, states were left with greater per-recipient funds, and had "nearly unlimited reach to improve poor people's lives"—including through the provision of tuition for postsecondary education—and yet most did very little (DeParle 2004, 215–16). The U.S. Department of Health and Human Services reported that in 2000, less than one percent of federal welfare funds were spent on education and training nationwide (Greenberg 2001).
5. The creators of the work-first slogan recognized this. See DeParle (2004).

CHAPTER 2

1. Other states used aggressive enforcement regimes to exclude women who, for example, were caught with a man in their homes who presumably was able to support the family (Abramovitz 1996). Whereas Mimi Abramovitz (1996) interprets these exclusions as means to balance the enforcement of both patriarchal standards of women's behavior and low-wage employment, Frances Fox Piven and Richard Cloward (1993) argue that man-in-the-house rules in particular were not about sexual behavior but were intended to enforce men's low-wage labor by preventing any ADC money from reaching unemployed men indirectly.

In either interpretation, the mechanism of enforcement was exclusion from benefits.

2. We distinguish here between the emergence of public job-training policy and the many strands of vocationalism (such as the 1917 Smith-Hughes Act, which provided federal funds for vocational education) that have strong connections to training and workforce development (see Grubb and Lazerson, 2004, chapter 3, for a discussion of these policy developments).

3. As in the New Deal, MDTA training programs were operated by local community-based organizations. Grubb and Lazerson (2004) argue that the MDTA was set up independent of schools in part to escape the negative reputation that vocational education carried at the time and also because it was thought that high schools were ill equipped to provide such training. In addition, Michael Katz (1989) and others (Weir 1992, 1993) note that that the War on Poverty used a similar approach because federal policymakers believed that success "required a new agency because it assumed the inertia and incompetence of the agencies that existed" (Katz 1989, 89). The Great Society programs were largely housed under the Office of Economic Opportunity (OEO), which was signed into law by Johnson as part of the Economic Opportunity Act of 1964. Indeed, community groups were engaged purposely because they provided "a method for 'shaking the system' and forcing change on reluctant school administrators, welfare and employment service officials, and even settlement houses and Community Chest leaders" (Katz 1989, 100).

4. The design and impact of JTPA are discussed in greater detail in chapter 5.

5. One influential example is David Ellwood's 1988 book *Poor Support.*

6. Many analysts point to the publication of Judith Gueron's *Reforming Welfare with Work* (1987), a summary of research conducted by the Manpower Demonstration Research Corporation (MDRC) on variations in welfare policy initiated by states in the 1980s, as a major factor in increasing the prominence of work in the welfare equation, specifically with regard to the Family Support Act (FSA) of 1988.

7. Clinton had been at the forefront on welfare reform in the 1980s as governor of Arkansas, and through his leadership in the National Governors Association (NGA) and the Democratic Leadership Council (DLC).

8. Of particular influence was "Principles for Real Welfare Reform," a 1994 position paper put out by Empower America, a Republican think tank led by such luminaries as the former secretary of Education William Bennett, the former secretary of HUD Jack Kemp, and the former congressman Vin Weber.

9. Hal Beder's (1999) summary of the results of twenty-two of the most credible outcome studies in adult education confirms many of these perceptions. Of the twenty-two studies, only five found earnings gains and only four, test-scores gains. Only three of the studies found an increase in rates of GED completion.

Julie Strawn (1998) and Strawn and Robert Echols (1999) echoed these findings in their reviews of the experimental literature on basic education. Fewer than half of the basic education programs for welfare recipients surveyed in the mid- to late 1990s increased either employment or average yearly earnings. Further, although these programs did increase the number of GEDs earned by participants, the majority of enrollees did not earn a GED, and few of the programs raised student test scores. Even when education and earnings impacts were found, there was no clear relationship between them, making it difficult for researchers to identify the causal links between basic skills education, test scores, and earnings (12–13).

10. A three-year evaluation of the JOBS programs revealed that those using human-capital development (HCD) strategies increased participation in ABE and showed small increases in employment and earnings that increased during the second year. Although the cumulative employment and earnings impacts were smaller for sites with human-capital approaches than for those using labor-force-attachment models (LFA), researchers noted that future trends were not clear. Earnings impacts for the HCD approaches had not caught up to the LFA strategies by the end of three years, but for some subgroups employment impacts in the HCD sites exceeded LFA impacts after two years (Freedman et al. 2000; Hamilton et al. 1997; Hamilton 2002).

11. As reflected in the slogan animating Washington State's Welfare Reform Program, called, tellingly, Work-First: "A job, a better job, a career."

CHAPTER 3

1. Indeed, policymakers have emphasized the economic and employment benefits of higher education far more than the "softer" benefits such as satisfaction or quality of life. This can be seen quite clearly in the growing influence of neoliberal philosophies tying education increasingly closer to employment (Slaughter and Leslie 1997). Yet even within this relatively narrow set of outcomes, the benefits of postsecondary education are clear.

2. The states are Arizona, Georgia, Iowa, Kentucky, Maine, Minnesota, Missouri, Nebraska, New Mexico, Rhode Island, Utah, Vermont, West Virginia, and Wyoming.

3. The states are Alabama, Arkansas, California, Illinois, and North Carolina.

4. Five states—Colorado, Florida, Maryland, New York, and Ohio—allow counties to decide whether postsecondary education can help meet work requirements.

5. That flexibility is, however, limited by two factors. First, PRWORA prohibits states from sanctioning a single parent with a child under the age of six who does not meet the work requirements because no child care is available. Second, PRWORA stipulates that states must use at least 70 percent of the mandatory and matching CCDF funds to assist families who are currently receiving public assistance, are attempting to transition off public assistance, or are at risk of becoming dependent on public assistance. This requirement represents an increase over prior spending on the title IV-A child-care programs—the former AFDC,

TCC, and At Risk Child Care programs—which were targeted to the same populations. Yet a sizable number of welfare recipients in some states continue to be placed on child-care waiting lists. Final TANF regulations provide a child-care protection clause which stipulates that a state may not reduce or terminate TANF assistance if a single parent of a child under age six fails to meet TANF work requirements due to an inability to obtain affordable, appropriate care within a reasonable distance from the home or worksite (Greenberg, Strawn, and Plimpton 1999). In fact, a state may be penalized by up to 5 percent of its TANF grant if it violates this requirement. States are required to inform families of this protection. But they can exercise their own discretion with regard to defining "affordable" and "appropriate" care, and must also develop procedures for determining a family's inability to obtain needed child care (Greenberg, Strawn, and Plimpton 1999). States consequently have considerable latitude with regard to implementing the child-care protection clause, and the choice of child care for families may well be either reduced or eliminated. And perhaps most important, failure to work because of a lack of child care does not extend the five-year total time limit for receiving federal assistance under TANF.

6. It is important to note that this is true in large part because federal philosophy regarding the care of poor young children has changed under PRWORA. In fact, federal welfare-reform legislation has resulted in several major changes in child-care policy (Greenberg 1998). Perhaps most important, this legislation removed welfare recipients' entitlement to child care, which had been guaranteed previously under the Family Support Act of 1988 (Greenberg 1998). Moreover, Congress now requires states to impose work requirements on welfare recipients with children below school age. And, perhaps most important, failure to work because of a lack of child care does not extend the five-year total time limit for receiving federal welfare assistance.

7. The powerful dilemmas faced by women trying to combine work, child rearing, and schooling have been documented in interviews with community college students in other research (see, for example, Gittell and Steffy 2000 and Matus-Grossman and Gooden 2002).

8. During fiscal year 1995, 1.9 million people, 43 percent of all Aid to Families with Dependent Children adult recipients, participated in the JOBS program nationwide. For fiscal year 1995, the average monthly percentage of JOBS participants enrolled in a self-initiated higher-education program was 7.5 percent. The percentage enrolled in an assigned higher-education program was 9.2. Twenty-three percent were enrolled in a high school, GED, ESL, or remedial education program, and 7.8 percent were enrolled in vocational training (U.S. Department of Health and Human Services 1999). These numbers are U.S. totals and were not broken down by state. These figures suggest that about 136,000 welfare recipients were enrolled in higher education through the JOBS program in 1995. Following reform, the comparable information provided at the federal level by the U.S. Department of Health and Human Services is based on the

number of TANF families that meet all family work requirements by participating in an approved work activity. For fiscal year 1997, this number of participating families was 520,237. We analyzed the Department of Health and Human Services data on the activities of these individuals. Adding all of the categories that potentially involve higher education (vocational education, job skills training, education related to employment, satisfactory school attendance, on-the-job training), other than job search, yields a total of 54,000 enrolled in higher education. Comparing this figure to the 1995 total suggests a sharp reduction, of 82,000, in the enrollment of welfare recipients in higher education, on the order of about a two-thirds reduction. This estimate is more conservative than that offered by David Manzo, who estimated that welfare reform may eliminate about 300,000 welfare recipients from educational programs across the country (Manzo 1997). (D. Manzo's figure may include secondary as well as postsecondary education—it is not clear from his account what types of schooling are included.)

9. Part-time students are often ineligible for financial aid. Thus, a large fraction of disadvantaged students, namely those who enroll in college part-time, will not appear in the financial aid statistics.

10. The 1999 National Household Education Survey asks for only the ages of all individuals living in the household. The 1995 National Household Education Survey does have a variable indicating whether there are children younger than ten in the household, but in neither case were we unable to determine whether the children are the offspring of the respondent.

11. The Center for Law and Social Policy released a revised list of state policies in June 2002, which was based on a May 2002 survey of states. We did not use this revised classification in our analysis because it did not correspond in time with our enrollment data.

12. Moffitt has compiled a very useful, state-level welfare policy database. More information can be found at http://www.econ.jhu.edu/People/Moffitt/Datasets.html.

13. The in-depth interviews we conducted in six states (see chapter 4) show that the state-level policy classification developed by CLASP does not completely correspond with the actual level of access to postsecondary education available to welfare recipients. Nonetheless, we expect that the CLASP measures should be related to enrollment patterns. In other words, a detailed, on-the-ground study in all fifty states would produce a classification scheme that would more closely match individual opportunities than that which CLASP has devised based on formal state policies. Thus, any effects we obtain will represent a lower-bound estimate of the impact of policy variation on access to higher education.

14. In additional analyses not shown, we included these policies retrospectively for 1995. We found a statistically significant effect, but the coefficients were smaller than those for 2000. This finding suggests that the same states that had more liberal policies toward welfare recipients in 2000 had other policies in effect in 1995 that also encouraged enrollments.

15. In the National Household Education Surveys analyses, in 1995, we coded women with children younger than ten in the household as mothers. In 1999, we classified as childless those for whom questions about children were coded as "inapplicable," and we assigned the balance to the category of parent. These are both imprecise measures but are the best we could do given the data limitations discussed earlier.

16. The effect of being African American rather than white is negative in the younger age group but not in the National Household Education Surveys sample as a whole. This difference may be related to the high rate of returning to school among African American women noted earlier. The explanatory power of the equation is greater for the entire sample than for the sixteen-to-twenty-four age group because the age measures explain more of the variance for the full sample.

Chapter 4

1. Bane and Ellwood both resigned in protest over Clinton's decision; for more see Jason DeParle (2004).

2. For the purposes of this data, college attendance is defined as enrollment in degree- or certificate-granting programs in two- or four-year institutions. GED, basic skills instruction, ESL, and general vocational education are not included.

3. Some states collect monthly average data, and others track recipients by year. Given the difficulty in obtaining state data, we were forced to accept what was available to us—thus, in three states the data are presented for a given month or monthly average, and in the other three states a yearly total is given; which it is, is indicated in the chart. It is inadvisable to compare states that use different lengths of time, but comparisons over time within state are valid, since both pre– and post–welfare reform data are given for the same type of time period (month or year).

4. In addition, the variable sources of the postsecondary data cause some difficulty in making comparisons across states. Specifically, in four states the data were provided by the state department of human services, which administers welfare. But the other two states' data were provided by very different agencies: in Washington it came from the state board of community colleges, and in Florida from the state FETPIP (Florida Education and Training Placement Information Program) system, which tracks longitudinal education data on program participants. Given the reasons already noted we suspect that these sources are more likely than state human services department to provide accurate estimates of college enrollment, but we were unable to use these sources in the other four states. If our data for Washington and Florida had been from human services departments in those states we might have received somewhat smaller numbers.

5. Initially, Massachusetts exempted certain categories of recipients from the work

requirements, including mothers of children under the age of six, but over time fewer recipients were exempted. Currently, only mothers of children under age two are exempted.

6. CSOs are the regional offices of the Washington Department of Social and Human Services.

7. In June of 2002, the state reduced funding for Work First training programs by $7.5 million, a smaller cut than many expected, given the state's budget woes (State of Washington, Work First n.d.).

8. Even lower numbers were reported in the Illinois Family Study, where only 2 percent of welfare recipients interviewed in 2003 reported being enrolled in postsecondary education in the past year (Lewis, Amsden, and Collins 2004).

9. See Evelyn Brodkin (1997) for more details on JOBS in Chicago. Under funding and evaluation pressures, caseworkers pushed the program more in the direction of job search and rapid labor-market attachment.

10. Since the recipient does not yet have a GPA during her first semester of school, her clock does not stop until the second semester, though she does not have to work in addition to attending school. The clock resumes during the summer months when the recipient is not in class.

11. The computer system used by caseworkers does not allow them to formally stop the sixty-month counter. Instead, local offices must identify clients who meet the criteria for having their clocks stopped and determine the number of months countered in error. Then they have to send paperwork to a central office on order to have the count adjusted.

12. In a qualitative study of fifteen Illinois welfare recipients, Sosulski (2004, 86) also found that only one was using the "college option" and had had her clock stopped.

13. Similarly, a survey of welfare recipients in California found that caseworkers discouraged college enrollment and successful achievement of educational goals, and that this was more common under TANF than under AFDC. Indeed, in that study one recipient reported that her caseworker was "really upset" that she had enrolled in college (Jones-DeWeever 2005, 20).

14. Massachusetts governors since 1991: William Weld (1991 to 1997), Paul Cellucci (1997 to 2001), Jane Swift (2001 to 2003), and Mitt Romney (2003 to present [2006]).

15. The report is available at http://www.masstaxpayers.org/ data/pdf/reports/execsum.pdf.

16. For more on these changes in Massachusetts, see the following webpages: http://massscorecard.org/MA-Senate_votes.htm; http://masstaxpayers.org/data/pdf/baulletines/Welftsmy.pdf; http://www.masslegalservices.org/ docs/2005-23.pdf.

17. Ten of the state's fifteen community colleges have participated at some point, eight initially implemented programs, and at this point only five colleges have programs.

CHAPTER 5

1. In this book "WIA clients" refers to adults only. WIA also covers dislocated workers and youth, but data on these groups are not presented, as we are primarily concerned with low-income adults with little work experience.
2. "Mandatory" one-stop partners are agencies that are required to offer services at the one-stop center. They are the Department of Labor (WIA Adult, WIA Dislocated Worker, WIA Youth, Employment Service [Wagner-Peyser Act], Trade Adjustment Assistance Programs, veterans' employment and training programs, Unemployment Insurance, Job Corps, Welfare-to-Work grant-funded programs, Senior Community Service Employment Program, Employment and Training for Migrant and Seasonal Farm Workers, Employment and Training for Native Americans); Department of Education (Vocational Rehabilitation Program, Adult Education and Literacy, Vocational Education); Department of Health and Human Services (Community Services Block Grant); Department of Housing and Urban Development (Employment and Training) (U.S. Government Accountability Office 2003).
3. Since one-stop staff most often are not involved in the provision of services at this level, individuals utilizing these services are not registered as WIA clients (U.S. Department of Labor 2003, 5). This is an important detail, since one-stops are not held accountable for the employment and earnings outcomes of clients who are not formally entered into the tracking system.

    Specific core services include job search and placement assistance, labor market information, initial assessment of skills and needs, information about available services, and some follow-up services to help customers keep their jobs once they are placed.
4. Since the delivery of intensive services is usually staff-assisted, this is the point at which individuals officially enter the system and become "WIA clients" (*Code of Federal Regulations*, 20CFR663.105). See note 6 for detailed information on these regulations.

    Intensive services are mandated to include the following (U.S. Department of Labor 2003, 5):

    1. Comprehensive and specialized assessments of the skill levels and service needs of adults and dislocated workers, which may include diagnostic testing and use of other assessment tools and in-depth interviewing and evaluation to identify employment barriers and appropriate employment goals
    2. Development of an individual employment plan, to identify the employment goals, appropriate achievement objectives, and appropriate combination of services for the participant to achieve the employment goals
    3. Group counseling
    4. Individual counseling and career planning
    5. Case management for participants seeking training services
    6. Short-term prevocational services, including development of learning skills,

communication skills, interviewing skills, punctuality, personal-maintenance skills, and professional conduct, to prepare individuals for unsubsidized employment or training

5. Not all training is provided by ITAs. WIA allows the following exceptions. First, on-the-job training and customized training can be provided through contracts with employers rather than funded through ITAs. Second, local areas can contract with community-based organizations and other entities to provide programs of demonstrated effectiveness to populations with multiple barriers to employment. Third, Local Workforce Development Boards (LWIBs) can contract for training services if there are too few providers in the area to fulfill the intent of ITAs (Perez-Johnson and Decker 2001). (See also *Code of Federal Regulations*, 20CFR663.400 and 20CFR663.430, for the specific rules; see note 6 for details). From October 1, 2000, to September 30, 2001, 75,963 adults received training under WIA, but only 55 percent received ITAs.

6. Regulations cited from the *Code of Federal Regulations*, title 20, volume 3, are as follows:

   20CFR663.105 (revised April 1, 2004), p. 746; available at http://frwebgate
      .access.gpo.gov/cgi-bin/get-cfr.cgi?TITLE=20&PART=663&SECTION=
      105&TYPE=TEXT.
   20CFR663.160 (revised April 1, 2004) pp. 685–86; available at http://frwebgate
      .access.gpo.gov/cgi-bin/get-cfr.cgi?TITLE=20&PART=663&SECTION=
      160&YEAR=2000&TYPE=TEXT.
   20CFR663.240 (revised April 1, 2004), p. 749; available at http://frwebgate
      .access.gpo.gov/cgi-bin/get-cfr.cgi?TITLE=20&PART=663&SECTION=
      240&TYPE=TEXT.
   20CFR663.250 (revised April 1, 2004), p. 749; available at http://frwebgate
      .access.gpo.gov/cgi-bin/get-cfr.cgi?TITLE=20&PART=663&SECTION=
      250&TYPE=TEXT.
   20CFR663.400 (revised April 1, 2004), p. 750; available at http://frwebgate
      .access.gpo.gov/cgi-bin/get-cfr.cgi?TITLE=20&PART=663&SECTION=
      400&TYPE=TEXT.
   20CFR663.430 (revised April 1, 2004), p. 751; available at http://frwebgate
      .access.gpo.gov/cgi-bin/get-cfr.cgi?TITLE=20&PART=663&SECTION=
      430&TYPE=TEXT.

7. For example, one board requires clients to write an essay about why they wanted "a particular training" before receiving it, while another requires clients to visit employers in fields they wish to pursue, and conduct informational interviews (U.S. Government Accountability Office 2005, 4).

8. Some important questions have been raised about the quality of the WIASRD data. In a recent report the U.S. Government Accountability Office (2005) called the data "incomplete" and "unverified" and not useful for cross-state or

even cross-locality comparisons because of "variations in data definitions" (4). This opinion of WIASRD is shared by the Department of Labor's Office of Inspector General, which attributes these flaws to "inadequate oversight of data collection and management" and to permitted flexibility in how states collect and report data on participant outcomes (U.S. Government Accountability Office 2005, 4). We fully recognize these flaws, but no other data source exists with which to evaluate the outcomes of WIA with regard to training and cross-state variation in training. (For their report on training the GAO did a web-based survey of 590 local WIBs [Workforce Investment Boards; see chapter 6 for detailed discussion], but those data are not publicly available and the survey was not designed to allow for cross-state comparisons). We support current efforts by the Department of Labor to improve data collection in WIASRD.

9. In this chapter we use the most recent year of available data on WIA because it is the most valid comparison to JTPA. Earlier WIA data exist, but do not reflect the full impact of the program because they were collected before WIA was fully implemented. See also note 13.

10. Only three states provide this information in their 2001 WIA annual reports.

11. Under JTPA the definition of a "disadvantaged" person at a particular point in time was being a member of a family whose income for the preceding six months was at or below the cut-off point for government welfare payments.

12. Reporting on low-income and TANF recipients is limited in federal WIA data to only those adult exiters receiving intensive services and training, so we do not know what percentage of those receiving core services only are low-income or receive TANF, and consequently we also do not know the proportion of low-income or TANF recipients in the overall WIA adult population. Overall, 10.1 percent of those receiving intensive services only were TANF recipients, and 11.1 percent of those receiving training were TANF recipients, and the 10.7 percent figure given in table 5.1 is a reflection of those two figures. This is not as informative as an overall figure for the proportion within the entire WIA adult population.

13. WIASRD data are what states use to create their annual reports to the federal government, but not all of the available data are contained in those reports. Thus, analyses of the raw data provide additional information unavailable to the general public. There is much suspicion among policymakers and practitioners about the reliability of both what is entered into the WIASRD system by local and state administrators, and what is reported out. The data received from the states hasn't been examined for its accuracy, but it is some of the only state-level data currently available that does not come from state reports.

14. Program year 2000 was the first year of WIA reporting for Illinois and Washington; it was the second for Florida, which was an early-implementation state. Thus, in Illinois and Washington, this program year likely contains some JTPA participants during this transition period.

15. Since program year 2000 was a JTPA-WIA transition year for Illinois and Washington, meaning that some JTPA participants were included in that overall num-

ber served, the increase in the number of WIA clients served over time may be even larger than it appears.

16. When comparing the data on the percentage in training in tables 5.3 and 5.4, bear in mind the time periods the data are from. Both of the program years (July 2000 to June 2001 and July 2001 to June 2002) presented in 5.4 occurred sometime before the reporting year 2001 presented in 5.3 (October 2001 to September 2002). Thus, although table 5.3 shows that 48 percent of WIA clients in Washington received training, and table 5.4 shows 73 percent and 56 percent, taken in chronological order these percentages are 73, 56, and 48—therefore indicating a linear decline over time.

17. Due to data limitations we cannot conduct the more relevant (and perhaps more revealing) comparison between low-income adults and those at other income levels. Only the total and low-income categories are available.

CHAPTER 6

1. Data from WIASRD (Workforce Investment Act Standardized Record Data) bear this out. Clients who entered WIA with preprogram quarterly earnings of $5,000 or higher suffered decreases in their earnings following program participation, ranging from $372 to $6,367, whereas clients whose last job paid less increased their quarterly earnings by $1,500 to 7,000 after exiting WIA (Social Policy Research Associates 2005, 17).

2. Adults are not counted toward the measures until they complete or exit the WIA program. Thus, if the caseworker sends his client into training, that client is still in WIA and does not get counted toward placement, positively or negatively, until she exits, at which point she will be counted in all measures: placement, retention, earnings, and credentials. The caseworker could send the client to training in the hopes that it would improve the client's chances of contributing positively to all measures (more employable, likely to stay employed, higher earnings, earned credential) without harming the caseworker's more immediate placement rate.

3. Many critics of JTPA argue that creaming occurred also under JTPA, which mandated performance-based contracts with training providers. Creaming of participants by providers had an effect on the job-placement success of service-delivery areas. In one state, Tennessee, it has been estimated that without creaming, placement rates would have fallen by 18 percent (Anderson, Burkhauser, and Raymond 1993). "Many of the original contracts encouraged providers to train those who were the most job-ready, because they rewarded providers on the basis of how many trainees they placed. This encouraged providers to cream off the easiest to serve, and led to severe criticism" (Osbourne and Gaebler 1992, 155). According to the authors of *Reinventing Government*, which laid the blueprint for much for WIA and welfare reform, the problem with JTPA's performance measures was that they were crude and underdeveloped. States could

avoid creaming, David Osbourne and Ted Gaebler suggest, by setting different performance goals and different reimbursement rates for different populations (1992), but these improvements do not appear to have been adopted in the federal WIA, and creaming continues.

4. Since 1997, workforce education at Florida community colleges has been funded on the basis of performance. Fifteen percent of the funds designated for community colleges have to be earned through positive program outcomes. Colleges earn points "when students complete training aimed at high-wage, high-demand jobs and when they are placed in such jobs" (Jenkins 2002, 2). It should also be noted that Florida community colleges earn additional performance dollars if they enroll and graduate disadvantaged students (target populations) in programs leading to high-wage jobs (this is along the lines of Osbourne and Gaebler's 1992 recommendations to prevent creaming). However, this provision does not appear to be successful. According to Davis Jenkins (2002),

> The new scheme does not seem to have had the effect of encouraging community colleges in Florida on a large scale to bridge disadvantaged students into training programs for high-wage jobs. According to an official at the Florida Department of Education, targeted disadvantaged populations account for less than 10 percent of all points generated in the performance-based funding system, while "regular Joes" generate over eighty points (20).

5. The $25,000 cost for training is most likely an exaggeration. Most individual training accounts are capped at approximately $1,500 per person.

CHAPTER 7

1. Julie is a welfare recipient who was interviewed as part of this study. Her name has been changed to protect her privacy.

2. Julie is not an anomaly. A recent study of welfare recipients enrolled in California community colleges found that nearly all understood the powerful connection between education and work and strongly desired a college education. Eighty-three percent of the women surveyed aspired to a four-year degree; only 15 percent intended to go no further than an associate's degree (Jones-DeWeever 2005, 28).

3. It should be noted that these transfer rates depend on the length of time allowed for transfer to occur. Paul Attewall and David Lavin's recent follow-up on a 1970 cohort of women who started studying at community colleges revealed that 31 percent ultimately completed a bachelor's degree, but nearly one-third completed that degree more than ten years after entry, and 10 percent completed it after more than twenty years (Attewell and Lavin 2003, 5).

4. For further information on efforts of these foundations and organizations to promote postsecondary access, see the relevant links at the following sites: http://www.luminafoundation.org/adult_learners/index.html; http://www.gatesfoundation

.org/Education/; http:www.nga.org/center/topics/1,1188,D_1507,00.html; http://www.ecs.org/ecsmain.asp?page=/html/issuesPS.asp; http://www.ecinitiatives.org/adult_learning/adultindex.asp; http:acenet.edu/programs/policy/projects/improving-lives.

5. The text of the speech at the Griegos Elementary School is available at http://www.whitehouse.gov/news/releases/ 2001/08/20010815-2.html. The text of the second speech is available at http://www.whitehouse.gov/news/releases/ 2002/07/20020729-6.html.

REFERENCES

Abramovitz, Mimi. 1996. *Under Attack, Fighting Back: Women and Welfare in the United States*. New York: Monthly Review Press.

Acs, Gregory, and Pamela J. Loprest. 2001. *Final Synthesis Report of the Findings from ASPE's Leavers Grants*. Washington, D.C.: Urban Institute.

American Association of Community Colleges. 2005. "Fast Facts." Available at: http://www.aacc.nche.edu/Content/NavigationaMenu/AboutCommunityColleges/Fast_Facts1/Fast_Facts.htm.

Anderson, Kathryn H., Richard V. Burkhauser, and Jennie E. Raymond. 1993. "The Effect of Creaming on Placement Rates Under the Job Training Partnership Act." *Industrial and Labor Relations Review* 46(4): 613–24.

Aronowitz, Stanley. 2000. *The Knowledge Factory: Dismantling the Corporate University and Creating True Higher Learning*. Boston: Beacon Press.

Aspen Institute. 2002a. *Measuring Up and Weighing In: Industry-Based Workforce Development Training Results in Strong Employment Outcomes*. Sector Policy Project, Executive Summary No. 3. Washington, D.C.: Aspen Institute.

———. 2002b. *Grow Faster Together or Grow Slowly Apart*. Report. Washington, D.C.: Aspen Institute.

Astin, Alexander W., Sarah A. Parrott, William S. Korn, and Linda J. Sax. 1997. *The American Freshman: Thirty Year Trends*. Los Angeles: University of California, Los Angeles, Higher Education Research Institute.

Attewell, Paul, and David Lavin. 2003. "The Value of Higher Education for Low-Income Populations: The Payoff for the Second Generation." Unpublished manuscript. CUNY Graduate Center. New York City.

Bailey, Thomas R., and Irina E. Averianova. 1999. "Multiple Missions of Community Colleges: Conflicting or Complementary?" Community College Research Center Brief no. 1. New York: Columbia University, Teachers College.

Bailey, Thomas, Davis Jenkins, and Timothy Leinbach. 2005a. "Community College Low-Income and Minority Student Completion Study: Descriptive Statistics from the 1912 High School Cohort." New York: Community College Research Center, Columbia University.

Bailey, Thomas, Davis Jenkins, and Timothy Leinbach. 2005b. "What We Know About Community College Low-Income and Minority Student Outcomes: Descriptive Statistics from National Surveys." New York: Community College Research Center, Columbia University.

Baker, Linda Renee, and Joseph Cipfl. 2001. "Letter Regarding Advancing Opportunities Program." Springfield, Ill.: Illinois Department of Human Services.

Barnow, Burt. 1989. "Government Training as a Means of Reducing Unemployment." In *Rethinking Employment Policy*, edited by D. Lee Bawden and Felicity Skidmore. Washington, D.C.: Urban Institute.

Barnow, Burt S., and Christopher T. King. 2001. "Publicly Funding Training in a Changing Labor Market." *Increasing the Effectiveness of Publicly Funded Training*. Washington, D.C.: Urban Institute.

Bassi, Laurie J., and Orley Ashenfelter. 1986. "The Effect of Direct Job Creation and Training Programs on Low-Skilled Workers." In *Fighting Poverty: What Works and What Doesn't*, edited by Sheldon Danziger and Daniel H. Weinberg. Cambridge, Mass.: Harvard University Press.

Bastedo, Michael, and Patricia Gumport. 2003. "Access to What? Mission Differentiation and Academic Stratification in U.S. Public Higher Education." *Higher Education* 46: 341–59.

Beder, Hal. 1999. *The Outcomes and Impacts of Adult Literacy Education in the United States*. Cambridge, Mass.: National Center for the Study of Adult Learning and Literacy.

Berg, Ivar. 1970. *Education and Jobs: The Great Training Robbery*. New York: Praeger.

Berkner, Lutz, Laura Horn, and Michael Clune. 2000. "Descriptive Summary of 1995–96 Beginning Postsecondary Students: Three Years Later." NCES publication no. 2000–154. Washington: U.S. Department of Education, National Center for Education Statistics, Institute of Education Sciences.

Bos, Johannes M. 1996. "Effects of Education and Educational Credentials on the Earnings of Economically Disadvantaged Young Mothers." Working paper. New York: MDRC.

Bowen, William, Martin Kurzweil, and Eugene Tobin. 2005. *Equity and Excellence in American Higher Education*. Charlottesville: University of Virginia Press.

Bowen, William, and Derek Bok. 1998. *The Shape of the River: Long-Term Consequences of Considering Race in College and University Admissions*. Princeton: Princeton University Press.

Brint, Steven. 2003. "Few Remaining Dreams: Community Colleges Since 1985." *Annals of the American Academy of Political and Social Science* 586(1): 16–37.

Brint, Steven, and Jerome Karabel. 1989. *The Diverted Dream: Community Colleges and the Promise of Educational Opportunity in America, 1990–1985*. New York: Oxford University Press.

Brock, Thomas, Mary Farrell, Daniel Friedlander, Gayle Hamilton, and Kristen Harkness. 1997. *Evaluating Two Welfare-to-Work Program Approaches: Two-Year Findings on the Labor Force Attachment and Human Capital Development Programs in Three Sites.* Report prepared for the U.S. Department of Health and Human Services. New York: MRDC. Available at: http: //www.mdrc.org/publications/ 203/abstract.html.

Brodkin, Evelyn. 1997. "Inside the Welfare Contract: Discretion and Accountability in State Welfare Administration." *Social Service Review* 71(March): 1–33.

Burke, Joseph, and Henrik Minassians. 2001. *Linking State Resources to Campus Results: From Fad to Trend. The Fifth Annual Survey.* New York: A. Rockefeller Institute of Government.

Campbell, John L. 2002. "Ideas, Politics and Public Policy." *Annual Review of Sociology* 28: 21–38.

Carnevale, Anthony, and Donna Desrochers. 2004. "Benefits and Barriers to College for Low-Income Adults." In *Low-Income Adults in Profile: Improving Lives Through Higher Education,* edited by Bryan Cook and Jacqueline King. Washington, D.C.: American Council on Education.

Center for Law and Social Policy. 2002. "Forty States Likely to Cut Access to Postsecondary Training or Education Under House-Passed Bill." Report. Washington, D.C.: Center for Law and Social Policy.

Chicago Jobs Council. 2003a. "Improving Our Response to Workforce Needs: Recommendations for Reauthorization of the Workforce Investment Act." Report. Chicago: Chicago Jobs Council. Available at: http: //www.cjc.net/publications/ wia_improving response_rpt.pdf.

———. 2003b. "From Safety Net to Self-Sufficiency: A CJC Proposal for a State Mixed Strategy Approach to Prepare TANF and Food Stamp Employment and Training Participants for Illinois' Skilled Workforce." Report (November). Chicago: Chicago Jobs Council. Available at: http: //www.cjc.net/ publications/ 1_Welfare_Reform_PDFs/From_Safety_Net.pdf.

———. 2005a. "Welfare-to-Work Group Meeting Summary." Report (January 21). Chicago: Chicago Jobs Council. Available at: http: //www.cjc.net/about/ documents/January.doc.

———. 2005b. "Welfare-to-Work Group Meeting Summary." Report (October 22). Chicago: Chicago Jobs Council. Available at: http: //www.cjc.net/publications/ 03_WkGrp_Meetings_WRW/WtW_Octobver_2004.pdf.

Choitz, Victoria, and Brian Bosworth. 2002. "State Scan of Higher Education Accountability Systems: An Interim Report to Workforce Connections of Southwest Pennsylvania." Report. Arlington, Mass.: Futureworks.

Chubb, John, and Terry Moe. 1987. *Politics, Markets and America's Schools.* Washington, D.C.: Brookings Institution.

Clark, Burton. 1960. "The 'Cooling-Out' Function of Higher Education." *American Journal of Sociology* 65(6): 569–76.

Clinton, William Jefferson. 1992. *Putting People First.* New York: Three Rivers Press.
———. 1996a. Untitled speech. Available at: http: //www.pbs.org/newshour/bb/election/june96/clinton_6-4.html.
———. 1996b. "Speech by President at Welfare Signing Bill." Available at: http: //www.clintonfoundation.org/legacy/082296-speech-by-president-at-welfare-bill-signing.html.
———. 1998. "Remarks on Signing the Workforce Investment Act of 1998." Speech, August 7, 1998. *Weekly Compilation of Presidential Documents*, August 10, 1998. Available at: http: //www.findarticles.com/p/articles/mi_m2889/is_n32_v34/ai_21118705.
Collins, Randall. 1979. *The Credential Society: A Historical Sociology of Education and Stratification.* New York: Academic Press.
Cook, Bryan, and Jacqueline King. 2004. *Low-Income Adults in Profile: Improving Lives Through Higher Education.* Washington, D.C.: American Council on Education.
Cox, Kenya Covington, and William E. Spriggs. 2002. *Negative Effects of TANF on College Enrollment.* Report. Washington, D.C.: National Urban League Institute for Opportunity and Equality.
D'Amico, Deborah. 1997. *Adult Education and Welfare to Work Initiatives: A Review of Research, Practice and Policy.* Washington, D.C.: National Institute for Literacy.
———. 1999. *Politics, Policy, Practice and Personal Responsibility: Adult Education in an Era of Welfare Reform.* Cambridge, Mass.: National Center for the Study of Adult Learning and Literacy.
Deil-Amen, Regina, and James Rosenbaum. 2003. "The Social Prerequisites of Success: Can College Structure Reduce the Need for Social Know-How?" *Annals of the American Academy of Political and Social Science* 586(1): 120–43.
DeParle, Jason. 2004. *American Dream.* New York: Viking Press.
DeRocco, Emily. 2002. "Statement by Emily Stover Derocco on Fiscal Year 2003 Request for the Employment and Training Administration." Available at: http: //www.usmayors.org/uscm/wash_update/workforce/derocco2002.pdf.
Dougherty, Kevin. 1994. *The Contradictory College: The Conflicting Origins, Impacts, and Futures of the Community College.* Albany: State University of New York Press.
———. 2003. "The Uneven Distribution of Employee Training by Community Colleges: Description and Explanation." *Annals of the American Academy of Political and Social Science* 586(March): 62–91.
Dougherty, Kevin, and Marianne F. Bakia. 2000a. "Community Colleges and Contract Training: Content, Origins, and Impact." *Teachers College Record* 102(1): 197–243.
———. 2000b. "The New Economic Development Role of the Community College." Community College Research Center Brief no. 6. New York: Columbia University, Teachers College.
Dowd, Alicia. 2003. "From Access to Outcome Equity: Revitalizing the Democratic Mission of the Community College." *Annals of the American Academy of Political and Social Science* 586(March): 92–119.

Duncan, Greg. 1984. *Years of Poverty, Years of Plenty*. Report. Ann Arbor: University of Michigan Survey Research Center.

Dyke, Andrew, Carolyn J. Heinrich, Peter R. Mueser, and Kenneth R. Troske. 2005. "The Effects of Welfare-to-Work Program Activities on Labor Market Outcomes." Unpublished paper, University of North Carolina, Chapel Hill, Department of Economics.

Edin, Kathryn, and Laura Lein. 1997. *Making Ends Meet: How Single Mothers Survive Welfare and Low-Wage Work*. New York: Russell Sage Foundation.

Ellwood, David. 1988. *Poor Support: Poverty in the American Family*. New York: Basic Books.

Ellwood, David T., and Thomas J. Kane. 2000. "Who Is Getting a College Education? Family Background and the Growing Gaps in Enrollment." In *Securing the Future*, edited by Jane Waldfogel and Sheldon H. Danziger. New York: Russell Sage Foundation.

Finegold, Kenneth, and Alan Weil, eds. 2002. *Welfare Reform: The Next Act*. Washington, D.C.: Urban Institute.

Freedman, Stephen, Daniel Friedlander, Gayle Hamilton, Marisa Mitchell, Jodi Nudelman, JoAnn Rock, Amanda Schweder, Laura Storto. 2000. *Evaluating Alternative Welfare-to-Work Approaches: Two-Year Impacts for Eleven Programs*. Report prepared for the U.S. Department of Health and Human Services. New York: MRDC.

Fremstad, Shawn. 2004. *Recent Welfare Reform Research Findings: Implications for TANF Reauthorization and State TANF Policies*. Washington, D.C.: Center on Budget and Policy Priorities.

Friedman, Pamela. 1999. "Post-Secondary Education Options for Low Income Adults." *Welfare Information Network: Issue notes* 3(12): 2–5.

Furstenberg, Frank. 1976. *Unplanned Parenthood: The Social Consequences of Teenage Childbearing*. New York: Free Press.

Gais, Thomas L., Richard P. Nathan, Irene Lurie, and Thomas Kaplan. 2001. "The Implementation of the Personal Responsibility Act of 1996: Commonalities, Variations and the Challenge of Complexity." Unpublished paper, Nelson A. Rockefeller Institute of Government, State University of New York, Albany. Available at: http://www.rockinst.org/publications/federalism/pr_act.pdf

Garrett, Geoffrey, and Barry R. Weingast. 1993. "Ideas, Interests and Institutions: Constructing the European Community's Internal Market." In *Ideas and Foreign Policy: Beliefs, Institutions and Political Change*, edited by Judith Goldstein and Robert O. Keohane. Ithaca, N.Y.: Cornell University Press.

Gilder, George. 1981. *Wealth and Poverty*. New York: Basic Books.

Gilens, Martin. 2003. "How the Poor Became Black." In *Race and the Politics of Welfare Reform*, edited by Sanford F. Schram, Joe Soss, and Richard C. Fording. Ann Arbor: University of Michigan Press.

Gittell, Marilyn, and Tracy Steffy. 2000. "Community Colleges Addressing Students' Needs: A Case Study of LaGuardia Community College." Report prepared for the deputy chancellor, Graduate School of the City University of New York. New York: Howard Samuels State Management and Policy Center. Available at: http: // web.gc.cuny.edu/Howardsamuels/ LagReport.pdf.

Goldrick-Rab, Sara, and Kathleen M. Shaw. 2005. "Racial and Ethnic Differences in the Impact of Work-First Reforms on Access to Postsecondary Education." *Educational Evaluation and Policy Analysis* 27(4): 291–307.

Goldstein, Judith. 1993. *Ideas, Interests and American Trade Policy*. Ithaca, N.Y.: Cornell University Press.

Goldstein, Judith, and Robert O. Keohane, eds. 1993. *Ideas and Foreign Policy: Beliefs, Institutions and Political Change*. Ithaca, N.Y.: Cornell University Press.

Golonka, Susan, and Lisa Matus-Grossman. 2001. *Opening Doors: Expanding Educational Opportunities for Low-Income Workers*. Report prepared for the National Governors Association Center for Best Practices. New York: MDRC.

Gordon, Linda. 1994. *Pitied but Not Entitled: Single Mothers and the History of Welfare*. Cambridge, Mass.: Harvard University Press.

Greenberg, Mark. 1998. "The Child Care Protection Under TANF." Washington, D.C.: Center for Law and Social Policy. Unpublished paper. Available at: http: // www.clasp.org/publications/ the_child_care_protect.htm

———. 2001. *How Are TANF Funds Being Used? The Story in FY 2000*. Report prepared for National Association of State Budget Officers (August 14). Washington, D.C.: Center for Law and Social Policy.

Greenberg, Mark, Julie Strawn, and Lisa Plimpton. 1999. "State Opportunities to Provide Access to Postsecondary Education Under TANF." Report. Washington, D.C.: Center for Law and Social Policy.

———. 2000. "State Opportunities to Provide Access to Postsecondary Education Under TANF." Revised 1999 report. Washington, D.C.: Center for Law and Social Policy. Available at: http: //www.clasp.org/publications/postsec_revised_200.pdf.

Gross, Steven, Kathleen Shaw, and Joan Shapiro. 2003. "Deconstructing Accountability Through the Lens of Democratic Philosophies: Toward a New Analytic Framework." *Journal of Research for Education Leaders* 1(3): 5–27.

Grubb, W. Norton. 1996. "The New Vocationalism: What It Is, What It Could Be." *Phi Delta Kappan* 77(8): 535.

———. 1997. "The Returns to Education in the Sub-Baccalaureate Labor Market, 1984–1990." *Economics of Education Review* 16(3): 231–45.

———. 2001. "Second Chances in Changing Times: The Roles of Community Colleges in Advancing Low Wage Workers." In *Low Wage Workers in the New Economy*, edited by Richard Kazis and Marc Miller. Washington, D.C.: Urban Institute.

———. 2002a. "Learning and Earning in the Middle." Part 1, "National Studies of Pre-baccalaureate Education." *Economics of Education Review* 21(4): 299–321.

———. 2002b. "Learning and Earning in the Middle." Part 2, "State and Local Studies of Pre-baccalaureate Education." *Economics of Education Review* 21(5): 401–14.

Grubb, W. Norton, Norena Badway, and Denise Bell. 2003. "Community Colleges

176

and the Equity Agenda: The Potential of Noncredit Education." *The Annals of the American Academy of Political and Social Science* 586(March): 218–40.

Grubb, W. Norton, Norena Badway, Denise Bell, D. Bragg, and M. Russian. 1997. *Workforce, Economic, and Community Development: The Changing Landscape of the "Entrepreneurial" Community College.* Berkeley, Calif.: National Center for Research in Vocational Education.

Grubb, W. Norton, Norena Badway, Denise Bell, Bernadette Chi, Chris King, Julie Herr, Heath Prince, Richard Kazis, Lisa Hicks, and Judith Combes Taylor. 1999. *Toward Order from Chaos: State Efforts to Reform Workforce Development Systems.* Berkeley, Calif.: National Center for Research in Vocational Education.

Grubb, W. Norton, and Marvin Lazerson. 2004. *The Education Gospel.* Cambridge, Mass.: Harvard University Press.

Gueron, Judith M. 1987. *Reforming Welfare with Work.* New York: Ford Foundation.

Gumport, Patricia. 2003. "The Demand-Response Scenario: Perspectives of Community College Presidents." *Annals of the American Academy of Political and Social Science* 586: 38–61.

Hall, Peter A. 1993. "Policy Paradigms, Social Learning and the State: The Case of Economic Policy Making in Britain." *Comparative Politics* 1(April): 275–96.

———. 1997. "The Role of Interests, Institutions and Ideas in the Comparative Political Economy of the Industrializing Nations." In *Comparative Politics: Rationality, Culture and Structure*, edited by M. Lichbach and I. Zuckerman. Cambridge: Cambridge University Press.

Hamilton, Gayle. 2002. *Moving People from Welfare to Work: Lessons from the National Evaluation of Welfare-to-Work Strategies.* Report. New York: MDRC.

Hamilton, Gayle, and Thomas Brock et al. 1997. *Evaluating Two Welfare-to-Work Program Approaches: Two-Year Findings on the Labor Force Attachment and Human Capital Development Programs in Three Sites.* Washington, D.C.: USDHHS and USDOE.

Harrington, Michael. 1962 *The Other America.* New York: Penguin Books.

Hasenfeld, Yeheskel. 2002. "The Making of the Black Box: An Organizational Perspective on Implementing Social Policies." Paper presented at the Workshop on Organizations and Social Policy. Chicago.

Hebel, Sara. 2003. "Unequal Impact: Community Colleges Face Disproportionate Cuts in State Budgets." *Chronicle of Higher Education* 48(38, May): A21.

Heller, Donald. 2002. *Condition of Access: Higher Education for Lower Income Students.* ACE/Prager Series on Higher Education.

Hirschman, Albert O. 1991. *The Rhetoric of Reaction: Perversity, Futility, Jeopardy.* Cambridge, Mass.: Harvard University Press.

Hoachlander, Gary, Anna Sikora, and Laura Horn. 2003. "Community College Students: Goals, Academic Preparation, and Outcomes." NCES publication no. 2003–164. Washington: U.S. Department of Education, National Center for Education Statistics, Institute of Education Sciences.

Hochschild, Jennifer. 1995. *Facing Up to the American Dream: Race, Class, and the Soul of the Nation.* Princeton: Princeton University Press.

Holzer, Harry, and Margy Waller. 2003. *The Workforce Investment Act: Reauthorization to Address the Skills Gap.* Research Brief. Washington, D.C.: Brookings Institution.

Horn, Laura, and Rachel Berger. 2004. "College Persistence on the Rise? Changes in 5-Year Degree Completion and Postsecondary Persistence Rates Between 1994 and 2000." NCES publication no. 2005–156. Washington: U.S. Department of Education, National Center for Education Statistics, Institute of Education Sciences.

Illinois Community College Board. N.d.. "Advancing Opportunities." Brochure. Springfield, Ill.: Illinois Community College Board.

Institute for Higher Education Policy. 2003. *Reauthorizing the Higher Education Act: Issues and Options.* Washington, D.C.: Author.

Jacobs, Jerry, and Rosalind Berkowitz King. 2002. "Age and College Completion: A Life History Analysis of Women Aged 15 Through 44." *Sociology of Education* 75(3): 211–30.

Jacobson, Louis S., Robert J. LaLonde, and Daniel G. Sullivan. 2001. "The Returns to Community College Schooling for Displaced Workers." Working paper. Chicago: University of Chicago, Harris School of Public Policy. Available at: http://harrisschool.uchicago.edu/About/publications/working-papers/pdf/wp_01_5.pdf.

———. 2005. "Do Displaced Workers Benefit from Community College Courses? Findings from Administrative Data and Directions for Future Research." Presented at the conference Effects of Community Colleges on the Earnings of Displaced Workers, sponsored by the Hudson Institute Center for Employment Policy. Washington D.C. (October 21).

Jenkins, Davis. 2002. "The Potential of Community Colleges as Bridges to Opportunity for the Disadvantaged: Can It Be Achieved on a Large Scale?" Unpublished paper. University of Illinois, Chicago, Great Cities Institute.

———. 2004. "A Bridge to Community College Career Programs for Adults with Poor Basic Skills." Available at: http://www.uic.edu/cuppa/gci/about/bios/documemts/A%20Bridge%20to%20Community%20College%20Career%20Programs%20for%20Adults%20with%20Poor%20Basic%20Skills.pdf (accessed June 2006).

Jones-DeWeever, Avis A. 2005. "Toward Self-Sufficiency: Accessing Higher Education Under Welfare Reform." Paper presented at the Association for Public Policy Analysis and Management fall conference. Washington, D.C. (November 3–5, 2005).

Kane, Thomas, and Cecilia B. Rouse. 1995. "Labor Market Returns to Two- and Four-Year College." *American Economic Review* 85(3): 600–28.

———. 1999. "The Community College: Training Students at the Margin Between College and Work." *Journal of Economic Perspectives* 13(1): 63–84.

Karoly, Lynn A., and Constantijn W. A. Panis. 2004. *The 21ˢᵗ Century at Work: Forces Shaping the Future Workforce and Workplace in the United States.* Santa Monica: RAND Corporation.

Katz, Michael. 1986. *In the Shadow of the Poorhouse: A Social History of Welfare in America*. New York: Basic Books.

———. 1989. *The Undeserving Poor: From the War on Poverty to the War on Welfare*. New York: Pantheon Books.

———. 2001. *The Price of Citizenship: Redefining the American Welfare State*. New York: Metropolitan Books.

Kienzl, Gregory. 1999. *Community College Involvement in Welfare-to-Work*. Washington, D.C.: American Association of Community Colleges.

Kingdon, John W. 1984. *Agendas, Alternatives and Public Policies*. Boston: Little, Brown.

Kirby, Gretchen, LaDonna Pavetti, Karen E. McGuire, and Rebecca L. Clark. 1997. *Income Support and Social Services for Low-Income People in Massachusetts*. Washington, D.C.: Urban Institute. Available at: http: //www.urban.org/url.cfm?ID= 310427.

Lafer, Gordon. 2002. *The Job Training Charade*. Ithaca, N.Y.: Cornell University Press.

Lavin, David, and David Hyllegard. 1996. *Changing the Odds: Open Admissions and the Life Chances of the Disadvantaged*. New Haven: Yale University Press.

Levin, John. 2001. *Globalizing the Community College*. New York: Palgrave Macmillan.

Levy, Frank, and Richard Murnane. 1992. "U.S. Earnings Levels and Earnings Inequality: A Review of Recent Trends and Proposed Explanations." *Journal of Economic Literature* 30(3): 333–1381.

Lewis, Dan, Laura Amsden, and Emily Collins. 2004. "The Two Worlds of Welfare Reform in Illinois: The Illinois Family Study." Fourth annual report from the Illinois Families Study. Urbana-Champaign, Ill.: University Consortium on Welfare Reform. Available at: http: //www.northwestern.edu/ipr/publications/papers/ IFSyear4.pdf.

Lin, Ann Chih. 2000. *Reform in the Making: The Implementation of Social Policy in Prison*. Princeton: Princeton University Press.

London, Rebecca. 2006. "The Role of Postsecondary Education in Welfare Recipients' Paths to Self-Sufficiency." *Journal of Higher Education* 77(3): 472–96.

Loprest, Pamela J. 2003. *Fewer Welfare Leavers Employed in a Weak Economy*. Report, no. 5 in series, "Snapshots of America's Families III." Washington, D.C.: Urban Institute.

Lurie, Irene. 2001. *Changing Welfare Offices*. Washington, D.C.: Brookings Institution.

Manski, Charles F., and Irwin Garfinkel, eds. 1992. *Evaluating Welfare and Training Programs*. Cambridge, Mass.: Harvard University Press.

Manzo, David. 1997. *The Influence of Federal and State Welfare Reform on Adult Education*. ED412–332. Available at: www.edrs.com.

Marini, Margaret Mooney. 1978. "The Transition to Adulthood: Sex Differences in Educational Attainment and Age at Marriage." *American Sociological Review* 43(4): 483–507.

179

Martinson, Karin, and Daniel Friedlander. 1994. *GAIN: Basic Education in a Welfare-to-Work Program.* Report. New York: MDRC.

Massachusetts Department of Transitional Assistance. February 2001.

Massing, Michael. 2000. "Ending Poverty As We Know It." *The American Prospect* 11(15): 30–38. Available at: http: //www.prospect.org/print-friendly/print/V11/15/massing-m.html.

Matus-Grossman, Lisa, and Susan Gooden. 2002. *Opening Doors: Students' Perspectives on Juggling Work, Family, and College.* Report. New York: MDRC.

Mayer, Susan, and Paul Peterson, eds. 1999. *Earning and Learning: How Schools Matter.* Washington, D.C.: Brookings Institution.

Maynard-Moody, S. 2003. *Beyond Implementation: A Sketch of a Theory of Policy Enactment.* Paper presented at the Annual Research Conference of the Association for Public Policy Analysis and Management. Washington, D.C. (November 6–8, 2003).

Mazzeo, Christopher, Sara Rab, and Susan Eachus. 2003. "Work-First or Work Only: Welfare Reform, State Policy and Access to Postsecondary Education." *Annals of the American Academy of Political and Social Science* 586(1): 144–71.

Melnick, R. Shep. 1994. *Between the Lines: Interpreting Welfare Rights.* Washington, D.C.: Brookings Institution.

Meyers, Marcia K., Norma M. Riccucci, and Irene Lurie. 2001. "Achieving Goal Congruence in Complex Environments: The Case of Welfare Reform." *Journal of Public Administration Research and Theory* 11(2, April): 165–201.

Mead, Lawrence. 1986. *Beyond Entitlement: The Social Obligations of Citizenship.* New York: Free Press.

Mezey, Jennifer. 2004. *Myths About the Adequacy of Current Child Care Funding.* Washington, D.C.: Center for Law and Social Policy.

Moffitt, Robert. 2006. Welfare Benefits Database. Available at: http: //www.econjhu.edu/people/moffitt/datasets.html.

Moore, Mark H. 1988. "What Sort of Ideas Become Public Ideas?" In *The Power of Public Ideas,* edited by Robert B. Reich. Cambridge, Mass.: Harvard University Press.

Moynihan, Daniel Patrick. 1965. *The Negro Family: The Case for National Action.* Washington: U.S. Department of Labor.

Murray, Charles. 1984. *Losing Ground: American Social Policy, 1950–1980.* New York: Basic Books.

National Center for Education Statistics. 1995. "Profile of Undergraduates in U.S. Postsecondary Education Institutions: 1992–93, With an Essay on Undergraduates at Risk." Publication no. NCES 96-237. Washington: U.S. Department of Education, National Center for Education Statistics, Institute of Education Sciences.

———. 1996 *National Household Education Survey: An Overview.* Washington: U.S. Department of Education, Office of Educational Research and Improvement.

———. 1997. "National Postsecondary Student Aid Study: 1995–96 (NPSAS: 96) Methodology Report." Publication no. 98073. Washington: U.S. Government Printing Office.

———. 2001. *National Household Education Survey*. Washington: U.S. Department of Education, Office of Educational Research and Improvement.

———. 2002a. "Chapter 5: Outcomes of Education." Washington: U.S. Department of Education, National Center for Education Statistics, Institute of Education Sciences.

———. 2002b. *National Postsecondary Student Aid Study: 1999–2000 (NPSAS: 2000) Methodology Report*. Washington: U.S. Government Printing Office.

———. 2003. *Condition of Education*. Washington: U.S. Department of Education, National Center for Education Statistics, Institute of Education Sciences.

National Center for Public Policy and Higher Education. 2000. "Measuring Up 2000: The National Report Card on Higher Education." Report. San Jose: National Center for Public Policy and Higher Education.

———. 2002. "Measuring Up 2002: The National Report Card on Higher Education." Report. San Jose: National Center for Public Policy and Higher Education.

———. 2004. "Measuring Up 2004: The National Report Card on Higher Education." San Jose: National Center for Public Policy and Higher Education.

———. 2005. "Policy Alert, November 2005." San Jose: National Center for Public Policy and Higher Education.

National Forum on Higher Education for the Public Good. 2003. "A Common Agenda." Report. Available at: http: /www.thenationalforum.org.

National Governors Association Center for Best Practices. 2002. *A Governors Guide to Creating a 21st-Century Workforce*. Washington, D.C.: National Governors Association Center for Best Practices.

Nora, Amaury. 1993. "Two Year Colleges and Minority Students' Educational Aspirations: Help or Hindrance?" In *Higher Education: Handbook of Theory and Research*, edited by J. C. Smart. New York: Agathon Press.

Orr, Larry. 2004 *The National JTPA Study: Impacts, Benefits and Costs of Title II Year-Round Programs: A Report to the U.S. Department of Labor*. Bethesda: Abt Associates.

Orr, Larry L., Howard S. Bloom, Stephen H. Bell, Fred Doolittle, and Winston Lin. 1996. *Does Training for the Disadvantaged Work? Evidence from the National JTPA Study*. Washington, D.C.: Urban Institute.

Osbourne, David, and Ted Gaebler. 1992. *Reinventing Government: How the Entrepreneurial Spirit Is Transforming the Public Sector*. Reading, Mass.: Addison-Wesley.

Patel, Nisha, and Julie Strawn. 2003. "WIA Reauthorization Recommendation." Available at: http: //www.clasp.org/DMS/Documents/1057258510.44/WIA_Recomm.pdf.

Patterson, James T. 1986. *America's Struggle Against Poverty*. Cambridge, Mass.: Harvard University Press.

Pauly, Edward, and Christina DeMeo. 1996. *Adult Education for People on AFDC. A Synthesis of Research*. Washington: U.S. Department of Education.

Pennsylvania Department of Public Welfare. 2004. *Job Retention Advancement and*

Rapid Re-employment Program. Available at: http://www.dpw.state.pa.us/LowInc/EduTrainWelRecip/003671359.htm.

Perez-Johnson, Irma, and Paul Decker. 2001. "Customer Choice or Business as Usual? Promoting Innovation in the Design of WIA Training Programs." Paper presented at the National Research Conference on Workforce Security Issues in the United States. Washington, D.C (June 26–27, 2001).

Peters, Howard. 1999. "Policy Memorandum re: TANF 60-Month Limit and Post-Secondary Education." Springfield: Illinois Department of Human Services.

Peterson, Janice, Xue Song, and Avis Jones-DeWeever. 2002. *Life After Welfare Reform: Low-Income Single Parent Families, Pre- and Post-TANF.* Washington, D.C.: Institute for Women's Policy Research.

Philippe, Kent A., ed. 2000. *National Profile of Community Colleges: Trends and Statistics.* 3rd edition. Washington, D.C.: Community College Press.

Pierson, Paul. 1993. "When Effect Becomes Cause: Policy Feedback and Political Change." *World Politics* 45(4): 595–628.

Piven, Frances Fox, and Richard Cloward. 1977. *Poor People's Movements: Why They Succeed, How They Fail.* New York: Alfred A. Knopf.

———. 1993. *Regulating the Poor: The Functions of Public Welfare.* New York: Vintage Books.

Presser, Harriet. 2003. *Working in a 24/7 Economy: Challenges for American Families.* New York: Russell Sage Foundation.

Prince, David, and Davis Jenkins. 2005. *Building Pathways to Success for Low-Skill Adult Students: Lessons for Community College Policy and Practice from a Statewide Longitudinal Tracking Study.* Report. New York: Columbia University, Teachers College, Community College Research Center.

Putnam, Robert. 2000. *Bowling Alone: The Collapse and Revival of American Community.* New York: Simon & Schuster.

Quadagno, Jill. 1994 *The Color of Welfare: How Racism Undermined the War on Poverty.* New York: Oxford University Press.

Ragin, Charles. 1987. *The Comparative Method: Moving Beyond Qualitative and Quantitative Strategies.* Berkeley: University of California Press.

Ragin, Charles, and Howard Becker, eds. 1992. *What Is a Case? Exploring the Foundations of Social Inquiry.* New York: Cambridge University Press.

Raphael, Steve, Michael Stoll, and Edwin Melendez. 2003. "Does Training Pay? Evidence from Programs for Economically Disadvantaged Adults in Massachusetts." Paper presented at New Tools for a New Era: The Symposium on Using Administrative Records to Fill the Information Gap. Sponsored by the Bureau of Labor Statistics and the Workforce Information Council. Washington, D.C. (July 23–24, 2003).

Reese, Ellen. 2005. *Backlash Against Welfare Mothers: Past and Present.* Berkeley: University of California Press.

Reville, Robert T., and Jacob Alex Klerman. 1996. "Job Training: The Impact on California of Further Consolidation and Devolution." In *The New Fiscal Federalism and the Social Safety Net: A View From California,* edited by James Hosek and Robert Levine. Santa Monica: RAND Corporation.

Rhoads, Robert A., and James R. Valadez. 1996. *Democracy, Multiculturalism, and the Community College: A Critical Perspective.* New York: Garland.

Roe, Emery. 1994. *Narrative Policy Analysis: Theory and Practice.* Durham, N.C.: Duke University Press.

Rogers-Dillon, Robin. 2004. *The Welfare Experiments: Politics and Policy Evaluation.* Palo Alto: Stanford University Press.

Rouse, Cecilia Elena. 1998. "Do Two-Year Colleges Increase Overall Educational Attainment? Evidence from the States." *Journal of Policy Analysis and Management* 17(4): 595–620.

Schram, Sanford F., Joe Soss, and Richard C. Fording, eds. 2003. *Race and the Politics of Welfare Reform.* Ann Arbor: University of Michigan Press.

Shaw, Kathleen M., and Sara Rab. 2003. "Market Rhetoric Versus Reality in Policy and Practice: The Workforce Investment Act and Access to Community College Education and Training." *Annals of the American Academy of Political and Social Science* 586(March): 172–93.

Simmons, Sarah. 2005. "Welfare (to School?) to Work: How Welfare Reform Affects Collegiate Attainment." Paper presented at the meeting of the Association for Public Policy Analysis and Management. Washington, D.C. (November 3–5, 2005).

Skocpol, Theda. 1992. *Protecting Soldiers and Mothers: The Political Origins of Social Policy in the United States.* Cambridge, Mass.: Harvard University Press/Belknap Press.

Slaughter, Sheila, and Larry L. Leslie. 1997. *Academic Capitalism: Politics, Policies and the Entrepreneurial University.* Baltimore: Johns Hopkins University Press.

Social Policy Research Associates. 1999. "PY97 SPIR Data Book." Prepared for U.S. Department of Labor, Employment and Training Administration, Office of Policy and Research. Oakland, Calif.: SPRA. Available at: http: //wdr.doleta.gov/opr/spir/spir97/nation97.pdf.

———. 2004. "PY 2002 WIASRD Data Book." Oakland, Calif.: SPRA. Available at: http: //www.doleta.gov/ performance/results/PY_2002_WIASRD_Databook.pdf.

———. 2005. "PY 2003 WIASRD Data Book." Prepared for the U.S. Department of Labor. Oakland, Calif.: SPRA.

Somers, Margaret, and Fred Block. 2005. "From Poverty to Perversity: Ideational Embeddedness and Market Liberalism over Two Centuries of Welfare Debate." *American Sociological Review* 70(2): 260–87.

Sosulski, Marya. 2004. "A Road to Inclusion: A Combined-Methods Analysis of Access to Post-Secondary Education for Women in the Illinois Public Aid System." Ph.D. diss., University of Wisconsin, Madison.

Spillane, James. 2004. *Policy in Practice: Where the Rubber Meets the Road.* Paper presented at the Education Finance Research Consortium Symposium. Albany, N.Y. (March).

Spillane, James, Brian Reiser, and Todd Reimer. 2002. "Policy Implementation and Cognition: Reframing and Refocusing Implementation Research." *Review of Educational Research* 73(3): 387–431.

State of Florida, Office of Program Policy Analysis for Government Accountability (OPPAGA). 2001. "Program Review: Workforce Development Education Program." Report no. 01-56. Tallahassee: Florida Department of Education.

State Higher Education Executive Officers. 1998. *State Survey on Performance Measures 1996–1997*. Denver: State Higher Education Executive Officers.

State of Washington, Board for Community and Technical Colleges. 2001. *Washington Community and Technical Colleges: Academic Year Report, 00-01*. Olympia, Wash.: SBCTC.

State of Washington, Work First. N.d. "Frequently Asked Questions About Workfirst." Available at: http: //www.workfirst.wa.gov/about/faq.htm.

Stein, Sandra. 2001. "These Are Your Title 1 Students: Policy Language in Educational Practice." *Policy Sciences* 34(2): 135–56.

———. 2004. *The Culture of Education Policy*. New York: Teachers College Press.

Stevens, David W. 2003a. *Mapping WIA One-Stop Client Flows*. Washington: U.S. Department of Labor, Employment and Training Administration, Office of Policy and Research,

———. 2003b. *WIA One-Stop Client Flow Demographics and Status*. Washington: U.S. Department of Labor, Employment and Training Administration, Office of Policy and Research.

Strawn, Julie. 1998. *Beyond Job Search or Basic Education: Rethinking the Role of Skills in Welfare Reform*. Washington, D.C.: Center for Law and Social Policy.

Strawn, Julie, and Robert Echols. 1999. *Welfare-to Work Programs: The Critical Role of Skills*. Washington, D.C.: Center for Law and Social Policy.

Teachman, Jay D., and Karen A. Polonko. 1988. "Marriage, Parenthood and the College Enrollment of Men and Women." *Social Forces* 67(2): 512–23.

Teles, Steven. 1996 *Whose Welfare? AFDC and Elite Politics*. Lawrence: University Press of Kansas.

Tennessee Higher Education Commission. 2004. "Performance Funding Standards 2000–01 through 2004–05." Available at: http: //www.state.tn.us/thec/2004web/division_pages/ppr_pages/pdfs/Policy/Performance%20Funding%20Standards%202000-05%20Cycle.pdf.

Thelin, John R. 2004. *A History of American Higher Education*. Baltimore: Johns Hopkins University Press.

Toner, Robin. 2002. "States Worry About Bush Welfare Rules." Available at: *New York Times On the Web*, February 2006, www.nytimes.com/2002/04/30/politics/.

Urban Institute. 2002. "Long-Term Welfare Recipients Are More Likely to Face Barriers to Work Than Other Welfare Recipients." Washington, D.C.: Urban Institute. Available at: http: //www.urban.org/uploadedPDF/900527.PDF.

U.S. Bureau of the Census. 1996. *Source and Accuracy Statement for the Survey of In-*

come and Program Participation 1996 12-Wave Longitudinal File. Washington: U.S. Bureau of the Census.

———. 2001. *Source and Accuracy Statement for the Wave 1–Wave 9 Public Use Files from One Survey of Income and Program Participation, 2001.* Washington: U.S. Bureau of the Census.

U.S. Census Bureau. 2003. *Current Population Survey: March 2002.* Washington: U.S. Department of Labor, Bureau of Labor Statistics.

U.S. Department of Education. 2003. *Digest of Education Statistics.* Washington: U.S. Department of Education, National Center for Education Statistics, Institute of Education Science.

U.S. Department of Health and Human Services. 1999. "Child Care in Pennsylvania: A Short Report on Subsidies, Affordability and Supply." Available at: http: // aspe.os.dhhs.gov/hsp/Child-Care99/pa-rpt.pdf.

———. 2003. "Indicators of Welfare Dependence: Annual Report to Congress." Available at: at http: //aspe.hhs.gov/hsp/indicators03/.

———. 2005. "TANF. Total Number of Recipients. Fiscal Year 2005." Available at: http: //www.acf.dhhs.gov/programs/ofa/caseload/2005/recipient05tanf.htm.

———. N.d. "Summary: Final rule: Temporary Assistance for Needy Families (TANF) Program." Available at: http: //www.acf.hhs.gov/programs/ofa/exsumcl.htm

U.S. Department of Health and Human Services, Administration for Children and Families, Office of Family Assistance. 2005. "SSP-MOE, Total Number of Recipients, Fiscal Year 2005." Table. Available at: Department of Health and Human Services website on February 2, 2006, at http: //www.acf.dhhs.gov/programs/ofa/caseload/2005/recipient05ssp.htm.

U.S. Department of Health and Human Services, Administration for Children and Families, Office of Planning. R. a. E. 2002. *Second Annual Report to Congress on the Temporary Assistance for Needy Families (TANF) Program.* Washington: U.S. Government Printing Office.

U.S. Department of Labor. 1998. "Key Features of the Workforce Investment Act as Compared to Current Law." Available at: http: //www.doleta.gov/usworkforce/archive/side by810.htm.

———. 2001. "Workforce Investment Act of 1998." Available at: http: //www .doleta.gov/usworkforce/wia/wialaw.pdf.

———. 2002. "Workforce Professionals." Available at: www.doleta.gov/usworkforce.

U.S. Department of Labor, Employment and Training Administration (DOLETA). 2002. "Workforce Investment System Initiative in Support of Homeland Security As It Relates to the Federalization of the Nation's Airports." Training and Employment Notice no. 4-02. Washington: DOLETA. Available at: http: //wdr.doleta .gov/directives/attach/TEN4-02.html.

———. 2003. "WIA PY 2001 Exiters, Adults—National Summary Report (Derived from PY 2001 WIASRD Records)." Table. Available at: http: //www.doleta.gov/ usworkforce/documents/annualreports/annual_report_2001.cfm.

185

———. 2004. "WIA PY 2003 Summary Report—Adults." Available at: http: // www.doleta.gov/performance/results/ WIASRD/PY2003/WIA_Summary_03_ adult.pdf.

———. N.d. "Working Partners, Welfare and Workforce Development: Glossary of Terms-Workforce Development." Retrieved July 31, 2003, from www.dol.gov/ asp/programs/drugs/workingpartners/wtw/gloss-wd.htm.

U.S. Department of Labor, Office of Inspector General. 1998. *Profiling JTPA's AFDC Recipients.* Report #06-98-002-03-340. Washington: U.S. Department of Labor.

U.S. Department of Labor Statistics. 2002. *Current Population Survey: Technical Paper 63RV, Design and Methodology.* Washington: U.S. Department of Labor.

U.S. Government Accountability Office. 1998. *Child Care: States Exercise Flexibility in Setting Reimbursement Rates and Providing Access for Low-Income Children.* Report No. GAO-02-894. Washington: U.S. Government Accountability Office.

———. 2001. *Workforce Investment Act: New Requirements Create Need for More Guidance.* Report no. GAO-02-94T. Washington: U.S. Government Accountability Office.

———. 2002a. *Workforce Investment Act: Improvements Needed in Performance Measures to Provide a More Accurate Picture of WIA's Effectiveness"* (February 2002). General Accountability Office publication no. GAO-02-275. Washington: U.S. Government Accountability Office.

———. 2002b. *Workforce Investment Act: Coordination of TANF Services Through One-Stops Has Increased Despite Challenges.* Report no. GAO-02-739T. Washington: U.S. Government Accountability Office.

———. 2003. "Workforce Investment Act. One-Stop Centers Implemented Strategies to Strengthen Services and Partnerships but More Research and Information Sharing is Needed." Report no. GAO-03-725. Washington: U.S. Government Accountability Office.

———. 2005. *Workforce Investment Act: Substantial Funds are Used for Training, but Little Is Known Nationally about Training Outcomes.* Report No. GAO-05-650. Washington: U.S. Government Accountability Office.

U.S. House of Representatives. 1998. "Workforce Investment Act Conference Report." *Congressional Record.*

Washington Work First. 2001. "Local Planning Area Performance Measures Report." Report. Olympia, Wash.: Employment Security Department.

Weaver, R. Kent. 2000. *Ending Welfare As We Know It.* Washington, D.C.: Brookings Institution.

Weir, Margaret. 1992. *Politics and Jobs.* Princeton: Princeton University Press.

———. 1993. "Ideas and the Politics of Bounded Innovation." In *Structuring Politics: Historical Institutionalism in Comparative Analysis,* edited by S. Steinmo, K. Thelen, and F. Longstreth. New York: Cambridge University Press.

Weir, Margaret, and Theda Skocpol. 1985. "State Structures and the Possibilities for "Keynesian" Responses to the Great Depression in Sweden, Britain and the

United States." In *Bringing the State Back In*, edited by P. Evans, D. Rueschemeyer, and T. Skocpol. Cambridge: Cambridge University Press.

Weiss, Janet A. 1990. "Ideas and Inducements in Mental Health Policy." *Journal of Policy Analysis and Management* 9: 178–200.

Wilson, William Julius. 1987. *The Truly Disadvantaged.* Chicago: University of Chicago Press.

Workforce Florida Inc. 2001. *Weekly Workforce Bulletin: Welfare Transition Reports for First Quarter 2001.* Tallahassee: Workforce Florida Inc.

Wrigley, Heide Spruke, Elise Richer, Karin Martinson, Hitomi Kubo, and Julie Strawn. 2003. *The Language of Opportunity: Expanding Employment Prospects for Adults with Limited English Skills.* Washington, D.C.: Center for Law and Social Policy.

Youcha, Geraldine. 2005. *Minding the Children: Childcare in America from Colonial Times to the Present.* New York: Da Capo Press.

Zwerling, L. Steven. 1976. *Second Best: The Crisis of the Community College.* New York: McGraw-Hill.

———. 1992. "First-Generation Adult Students: In Search of Safe Havens." In *First-Generation Students: Confronting the Cultural Issues. New Directions for Community Colleges*, special issue (no. 80), edited by L. Steven Zwerling and H. B. London. San Francisco: Jossey-Bass.

INDEX

Boldface numbers refer to figures and tables.

ABE (adult basic education) programs, 33, 83, 151–52, 158–59*n*9, 10

Abramovitz, M., 157*n*1

access, to postsecondary education. *See* postsecondary education, access to

accountability and outcomes: under CETA, 98, **99**; creaming practice, 128–31; under JTPA, **99**, 100; Massachusetts community colleges, 91; state universities, 108; under WIA, 97, **99**, 101, 106–7, 124, 128–32, 135, 138, 139, 148

ADC (Aid to Dependent Children), 19–20

adult basic education (ABE) programs, 33, 83, 151–52, 158–59*n*9, 10

Advancing Opportunities (AO) program (Illinois), 79, 91–92

advocacy groups, 20, 79, 85, 88–89

AFDC (Aid to Families with Dependent Children). *See* Aid to Families with Dependent Children (AFDC)

African Americans: ADC eligibility, 20; college access and growth of middle class, 37; college enrollment, 55, 57, 59–60; community college enrollment, 11; discrimination, 20; JTPA

services, **110**; as public image of typical welfare recipient, 20–21; WIA services, **110**, 119–22, 146

age, college enrollment by, **52**, 56, 59

Aid to Dependent Children (ADC), 19–20

Aid to Families with Dependent Children (AFDC): college enrollment data, 62, 66, 67, **70, 72, 73**; education and training under, 27, 33, 46; eligibility, 20, 27; elimination proposals, 28; in Illinois, 79, 92; JOBS program participation, 160*n*8; number of participants, **69**

American Council of Education, 153

American Dream, 3, 142

Aronowitz, S., 137

associate's degree programs: and earnings, 6, 38; enrollment trends, 60

Attewall, P., 168*n*3

bachelor's degree programs: and earnings, 6, 38; enrollment trends, 60; and unemployment, 37–38

Baltimore, welfare recipient study, 29

Bane, M., 64

Barnow, B., 107